CHRONIC PEDALITIS

One Man's Affliction

Tom Waite

This edition:
ISBN 978-0-9835397-5-9

Published in the United States of America.

Tom Waite
2014

Acknowledgments

I thank the fine folks at Queen Bean Café and Serrano Social Club (now Preservation Coffee & Tea), my primary and secondary writing spots. (Tertiary spots shall remain unnamed.) I especially thank baristas of Ashleigh, Sylvia, Debbie, Anna, Toni, Brady, Candace, and Beth varieties. This may be the caffeine talking, but you always made me feel welcome.

I thank all of the road angels who tried to rescue me along the way. You know who you are. And you know I love you like a strong tailwind.

I thank all of the bike-shop wrenches/mensches who put me back on the road, especially Lee Huston, El Tobo, Sasha of Citizen Chain, Bob of the Breckner variety, Donnie Collins, Mike Busa, and Brandon Groff (who still covets the Pugsley he built up for me).

I thank all of the Car People who obeyed one or more of the Commandments of Safe Driving while whizzing by my fragile frames of calcium and steel (i.e., $Ca_{10}(PO_4)_6(OH)_2$ and chromoly, respectively).

Finally, I thank K. Cardin, J. Goodell, P. Kotz Welch, A. Marshall, J. Martel, L. Jennings-Matthews, R. Stephens, L. Waite, and especially B. Fenster (stay-at-home cyclist extraordinaire) and J. Bailey for providing inspiration, test-riding the manuscript, and otherwise making the journey worthwhile.

thanks thanks thanks
thanks thanks
thanks

Contents

HAPPILY
EVER
AFTER

Chapter 1

Homeland Insecurity

Or How *Not* to Keep a Low Profile

I divorced my last vehicle years ago, vowing never to get remarried. I gave the carbon-spewing beast to charity, effectively revoking my own driving privileges, and then pedaled away to permanent car-freedom. I did so as a conscientious objector. By minimizing my carbon footprint, I hoped to slash my personal contribution to global warming, the extinction crisis, and warfare.

You may say I'm an insufferable zealot. I prefer eccentric purist. Call me what you will, I felt full of righteousness to opt out of the car culture once and for all. And I felt a surge of childlike joy. Even though I'd already been mostly living on my bike for years, it still felt like the first day of summer vacation. Look ma, no gas!

I'm glad to report I've remained virtually monogamous ever since, devoted to the bicycle as my sole conveyance. And it's been conjugal bliss. Of course, as in any marriage, there have been a few bumps in the road. But I'm getting ahead of myself.

As a key feature of my green lifestyle, I pedal everywhere. If I feel like going to a Red Sox game in Boston or homesteading at my backwoods log cabin in Canada or visiting my old stomping grounds in Alaska or hearing a newgrass band along the Erie Canal in New

York or birding near San Francisco or attending a reunion in Maine, I simply get on my bike and pedal. No matter the weather or season. No matter the road conditions. (If the snow gets really deep, I switch to my winter bike, a Pugsley, and pass snowplows.) I pedal. No excuses. No exceptions.

Actually, I do make rare exceptions to my just-pedal rule. If a friend or family member utters one of the *d*-words — death, divorce, dementia, diagnosis, or disease — I relax and get off my high steel horse. I head straight to the nearest train depot, airport, bus station, or ferry terminal. I grudgingly stray from my greener-than-thou lifestyle. In times of crisis, I'm a willing accomplice, guilty as charged.

But even when someone dies, I take my bicycle with me. Just as an avid birder would always bring binoculars, even to the cemetery, I'm not about to ditch my bike. But while it's straightforward to bring your binoculars, it's not always so convenient to bring your bike. Sometimes, it seems it would be easier to smuggle three cats in your overcoat, as one of my former graduate students did when she flew, pre-9/11.

Consider yourself forewarned:

Traveling with your bike may make you conspicuous, triggering unwanted attention. Put yourself in my place. You may not feel sociable, particularly in your time of grief. You may want to keep a low profile, to be left alone. Luckily, you're savvy enough not to show up at the airport in your skintight cycling costume looking like a MAMIL (middle-aged man in Lycra). You've packed away your helmet, fingerless gloves, neon shirt, tights, and cycling shoes. You don't look like a raging velophiliac. You look like an ordinary citizen, maybe even a responsible adult. And yet you have that bike-as-baggage problem. This alone will make you conspicuous, perhaps even more so than when you're pedaling and trying to be as conspicuous as possible.

By the way, when you're pedaling you only *think* the Car People appreciate your conspicuousness. They don't. They actually see you as a puffy Lance wannabe in neon and tights. They're not celebrating you for being cool and doing your small part to make the world a greener, saner, safer place. Quite the contrary, they tend to utter stuff like "loser," "nice tights," or "get on the fucking sidewalk, bitch!"

Which reminds me: As Art Buchwald once joked, Americans can forgive a fellow citizen who commits an unspeakably heinous atrocity, unless that atrocity happens to be refusal to use an automobile. In the good ole U.S. of A., if you're not one of the Car People, you might as well be a donut.

Even Lance will be forgiven, eventually. After all, despite how much we resent him — for enhancing his performance pharmaceutically, centrifuging his blood, lying his gaunt face off roughly 8,492,538 times, threatening snitches, consorting with Dubya, wearing tights in public and kissing Cheryl Crow in private — the fact remains: he owns and operates a fleet of vehicles. (Don't get me wrong, the French will never forgive him.)

I've always found it problematic to travel *with* my bicycle. At best, I've encountered subtle resentment and suspicion, as expressed by eye rolls and snide remarks. At worst, I've found myself being treated as a pariah, persona non grata, and even an Orwellian person of interest.

Here's a prime example:

It's a Tuesday in June in the latter part of the first decade of the 21st century. Having just got word that a friend in Maine is going through a midlife crisis, I power off my laptop and face the unhappy prospect of not spending all day "working" on yet another manuscript (i.e., incipient peer-reviewed scientific journal article destined to attract a single-digit readership). I'm a workaholic extraordinaire and it's not easy to descend from the ivory tower and enter the real world, the one outside academia. I'm not happy, but duty calls. It must be done. But, hey, I think, I'll take advantage of the crisis and turn my trip into a mini bike tour, while still visiting my friend in need. And because I'll have my laptop in a pannier, I'll be able to obsess over work whenever I'm not pedaling.

So, I pack my bike in a big fancy bag, phone a cab, and head to the airport in Columbus, Ohio. On the way across town, I refrain from booting up and pecking away at the keyboard. Instead, I chat up the cabbie. I guess his place of origin, "Are you from Somalia?"

He looks at me in the rearview mirror and says, "Ethiopia."

Later I ask if he dislikes anything in particular about living in the States. Without hesitation, he zings me: "Everyone asks if I'm from Somalia."

He laughs and says the worst thing is living among people who suspect him of being a terrorist. I do my best to commiserate and then I give him an obscene tip, as reparation for my faux pas.

At the airport, I head straight to the ticket counter for Skybus, a new fly-by-night airline whose hub happened to be Columbus. I'm hoping to get a super cheap fare to "Boston."

> Skybus had an innovative approach. They offered the cheapest fares in the business, with tickets starting at $10 (for the first few seats on each flight) and sliding to a max of $49 (as occupancy approached capacity). But they flew their frugal passengers to decommissioned military airports, located safe distances from major urban areas. So a passenger could fly from Columbus to "Seattle" for 1000 pennies (or a roll of quarters). When the plane landed in Bellingham — 99 miles north of the airport in Seattle — the passenger would be offered a "free" shuttle ride to the original destination.

Because I was booking the flight just minutes before takeoff, I had to pay full freight. I didn't mind. I'd just paid that much for a cab. I also didn't mind that the flight to Boston would actually deliver my bike and me not in Boston or even in the Commonwealth of Massachusetts but in Portsmouth, in the State of New Hampshire, 56 miles north of Boston's Logan Airport. I was headed to Maine, so landing in Portsmouth was fine by me.

An hour and a half after takeoff we start the descent. I study the lay of the land, making a mental note of the general direction of three bridges that span the Piscataqua River and so connect Portsmouth, New Hampshire with Kittery, Maine. With that sketchy cognitive map and my penchant for bushwhacking, I'm ready for my bike trip — except for one unresolved trivial detail.

We deplane on the tarmac and get herded to the terminal building. In keeping with its status as a former Air Force base, the building's no more elaborate than a box of cinder blocks. Once inside, I check out the scene. There's a tiny counter for rental cars, two coin-op machines, and a single conveyor belt for luggage.

While the baggage handlers are mangling our stuff, I begin making myself conspicuous. With a full beard, I start casing the joint, searching corridors, opening doors, all the while talking to myself under video surveillance. I'm not saying "Praise be to Allah." I'm not ranting about infidels of The West. I'm not using terms like jihad or fatwa. I'm not wearing a Bin Laden T-shirt. And yet I'm keenly aware my behavior could raise suspicion.

Why was I drawing attention to myself? I was simply looking for a locker or a storage room where I might be able to stash my bike bag while touring around Maine for a couple of weeks. (I'd chosen a bag rather than a rigid bombproof box figuring a bag would be more readily storable.) Not surprisingly, I found nothing promising.

Suddenly, the conveyor belt started moving and the first piece of luggage to appear was my big blue bike bag. I grabbed it by its deluxe handles and pulled it along its deluxe wheels out of the terminal building and onto a soft bed of white pine needles.

I unzipped the bag to find my bike intact, spokes and all. I popped on the wheels, attached the brake cables and handlebars, and slid the seat post into place. In minutes, I had a reassembled bike.

It was 9:40 AM, a criterion morning: 72°F, not a cloud in the sky, with a moderate southerly breeze, a tailwind. I was chomping at the bit. I ducked behind the bike bag and did a quick change into my MAMIL costume, presumably while under video surveillance. Barring any SNAFU, like getting busted for public nudity, I'd be 88 miles up the coast, visiting my sister in time for dinner.

BUT I STILL HADN'T FIGURED OUT WHAT TO DO WITH THE BIKE BAG.

I took a risk and left the bike and bag "unattended" while I went back inside to ask for advice. I approached a gaggle of uniformed yet uninformed TSA guys, a triumvirate of beefy burritos of manhood. They looked like brothers, all in their 30s and all sporting the same compensatory mustache. I mentioned my dilemma. I hinted it would be ideal if I could store the bag at the airport for a couple of weeks. One of the triplets rolled his eyes for the comedic benefit of his cronies and said, "We don't babysit your luggage, dude."

"No, of course not," I said. "Sorry to bother you. I'll figure something out."

They were still laughing as I wandered back outside to weigh my options. I was laughing too, not with but at the clonal thinkers with matching mustaches.

Let's see, what to do, what to do. I considered several possibilities.

Plan A: I could discard the bag, but it was new and worth $400 (i.e., 20 round-trip flights to "Seattle"). There's no way I was going to toss it. Besides, that could raise suspicion. Just my luck, I'd get nabbed for illegal dumping. Assuming I got charged with a misdemeanor,

I'd be incarcerated for no more than 12 months, but the fine could be substantial. Not worth the risk.

Plan B: I could hide it in the forest nearby and hope for the best. But, again, it was worth $400 and I didn't want to get busted for illegal dumping.

Plan C: I could stash it *temporarily* and pedal to a hotel and make a reservation to stay there on my way back through town and ask them to store it for me. But how could I get the bag to the hotel? I could hire a cab, of course, but I was anxious to return immediately to my carbon footprint-minimizing lifestyle.

Plan D: I could stash it for the hour or so it might take to pedal over to the Greyhound bus station and back — to see whether the lockers there were big enough to accommodate my bag. Then I could schlep it on my back to the bus station. I might even be able to trolley it behind my bike, if I pedaled slowly and the pavement was smooth. Worst-case scenario: I could put my bike back in the bag and walk it over to the bus station, which should take less than an hour. One way or another, this seemed like a pretty good plan.

But I still had to decide where to store the bag for the next hour. Suddenly, I noticed a bike rack next to the entrance to the terminal building. And then, in a flash of brilliance, I convinced myself that locking my bike bag, which was clearly labeled with the word "Bicycle," with my bike lock to the bike rack made perfect sense. After all, what are bike locks for if not partly to lock bike bags to bike racks when the need arises? I would hide it in plain sight. What an elegant solution! It all seemed permissible, if not fully legitimate.

Meanwhile, I was not oblivious to the possibility, however remote, that the mustache men might find fault with this rationale. I'd heard about 9/11 ad nauseam. (I first learned about it while pedaling through traffic with passing cars blasting their radios.) And I'd been exposed to those incessant announcements in airports that unattended luggage will be confiscated. (Over the years, I'd heard this announcement and its variants about 3,825 times, in 13 languages, all over the world.) I'd been warned, incessantly. But I'd never heard an announcement specifying dos and don'ts regarding bike bags per se.

I rationalized that I wasn't really leaving my baggage unattended. I was locking it *outside*, to a bike rack that wasn't even touching the building. It was a good human body length away, a reasonably safe distance, I thought.

Even though it seemed unlikely anyone would even notice the bag, I left the luggage tag with my contact info dangling for anyone to see. I even left the bag partly unzipped so any curious mustache guy could readily inspect the contents. And then off I sped, just for an hour or so.

I headed in the general direction of the bridges, toward Maine. This proved to be easier said than done. I did a few miles of extraneous warm-up pedaling, trying one road after another. Eventually, I happened upon a decrepit bike path. It was cracked with weeds growing in profusion, but I figured it would lead me downtown. Sure enough, a few minutes later I arrived. And then I spotted one of the bridges. Impulsivity is my middle name and the next thing I knew I was sprinting across the bridge, entering the State of Maine at 30 mph, 5 mph over the posted speed limit.

I hit the brakes to reduce the risk of getting hassled by an overzealous local cop. (I seem to get in a lot of trouble on bridges. Apparently you're supposed to ride in an official shuttle vehicle and not sprint into a nation state on your own pedal power. Whatever.)

No blue lights flashed as I "banged a right" (as Mainers say) onto old US Route 1A, the scenic coastal route. I flew northward, aided by a strong tailwind and my own manic energy. I was so glad to be back in my home state, the self-proclaimed utopia where signs on the highway brag: "MAINE: The Way Life Should Be." A wave of euphoria came over me. I pedaled on, secure in the notion that all was right with the world.

Forty minutes later, I arrived in historic York, just a dozen miles from the bridge. This quaint village — first "settled" by interlopers from across the pond circa 1624 — is so historic that practically the entire place, 1700 acres' worth, is designated as a Historic Place on the U.S. National Historic Register.

I pulled into the "Bagel Basket," which — how apropos — is situated in a historic house. I went in and got in line behind a few fellow citizens of the summer complaint variety (i.e., affluent folks from unsavory places like Massachusetts and Connecticut). A little eavesdropping and I soon discovered these humans were all locals. I was blown away by the less-than-overwhelming diversity of the town, a culture shock I experience every time I return to Maine, where nearly every town remains in a virtual tie for The Whitest Place on Earth.

I ordered a four-shot cappuccino and a sun-dried tomato bagel with chive cream cheese. I found a shady spot out front and settled in for brunch. It was a perfect start to a perfect day, the first day of my own private

Tour of Maine. How could anything go wrong? No acts of God would intervene. Not today. No way.

I sat for a few minutes pondering the history of York, the British invasion, the systematic assimilation/annihilation of the Abenaki, the fact that Mark Twain used this village as a summer writing retreat. I was wondering whether Twain wrote "The Taming of the Bicycle" here and why immigration has been so sluggish, when something broke my reverie.

It was a helicopter!

How bizarre! I immediately realized it must be an air ambulance returning to the hospital across the street. But it didn't land. It circled the neighborhood and still didn't land. It kept circling.

How rude! I thought, "I bet Mark Twain never had to put up with a racket like this."

> The scene reminded me of my years as a grad student living in a lively part of Columbus. It was a not-yet-gentrified neighborhood with drive-by shootings, drug-dealing, hookers performing $10 tricks behind White Castle, homeless guys who camped around the Golden Goat cans-for-quarters machine and left used condoms in the back of my vehicle and lined up to donate blood-for-cash every morning. Nightly, a police helicopter circled overhead for hours shining its beam and creating the illusion that everything was marginally under control. But, hey, the rent was cheap.

But a circling helicopter here? It didn't fit. I might have been clueless, but give me a little credit: at least I noticed the incongruity. I recognized the helicopter was totally out of place in idyllic York, where the homeless population was nearly one, the crime rate was negligible, and the local authorities spent their time eating bagels rather than donuts — when they weren't retrieving white kittens from historic trees along the historic streets.

The most plausible explanation, I thought, was that this was York's first ever helicopter-based manhunt and the culprit must be some homicidal knucklehead from out of state who'd gone postal and was now fleeing. I scanned the area searching for the armed fugitive about to get his comeuppance. I imagined the authorities would be taking this guy out any minute now.

As the helicopter continued circling, I started to get a creeping sense that I was overlooking something crucial. But to crack this case, it looked like I would need one of those Eureka moments.

At this point, **I checked my phone.**

Oh no! I'd missed eight calls from the same unfamiliar number. This couldn't be good. Ordinarily, I ignored all missed calls, but I decided not to ignore *these* calls. I hit the call button: it was some ferocious guy with TSA or Homeland Security. Holy crap! He skipped the pleasantries and launched straight into bellowing. He was furious, to put it mildly. My head started spinning. I felt a full-blown panic attack coming on.

He said something about having called in the *bomb squad*!

I was immediately contrite. I apologized profusely. All I could think was:

I'm going to Guantanamo — for 12 years.

The guy kept yelling: "Why?! Why would you do such a stupid thing?! We not only had to call in the bomb squad, we also had to evacuate the airport. We had to divert a flight. All because of your stupid stunt! What's wrong with you?!"

These were not rhetorical questions. I had some explaining to do. I tried to reassure him that while I do irrational things virtually every day, I'm harmless.

He said, "We know. In the time it took for you to get your head out of your ass and call us back, we ran a background check. And we don't do a Google search, if you know what I mean. We know everything. We know where you live, what you do for a living. We know everything there is to know, including that recent speech on the statehouse lawn. We've already determined that you're basically harmless."

I didn't think it was in my best interest to mention that I was in the early stages of Huntington's disease, which improves one's capacity for irrational decision-making. But they probably knew that too. Surely, they had a team of their best and brightest reading through every e-mail and text message I'd ever sent or received. Big Brother was now watching.

"And why the hell didn't you answer your phone? You left your number, but then you went silent!"

I refrained from mentioning that it's unsafe to pedal-and-talk and that I didn't hear my phone because it was in a pannier. I just kept apologizing.

We kept "chatting" and when his tone eventually softened, I asked, "Does this helicopter circling right over my head have anything to do with this incident?"

"What do you think?!" he bellowed. "And what are you doing now? Why did you stop there?"

"Uh, I'm having a bagel," I said sheepishly. (To my credit, I didn't say I was "having brunch.")

This *really* pissed him off, disproportionately, I thought. You too may think he overreacted, but read on. I haven't even shared the worst part of the story yet.

Consider it from his perspective. A Ted Kaczynski look-alike shows up at the airport. He cases the joint, leaves a putative bomb, and then sprints away on a bicycle. But that's when it gets interesting. Based on eight triangulations of his cell phone signal, the bicycle-bomber then sprinted up the coast straight toward the Bush presidential compound in Kennebunkport — where Dubya was scheduled to arrive the next day! (This was back when he still visited Kennebunkport, his dad's "Camp David," and hadn't yet devoted himself to riding his mountain bike and listening to country music on his iPod during frequent junkets on the ranch in Crawford, Texas.) When I returned the call, I was 22 miles from the compound. I'd be arriving in just over an hour at the easily penetrable checkpoint to Walker's Point, where the compound sits in plain view, perched conspicuously on the Atlantic Ocean (a la Guantanamo). No wonder the guy was mad.

But was he mad enough to have me taken out? Was there a red laser dot pointed at my helmet by the sniper in the helicopter circling above?

Gradually, he softened again. He even offered to let me retrieve the tools that came with the bike bag. The bomb squad had salvaged these odds and ends after blowing up the bike bag, and despite my egregious act, I would be allowed to reclaim my property. He gave me an address where I could pick up these items. (This seemed like a transparent way of getting me to turn myself in.)

At this point, I goofed. I pissed him off again, this time by asking about the bag. He got angry and said I obviously still didn't appreciate the gravity of what I'd done and that the bag had been blown up by the bomb squad. And then I made matters even worse. I said something along the lines of: "I know it was blown up, and it's probably in really bad shape, but maybe I could salvage it. Maybe I could patch it with duct tape and get some more use out of it."

This infuriated him. He re-emphasized that the bomb squad had blown up my bike bag. He said there was nothing recognizable left of it. That every last bit of material that had once been the bag was now dust, powder. That there was nothing left to patch. There was no bag! Period!

I daydreamed: So much for the manufacturer's warranty and hyping of the virtually indestructible, specially reinforced ripstop fabric. Stronger than a parachute? Please.

I apologized yet again. I thanked him for his patience. I thought about GITMO. I wondered whether I'd be allowed to ride a bicycle in my cell.

Eventually, with no further admonishment, he let me go.

The interrogation was over. As far as I could tell, I was not to be apprehended or incarcerated. My injudicious acts had surely triggered Homeland Security to elevate the threat-level to Orange or even Red. And now I was apparently wasting the guy's time, annoying him with excessive apologies. I was free to go, on my own recognizance, and I didn't even have to pay a fine? Go figure.

Relieved, I hopped on my bike and pedaled northward, up the coast. But with a renewed appreciation for the virtue of exquisitely rational cognizing, I prudently chose US Route 1, not 1A, and thereby skirted around Kennebunkport. I didn't want to press my luck.

Hours later, I arrived at my sister's place and regaled her with my latest you-won't-believe-what-I've-done-now tale. She laughed herself silly and said, "That story would have been even better if the evening news showed footage of you sitting there eating a bagel with a laser dot dancing around on your helmet, especially if they showed your face when you made the phone call. You could have gone viral."

During the night she left a note for me on the kitchen table. It said, "I can't sleep. I'm pretty sure I heard a helicopter. They must know I'm 'harboring' you. Sorry, but I'm afraid I must ask you to leave ASAP. P.S. Just kidding, you can stay till they take you away."

I left after breakfast and spent the next couple weeks visiting my friend in need and pedaling around Maine dogged by the fear that the authorities were monitoring me. I feared they were going to drop out of the sky and nab me when I least expected it. Was Big Brother now watching my every move? What do they say, it's only paranoia if it's untrue?

And I spent lots of pedaling time cogitating over the mystery of why they simply let me go in the first place. And why was there no digital footprint. Why did they keep the incident a secret?

Maybe they were embarrassed. Is that why they didn't even take me into custody for "questioning?" Is that why they didn't feed my story to the media? They could have portrayed me as even more clueless than those fools who try to board planes with their favorite pocket knife or cigarette lighter.

Or maybe they treated my unattended bag as an excuse to run an impromptu bomb squad drill. If so, I've apparently done my small part to make air travel safer in this post-9/11 world. You're welcome America!

~

Fast forward two weeks:

I returned to the scene of the crime, but without my bike, which I'd judiciously sent back to Ohio via UPS. That's right, I went back to Portsmouth International Airport, but not to retrieve my tools and not because it was the most sensible way to get back to Columbus. No, I boldly returned to the scene out of perverse curiosity, for two reasons. First, I was anxious to find out whether I was now on the Terrorist Watch List or the No Fly List. At best, I thought they'd let me fly after subjecting me to an interrogation and a body cavity search. And I figured they'd treat me to these indignities for the rest of my life. So, I was pleasantly surprised when the security folks waved me right on through. They didn't even make eye contact. Who's clueless now?

The second reason I returned to the scene of the crime was to inspect my handiwork. Mainly, I wanted to see the crater left behind when the bomb squad blew my bike bag to smithereens. I arrived on foot, having walked from downtown Portsmouth, as if to draw even more attention to myself. (Despite the fact that we're the only obligately bipedal primate species, walking any appreciable distance is even more suspicious than pedaling.) As I approached the entrance, I could see that the bike rack was MIA, but the ground was pristine. There was no evidence of an explosion. No crater. No charred vegetation. Nothing.

I was baffled. I couldn't figure out why the bombing of my bike bag hadn't left even a trace of evidence.

Not surprisingly, when I told this story back at the university, one of my colleagues helped me see the colossal flaw in my logic. He said, "No offense, Tom, but why would you look for evidence of an explosion at the place where you left the bomb decoy? What do you think the bomb squad does? Do you really think their job is to aid terrorists by detonating their bombs where they leave them and thereby blow up the intended target? Do you really think they would blow up the airport *for* you?"

"No, no, of course not, now that you put it like that. I don't know what I was thinking, obviously. But tell me, what *did* they do? How did they blow up the bike bag?"

This guy's a walking Wikipedia. He knows just about everything there is to know, plus lots of other stuff. He's a know-it-all's know-it-all and I mean that in a good way. So he offered a detailed description along the lines of:

The bomb squad probably used a robot to do an initial inspection. Then they presumably used a remote-controlled crane to put the entire bike rack with the bike bag and the locked-up bikes into a containment vessel, maybe a big hemispheric chamber on a flatbed. Then they probably transported the contents to a bombing range. And only then, when the bomb was nowhere near the airport, they would have blown it up, bike bag, bike rack, and bikes.

Then he asked, "By the way, how many bikes were locked to the rack?"

At this point, my regret shifted. Naturally, I still feel bad about the bomb scare. I feel bad that I singlehandedly activated the Homeland Security apparatus. I feel bad that I caused an airport evacuation and a flight diversion. I feel bad that I ran up a tab of hundreds of thousands of U.S. dollars, at the taxpayers' expense. But what I feel worst about is that I caused the destruction of two bicycles. For that crime alone, I should have been put on a watch list, the Bicycle Security Watch List. And yet, I apparently didn't even make it onto Homeland Security's Terrorist Watch List or even their Clueless Bearded Bastard Watch List. Go figure.

Addenda

I've returned several times to the bagel shop, never to the airport. I've never again used a fancy bike bag. (To this day, I maintain a strong preference for recyclable *cardboard* bike-boxes.) And I've never again triggered mobilizations of bomb squads, evacuations of airports, or diversions of flights.

Admittedly, I've had some self-imposed difficulties when crossing international borders. Hint: When they ask you where you live, don't say "Earth." Don't brag about your peripatetic lifestyle, about being an inveterate velophiliac, a cyclonomad. Don't tell them you've been traveling nearly continuously for several years and have no fixed address. They do *not* want to hear this. They will not be amused or impressed. They will detain you for hours, until you've answered all of their questions in ways they deem acceptable.

While I've made some minor blunders and attracted the wrong kind of attention on occasion, never again has a helicopter circled overhead. Never again have I been the target of a man hunt. Never again have I been mistaken for a would-be presidential assassin, terrorist, traitor, fugitive, or even run-of-the-mill anarchic bomber with anti-American tendencies. But the next divorce or diagnosis or death in my family or circle of friends can't be too far off, so stay tuned.

And don't stray from your luggage.

~~~

In the aftermath of the bombing at the 2013 running of the Boston Marathon, I pledge to be as benign as possible. And I hereby retract all glib remarks. *Mea culpa.*

Upon further reflection, I must share my evolutionarily inspired take on the bomb scare I caused 66 cycling miles from the finish line of the Boston Marathon. The defense system at the airport resembles the evolved defense system of the human body, which operates like a smoke detector. Your body often perceives even a slight insult as a potentially fatal raid and launches what feels like an all-or-none defense — with uncontrollable coughing, explosive spewing from the digestive track, high fever, debilitating weakness and fatigue. Why does your body's natural defense system react in such an extreme way?

This apparent paradox is easily resolved if you think about an actual smoke detector. Its purpose is to save your life by warning against a potentially deadly house fire and to do so without fail. Because the cost of failing to detect a real fire is nothing short of catastrophic, the gadget is designed to overreact when you scorch toast. As far as the smoke detector is concerned, where there's smoke there's fire. In signal-detection jargon, we're okay with the fact that nearly every blasting of our ear drums turns out to have been yet another false positive. That annoyance we accept as a small price to pay for protection against the rare but deadly house fire.

By extension, TSA's seemingly extreme overreaction is precisely what we'd expect. In defense of their evolutionarily relevant defense system, the cost of failing to detect a real bomb at an airport (i.e., mayhem and terror) typically vastly exceeds the cost of a false positive (i.e., a big pile of cash). And when the cost of failing to detect a real bomb exceeds the cost of calling in the bomb squad, don't we expect false positives to be prevalent? (If I had TSA's parameter estimates, I could solve the underlying equations and predict false positives for a whole suite of plausible scenarios.) Suffice it to say, if you leave a bike bag, you should expect to mobilize TSA's defense force and trigger an all-or-none response, like a massive allergic reaction.

With this perspective permeating my every thought for decades, I should've known better. I shouldn't have been so cavalier as to set off the smoke detector and then flee the scene. And the truth is: I did know better. Leading up to the moment when I "temporarily" locked the bag to the rack, I wondered whether TSA had yet begun applying evolutionary game theory — like my colleagues and I would have done — to the problem of optimal allocation of limited resources in the context of airport security. Simply put, an optimized defense system would randomize *sensu stricto* patrolling and monitoring, making it truly unpredictable and hence hard to cheat.

My hunch was that Bubba and his clones weren't using game theoretic algorithms to tailor their defense system and thereby minimize the risk presented by bike-bag bombers and other evil-doers. I suspected they were using a haphazard approach. I imagined they were understaffed. I figured security at this miniature airport would be lax compared with, say, LAX or Chicago O'Hare, major airports where I wouldn't dream of leaving a decoy bomb for even a nanosecond. Basically, I thought I'd get away with it.

Once again, I apologize.

🚲 🚲 🚲 🚲 🚲

Chapter 2

Marry Your Bike

And Live Happily Ever After

To marry your bike — truly, madly, deeply — you must divorce your car. But I warn you: Divorcing your car can be like quitting smoking. Like the smoker who jokes about how easy it is to quit — so easy that she's successfully done so 47 times — I was so good at divorcing my car that I got remarried repeatedly. I was one of the Petroleum People and a serial monogamist to boot.

Let's see, I divorced my first car, a Plymouth Duster, back in the 70s. That marriage was a mistake. I was too young, 16, and she was too old. I had to start her using a screw driver to arc across her alternator bolts, pump her brake pedal furiously to avoid rear-end collisions, refill her leaky radiator at every opportunity, and stay under 48 mph to keep her front end from shimmying. Plus, she had to have a lot of work done at the body shop. Claiming irreconcilable differences, I gave that bucket of bolts to my sister in favor of pedaling and hitchhiking. Claiming failure to consummate, my sister kicked her to the curb a week later.

Next, I divorced a Subaru Something-or-Other, which I owned and operated for just a few weeks while running a fish hatchery and doing marine biology research in Maine. That was the first in a series of utilitarian car-marriages. She was a research vehicle. Our brief coupling ended in annulment, when I swapped her with my own father for a canoe paddle and a pair of snowshoes. (For the compulsive score-keepers among you, yes, that makes two creepily nepotistic/incestuous splits in a row.)

A year later, I got hitched to a little Toyota pickup so I could drive to Alaska to do my PhD research. Abandonment led to another annulment. I left that vehicle parked curbside for months, until the police, unbeknownst to me, impounded her and then auctioned her off.

Years later, I got hitched to a little Nissan pickup. That was a wildly successful marriage. I used her to transport my mountain bike to and from Alaska for several years. But she made me a widower. I almost lost her initially when a fellow citizen who sold homemade pharmaceuticals filled her full of lead. I kid you not, to punish me for monopolizing a coveted parking space, he shot out her radiator from point blank range. A year later, I did lose her, in a fatal crash, courtesy of a driver who made an injudicious left turn in the face of oncoming traffic. I unceremoniously buried her compacted remains in a landfill.

Okay, that's more than enough ancient history about my exes. This is supposed to be the happily-ever-after story of my final car-divorce and simultaneous bike-wedding.

Here goes:

After decades of failed divorces, I got car-married for the last time, nearly 20 years ago. What possessed me to do it? Well, this decision was precipitated by precipitation. You see, I bought a Nissan Pathfinder with 4-wheel drive capability to serve as my research vehicle because I'd landed a faculty position at Michigan

Technological University in the oh-so-snowy Upper Peninsula of Michigan, on the shore of Lake Superior, 550 miles north of Detroit.

I'd heard all about the region's infamous lake-effect snows, which make Buffalo and Syracuse look about as snowy as Orlando and Miami. And yet I remained overconfident. Because I'd grown up in Maine and spent a decade in Alaska, I thought I knew a thing or two about driving in snow. I was wrong. Even with chains on the tires and a shovel onboard, I was unprepared.

I got mired in a massive drift in the first blizzard and had to abandon the vehicle for two days. My one-story house got entombed, with me inside. I tunneled my way out a window on the leeward side of the house when the blizzard stopped and snowshoed down the road to dig out my vehicle. It was completely buried. Two pre-teen sisters of Finnish descent took pity on me. They brought me coffee and cookies and helped me shovel. Eventually, we unearthed the vehicle and I drove off, none the wiser.

I now realize I could have saved myself a lot of trouble by pedaling. My not-yet-invented winter bike, the Pugsley, has 4-inch-wide knobby tires. It's the Hummer of bicycles. If I'd had that bike at the time, I could have simply pedaled to campus and spent the day doing science. Instead, I squandered the day shoveling.

Winter bikes weren't commercially available yet. When they did become available a few years later, an intrepid Michigan Tech undergrad was photographed pedaling through a snowstorm. It was the first day of deer-hunting season and he'd had success. But as a hardcore cyclist, he didn't follow the standard protocol. He didn't tie the deer carcass to the top of a truck and parade around town. Instead, he showed off his manly prize by pedaling around campus with the carcass draped around his neck.

The snow kept coming. I counted 48 consecutive snowy days. And then I lost interest. By the end of the winter, in late April, we'd been treated to nearly 27.4 feet total accumulation. I can vouch for the claim that the Michigan Tech campus gets more snow than any other university campus in the USA, including the University of Alaska campuses in Anchorage, Fairbanks, and Juneau. So now you know why Michigan Tech boasts an on-campus downhill ski slope but no baseball or softball program.

Flash forward to April 22, 2013: Speaking of bicycling and Michigan Tech University, you've probably heard the big news? The august body known as the League of American Bicyclists has just added Michigan Tech to its list of Bicycle Friendly Universities, making it the 58th such honoree scattered among 30 states. Not showing off, Michigan Tech was awarded this honor not at the Diamond or Platinum or Gold or even Silver level, but rather at the least prestigious Bronze level. Apparently, in the area of bike friendliness, Michigan Tech still has some improving to do.

The next winter was a dud. We got just 14.6 feet of snow. That was a major letdown, so much so that I didn't even stay for a third winter. Instead, I accepted a tenure-track offer at Ohio State University and moved back to the unsnowy southern flatlands, where I'd immediately resume living on my bike. But first I had to replace it because 17 minutes after arriving on the OSU campus, my bike was stolen. I phoned the campus police and told my story. The dispatcher laughed and said, "Welcome to Ohio State!"

I asked him to guesstimate how long it might take to recover my bike. He laughed again. I asked how long it had been since the campus police last returned a stolen bike. He said he didn't know, but he'd only been in that job for 20 years. I ran straight over to a nearby bike shop and, minutes later, pedaled back to the Pathfinder. Surprisingly, it was still there. It hadn't been stolen or even vandalized, but someone had placed a parking ticket under a windshield wiper — on a Sunday no less. Welcome to Ohio State!

I didn't divorce the Pathfinder right away because I continued to use it as a research vehicle in Ontario, where it snows aplenty. But I did begin plotting my divorce, as the final step in my green-lifestyle conversion. I'd already installed photovoltaic panels on my roof, begun growing much of my own food and heating the house with a corn-pellet stove. I was happily homesteading in plain sight, off the grid in the middle of the city. But I also had that damn vehicle parked in the driveway. It was an eyesore and sent all the wrong messages. It had to go. Besides, I was living on my bike and only using the vehicle once a year for a month-long field season in Ontario.

One day in May, I threw my mountain bike into the back of the vehicle and drove to the nearest office of Volunteers in Service to America (VISTA). I walked in and asked the woman working there, "Do you accept vehicle donations?"

"Sure do," she said, "Fill out this form and we'll auction off your car and use the money to support our programs."

Naturally, I was uncomfortable with the fact that my vehicle would remain in circulation. I wanted to put a bullet through her radiator and bury her carcass in the backyard. But I consoled myself that the proceeds would go to a good cause and that my vehicle would be off the road in a few years.

A few minutes later, I handed her the completed form and the title. She thanked me and handed me a receipt, which I would use months later — like a money-grubbing fool — as evidence of my tax-deductible donation.

Then she asked, "Don't you need a ride home?"

"No thanks, I brought my bicycle."

"Are you sure? It's too dangerous to bike around here."

"Yeah, I'm sure. I bike everywhere. I'll be OK."

> This was my standard line, but whenever I uttered it I would instantly recall episodes when I regretted my bold approach. Once I got caught in the middle of a wild scene, where four members of a gang started beating an old man and then turned their attention to me when I tried to intervene. They chased me and threw tennis ball-sized rocks at me. I escaped unscathed. Badly shaken and yet undeterred, I had another close call later that same night. I escaped three would-be muggers on a bridge. In all such cases, I was emboldened by my ability to escape by simply sprinting away on two wheels. I felt invulnerable. I still do, more or less.

So, in less time than it would have taken to butcher the National Anthem, I'd completed the transaction. But then as I was starting to pedal off, the VISTA woman came running after me. She wanted me to reconsider. She said, "Are you sure about this? I just looked up the Blue Book value. It's worth over $16,000!"

Maybe she wanted to avoid the hassle of my getting donor's remorse and then returning to reclaim my vehicle. She apparently thought my act of generosity was excessive. Maybe she thought I was unstable. Maybe she thought I should gift the vehicle to her personally. I don't know what she was thinking, but I assured her I knew what I was doing and that she was doing me a big favor. And then, never looking back, I pedaled off.

Good riddance! No more gas, brake, or clutch pedals for me. I would be a permanent purist, pushing only pedals of the self-propulsion variety.

~

I went through that final car divorce over a decade ago. And I've never for one second regretted my choice. I've never missed having a vehicle or even a driver's license. I have a license to pedal. And I'm lucky enough to be able-bodied and retired as well. For me, that makes every day a Car Free Day. Mine is a Car Free Life. And it's a celebratory one at that.

I'm happily married to my bicycle partly because the cause is just. I didn't adopt this lifestyle to show off, to create opportunities to proselytize. I did it for my own ethical reasons. I did it to compensate for decades' worth of accumulated green guilt. As someone once said, to be an ecologist is to live alone in a world of wounds. I knew all too well that I was floating face down in my own hypocrisy. I knew the connection between our carbon footprint and the impending global extinction crisis. Ecologists widely agree that we're on the verge of driving most species to extinction. This is nothing short of a biotic holocaust and we're the perpetrators. First, we appropriated natural ecosystems worldwide. Then, we caused global warming. The combined effect will be devastating, especially if we refuse to hold ourselves accountable and do something epic about it.

One thing we could do is eliminate gasoline subsidies. The American addiction to gasoline is aided and abetted by these government handouts. We enable each other's addiction by using our tax dollars to keep the price artificially low.

The *real* price of a gallon of gasoline vastly exceeds what Car People pay at the pump. The enormous discount is covered by subsidies, which deceive us into thinking that gasoline is virtually free. Imagine how expensive it would be if we paid *at the pump* the hidden costs of: our permanent military presence in the Persian Gulf, road construction and maintenance, each other's hospital stays, and pollution abatement including putting the global warming genie back in the bottle. Imagine the astronomical price tag on that last line item, if it even proves to be doable.

Americans are notorious for *hating* government handouts — unless of course they benefit from them personally. And yet how many motorists would like to pay $30 or more per gallon of gasoline? And how many car-divorces would ensue?

> Caveat: Cycling isn't "free" or innocent. Our reliance on the petrochemical industry is imbedded in

cycling. While my bicycle lacks a gas tank, indirectly it's a real gas guzzler. Think of the mining of the raw materials, the manufacturing and transport of the frame and parts, the maintenance of my sweet ride. It's all oil-dependent. What's more, even the operation of it, the pedaling, has a carbon footprint. Think of all the extra pizza I consume to fuel my excessive pedaling. And think of all the carbon-spewing that underlies my refueling stops.

Imagine the carbon footprint of a transcontinental tour. If you luxuriate along the way — staying in motels, eating in restaurants, taking your own sweet time — your cycling footprint could conceivably be bigger than, gulp, an RVer's.

Tired of wallowing in my own green guilt, I went cold turkey. I quit, once and for all. No more car ownership for me. Hell, I go years at a time without even accepting a ride in a gas-powered vehicle. The most recent instance of this happened when I got scraped off the pavement and put in an ambulance after getting smucked by a truck. But that's another story.

~~~

While living on my bike, I don't wear this underlying rationale on my sleeve. Most folks apparently assume I'm riding for health or financial reasons. They usually say, "Well, that's a great way to stay in shape" or "You must save a lot of money on gas." I usually play along.
This sort of attention routinely catches me off guard. While people I meet along the way almost always think my carfree lifestyle is unusual, I don't see it that way. I see it from a global perspective and so tend to think of myself as mainstream. The majority of people on Earth, like me, are carfree. Half of all people have less than $5

US per day in purchase power, so they're not driving anywhere. They walk, like our ancestors did. And if they're really lucky, they "cheat" by pedaling.

My car-free lifestyle also reflects the historical reality of humans. Imagine modern human history, about 250,000 years, condensed into a day. We got cars within the last minute. They're a modern contrivance — like the bicycle — and in no way define us.

From this perspective, it's not preposterous that someone like me would choose this lifestyle. It's not even improbable. We The Carfree People are in the majority. And we modern humans have been carfree for 99.95% of our history. On a macro scale, in both space and time, I'm hardly an outlier. I couldn't be more ordinary.

What's unusual, admittedly, is that I've chosen to live on a bike even though I have the financial wherewithal to drive a new luxury automobile. I'm not a homeless drifter (not that there's anything wrong with that). I'm an unencumbered, privileged adventurer with an incurable case of wanderlust. I'm independently wealthy, partly because I no longer spend $100,000 per decade to own, operate, maintain, and insure an automobile. I'm free to pedal and even free of the financial burden. But that's just a side bonus. My main motive was to live in an environmentally ethical way.

As a most welcome byproduct, I get to live like a 12-year-old. And I don't even have to get up at 4:45 AM to deliver newspapers, which is good because I also don't have a curfew or a regular bedtime. Of course, there isn't much trout-fishing or baseball-playing, but it still feels like those carefree, carfree halcyon days as a tweenager, when I traveled everywhere by bicycle.

I'm living the dream. And I have every intention of staying married to my bicycle, happily ever after, till death do us part — until I get smucked by another truck.

Disclaimer

Like virtually every serious cyclist you've ever known, I'm not strictly monogamous. Admittedly, I've been a serial monogamist, getting remarried to a bicycle within minutes of the most recent widowing (e.g., when my bike gets demolished by a head-on collision or "borrowed" by a disreputable teenager with bolt cutters). Typically, I've been a bigamist, married simultaneously to an all-purpose commuting/touring bike and to a winter/mountain bike. Occasionally, I've been polygynous, when having an affair with a third bike. Rarely, I've dabbled in polyamory and even bike-swapping.

And except for the time I mailed my bike from Maine to Georgia and then walked the Appalachian Trail to reunite, I've never been celibate. Even then, I was in a committed long-distance relationship. And I had no meaningless bike flings along the way. None.

These days, while my winter bike hangs in storage in my cabin in Canada, I'm happily married to a Surly Long Haul Trucker. And I have the paper to prove it!

🚲 🚲 🚲 🚲 🚲

Marriage Certificate

This is to Certify that

__Tom Waite__ AND _Surly Long Haul Trucker_
Passenger/Motor   Conveyance Sublime

Were Wed

By: Lee Huston, Owner/Velophile/Wrench/Mensch

At: Center Street Bikes, Brunswick, Maine, USA

Chapter 3

Of Course the Danes are Happy: They Pedal!

Or Do They Pedal Because They're Happy?

"[The bicycle] is proof that God loves us and wants us to be happy."

> — Adaptation of Ben Franklin's quip about beer, which he presumably made while under the influence of beer

"But they're SOCIALISTS! Of course they're happy, they have everything given to them. It's not right. Only rich people deserve to be happy. If we allow common people to be happy then what good will it be to be wealthy? People will just do what they want without doing things for rich people. Society will crumble."

> — Comment on Rachel Maddow's blog posted on *The HuffPost Social News*

The Danes have achieved global domination in two key areas, happiness and pedaling. Ever since the inception of Global Happiness Surveys in 1973, they've blown away the competition. And their habit of commuting by bicycle is likewise world class. On the global stage, these ordinarily reserved Scandinavians are really hogging the limelight.

For stereotypical Yanks, these facts raise all kinds of uncomfortable questions. For starters, they'd like to know:

- Who are these Danes and where are they from?
- How can they be happy when they're not even free?
- Where do they get off outcompeting the U.S. of A. in *anything*?
- Don't they know *money* buys happiness?

And the most uncomfortable question of all: **Where does the USA rank in the happiness surveys?**

Surely, we're Silver or Bronze Medalists, right? Not quite. Turns out, we're way down the list. And before you go blaming our lousy scores on some conspiracy, yet another manifestation of pandemic anti-Americanism, you should know this is *self-reported* happiness. When asked to pick a number between 1 and 10 to indicate how happy we are, we Yanks can't even fake it.

How bad is it?

Well, believe it or not, we really *suck* at happiness. We're #23! That happens to be the glory number to wear on a basketball uniform these days, thanks to Michael Jordan. But in virtually every other context and especially on global lists, we like to be #1. Number 2, by American standards, is wholly unacceptable. If you're American and you finish 2nd, you might as well be a croissant. Anything other than 1st place is considered losing.

Recall (Norwegian-born) Knute Rockne's take: "Winning isn't everything; it's the only thing."

And recall Nancy Kerrigan's meltdown after "winning" the silver medal in figure skating in the 1994 Winter Olympics, in Lillehammer, Norway. She was caught on camera dissing her opponent and then she skipped the closing ceremonies, opting to bolt for a $2 million payola at Disney World, where she was caught dissing the Disney event. (Never mind that the Gold Medalist, Oksana Baiul, gave a transcendent performance.)

Norway, by the way, happens to be one of several northern European countries that kick USA's ass in raw happiness as well as in a new prosperity index that accounts for both wealth and happiness. In the most recent prosperity survey, Norway won Gold, edging out Denmark and Sweden. Neighbors Finland and the Netherlands finished in the top 10. (USA finished 12th, well behind its hat, a.k.a. Canada.) Let's hope Denmark doesn't have a meltdown and start badmouthing its happy neighbors, including the Netherlands, whose folks rival the Danes in cycling (and even take the Gold for bicycles owned per capita, at a whopping 0.99).

While Yanks suck at happiness, we haven't lost our grip on other areas of global domination. Off the top of my head, I'm pretty sure we're still #1 in:

- Aggregate wealth (check)
- Military spending (check)
- Car ownership (check)
- Gun ownership (check)
- Incarceration rate (check)
- External debt (check)
- Carbon footprint (check)
- Mathematics (check)

Just kidding with the last bullet point. As the whole world has known for decades, Americans *suck* at math. (We placed 32nd in a recent survey.)

> Alarmingly, two-thirds of high school graduates these days lack basic skills. Of course, this will be lost on them because they suck at fractions, basic probability statements, decimals, percentages and the like.

Eventually, the news that Yanks suck at math seeped into societal consciousness even *within* the USA. And there's been lots of hand-wringing ever since, especially among educators and politicos. In keeping with our obsession with being #1, we've been tripping over ourselves trying to climb the math ranks. There have been Presidential commissions and task forces and endless studies by academics aimed at getting to the bottom of this crisis. It's become something of a national pastime to fret about it and throw money at it. And yet We the People of Yanklandia continue to get our unmathematical butts kicked by the likes of Liechtenstein, Luxembourg, and of course Denmark, and even France.

The vast majority of Americans seem unfazed. Maybe they're fatigued by all of this bad news. They seem to share Teen Talk Barbie's view that "Math class is hard" and don't seem to give a rat's lower GI tract over our abysmal performance in math. Apparently, they just don't care.

> I'm waiting for the day when results from the first global survey of reading comprehension in *English* are publicized. How many of those postage stamp-sized Euro countries will kick our Anglo butts in *our*

official language? Will Swedes and Finns and Norwegians and Danes outperform us? Yes.

Sucking at math is one thing, but will "real Americans" be so blasé when they realize we also suck at *happiness*? Don't they still believe happiness is the ultimate goal in life, the *raison d'ete*, and the logical outcome of successfully pursuing the American Dream?

Will they see our mediocre happiness scores as a sign that our reign as the world's self-proclaimed Superpower is coming to its inevitable end? Surely, to finish so far down in the happiness ranks will be totally unacceptable, *n'est-ce pas*?

All of which begs the question: what's the point of being *nouveau riche* and having all that stuff — a big screen TV in every room and a personal automobile for each adult and adolescent member of the household — if we're not happy?

And how did it get to this? Have we Yanks been duped, by each other perhaps? Yes, I think so. And because I don't hate math, I feel qualified to share a most inconvenient insight: our 23rd place finish was misleadingly optimistic. Adjusted for wealth, **Yanks are in a virtual tie for the *un*happiest country.**

Take a gander at the graph, which shows the relationship between personal wealth and happiness in the USA and 11 benchmark countries (10 rich countries from Western Europe plus Canada). In geekspeak, regressing happiness on per capita parity purchase power (PPP) reveals that the USA has the 2nd biggest negative residual. Translation: Yanks are the 2nd unhappiest country adjusted for wealth.

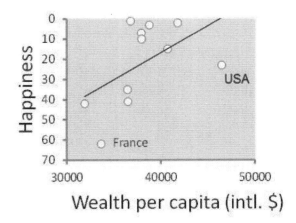

Only the French are more miserable relative to wealth and only slightly so.

> Fittingly, *malaise*, *misérable*, and *morose* are French words. And those are just the *m*-words. Is it any wonder the French have an etiological monopoly on English words connoting unhappiness? How *à propos*!

Why are the French so *misérable*? Isn't it obvious? It's clearly because:

> 1) While they're pedaling fools compared with Yanks, they don't pedal nearly enough.

> 2) They envy other Euros (of the tame and upright ape variety) for having more Euros (of the coin variety).

> 3) They waste too much emotional energy loathing a certain American for dominating the Tour de Lance.

4) They feel remorseful for condescending to American tourists in Paris.

5) They regret denying the American military permission to use their airspace.

That, *mon ami*, is a quintuple whammy (*une poisse quintuple*). Of course, multitudes of literate French will now accuse me of x, y, and z. They'll denigrate me for being a *xénophobe*, a *Yankee*, and a *zélote*. *C'est la vie.*

> Which reminds me: In the world according to Yank comedian, Steve Martin, the problem with the French is they have a different word ... for everything. Strictly speaking, he was wrong, as the examples above show. But he was right that Anglophones should squelch any temptation to speak *en Français*. If you try to order a cheese omelet, you'll butcher it and end up saying you'd like to massage the server's grandmother. But I digress.

Okay, that's more than enough obsessing over the French. *Je m'excuse* (I apologize).

Besides, what inquiring minds really want to know is: how could Americans emulate the Danes and their neighbors to become happy too?

~~~

I see three obvious pathways to improved happiness in the Land of Yanks.

Option A: We could commission endless studies, squandering lots of tax dollars. We could study the problem to death for decades and never accomplish a thing, other than to slide further down the slippery slope.

Option B: We could undergo a hegemonic shift and adopt wholesale the Danes' brand of socialism, with a universal safety net that puts theirs to shame.

Option C: We could just pedal.

This last option isn't as absurd as it sounds considering that daily biking distance (r^2 = 0.33) is a much better predictor of happiness than is PPP (r^2 = 0.04). (The latter statistic means that 96% of variation in self-reported happiness across nation states is explicable by something *other* than personal wealth.) So, just in case there's even a weak causal linkage underlying the correlation between pedaling and happiness, we should probably play it safe and pedal a helluva lot more. On this basis, I tentatively recommend option C.

But would it work? Can we simply pedal our way to happiness? Maybe not, but isn't it worth a try? What's the worst thing that could happen? Our friends from Denmark suggest, pessimistically, that we might become a little less *miserabel* (miserable) and a little less *overvægt* (overweight). I suggest, optimistically, that we could climb the happiness ranks, leapfrogging our way to medal contention in one short decade.

And we unhappy Yanks are perfectly positioned to do so. We already own well over 100 million bicycles. We love to *own* them (currently, at a rate of about 50 full-size bicycles per 100 licensed drivers), though admittedly not as much as we love to own guns (89 per 100 residents) and cars (80 per 100 residents). We just don't like *pedaling* our bicycles, even under ideal conditions.

Adult Yanks mostly use their bikes recreationally. They use them as car-roof ornaments, as status symbols. These Yanks like to honk at me as they speed by, as if to say, "Hey, we're kindred spirits."

My private reaction when I'm not feeling gracious: "You *own* a bike; I *pedal* one. You use your bicycle to accessorize your vehicle; I don't even own a vehicle. What we really have in common: like most American adults, we both own a bike. But, hey, that's a start."

An alarmingly big fraction of the adults I meet in the states tell me they used to ride a bike, but it now has a flat tire. Apparently, I'm just supposed to nod, to acknowledge their bad luck.

Yanks also love to buy little bicycles for their children (who would sue otherwise), but then they don't let them ride them to school. And they don't bother fixing flat tires. And so the children become car addicts at an early age.

To emulate the Danes, we Yanks need to embrace the notion that the bicycle is a legitimate mode of transportation rather than a piece of recreational equipment or car-bling or a child's toy or the last resort of the homeless.

We need to use bikes for transportation, like the Danes and like handfuls of fellow Americans who happen to live amid the intelligentsia in towns like Palo Alto, Berkeley, Davis, Eugene, Portland, Seattle, and Bellingham.

I was raised in a little town in a vacuum of intelligentsia, where the grand total of adults commuting by bicycle was precisely zero. Last summer, I pedaled cross-country and reassessed the bike-commuting community in my hometown. It didn't take long to do a complete census.

I could be in one of those pedaling paradises now, pecking away at this keyboard. Instead, I find myself temporarily holed up in Modesto, California, where I'm jotting down these tales and plotting to travel far and wide again soon. For now, this place will suffice, even though the cycling community consists mainly of 379 homeless guys ... and me.

Overall, USA's in a virtual tie for last place in bicycle commuting (~0.5% of trips). A Yank's well over 100 times more likely to drive than pedal to work or school.

And the central tendencies in per capita daily bicycle-commuting distance will make you shake your head:

- Median (middle) = 0 nanometers
- Mode (most common) = 0 nanometers
- Mean (average) = roughly twice or thrice the length of a bicycle

Those facts should suffice to convince any skeptic. But to hammer home the point that Yanks hate to commute by bicycle, I offer this truly cringeworthy factoid:

An American is more likely to spend a given day in prison rather than spend even a second of that day on a bicycle!

By the way, we lead the world in imprisonment rate, at 756 per 100,000, eking out the likes of Russia, Rwanda, and Cuba. But, hey, as the jingoistic lyric goes, "at least we know we're free."

In Denmark, by contrast, a resident is *much* more likely to commute by bicycle than to spend the day in prison. With an imprisonment rate of 63 per 100,000, a Dane is easily 100 times less likely than a Yank to be incarcerated and nearly 100 times more likely to be on a bicycle.

> I'm not trying to imply that pedaling will keep you out of the Big House. But if you do find yourself incarcerated and you happen to be in Brazil at the time, take advantage of their program whereby producing electricity by pedaling will get your sentence reduced.

Clearly, Yanks have plenty of room for improvement in the cycling arena. Pedaling only a few centimeters a day, on average, we lead the world in room for improvement. We're #1.

~~~

How much cycling do the mythologized Danes actually do?

Well, consider the capital city, Copenhagen, where more people commute by bicycle than in all 25,375 municipalities of the USA combined. According to the Official Website of Denmark, Copenhagen's widely regarded as the Most Bikeable and hence Most Livable City in the World. And as if that isn't enough head-swelling recognition, it was recently designated the first Bike City of the World. Other cities are clamoring to get added to this exclusive list of one.

They're seeking ways to emulate Copenhagen, where:

- 40% of commuters cycle
- 400 km of designated bike paths exist
- 40,000 cyclists daily use the busiest bike routes

And those are just the factoids beginning with 40!

The most eye-popping fact of all: Copenhageners pedal, in aggregate, 1.2 million kilometers daily!

> Yanks who don't suck at math will readily convert that to $4.7{\times}10^{10}$ inches or, I suppose, ~750,000 miles.

That's the equivalent of two round-trips to the moon or 28 trips around Earth, which happens to match my projected lifetime total. So far, I've done about a third of that distance, which leaves me about a half million miles to go. If I average 50 miles per day, I could match the daily Copenhagen total in about 27 years. Clearly, I'd better stop squandering valuable cycling time with this sedentary writing pursuit.

> Alternatively, I could mimic A.J. Jacobs who recently wrote a book about fitness, *Drop Dead Healthy*, while walking on a treadmill. I'm pretty good at texting while pedaling, but I don't know about writing an entire book. Sounds unsafe. If I'm going to attempt a stunt like that, maybe I should switch from my "crotch bike" to a recumbent trike.

> Or, I could mimic Bob Fenster, author of *Duh!* He's pedaling to the moon and back without ever leaving his home gym. Approximately daily, he reclines on his turbo recumbent Exercycle and churns out big miles. Safety first, Bob!

Let's imagine *you* wish to match the Copenhageners' collective daily mileage over the course of *your* lifetime, but you don't have the luxury of spending several hours daily pedaling. Let's assume you pedal a modest 10 miles per day, on average, starting on your 40th birthday (i.e., coinciding with the beginning of your first mid-life crisis). To achieve your lofty goal, you must live to be the ripe ole age of 245. Good luck with that.

Don't be deceived. I've intentionally perpetuated the myth that Danes pedal a helluva lot more than they really do. The astronomical figure 1.2 million kilometers per day works out to **only** 1.7 kilometers *per person* per day or just a shade over a mile and hardly worth boasting about, right? While collectively Danes do a lot of pedaling, individually they hardly pedal at all. The typical Dane on a typical day does a bit of light pedal pushing, barely enough to power a 100-watt light bulb for a few minutes.

> When I pedal that distance at a steady 12 mph on flat terrain, it only takes me 5 minutes, I don't break a sweat, my breathing is normal, my heart rate never goes above 90 bpm, and I only burn a few dozen extra calories. This minimal energetic expenditure could be recouped by consuming half a tablespoon of peanut butter or half of one of those little fun size Snickers bars or a swig of Gatorade.
>
> A typical trip by a typical Dane increases her or his energetic expenditure by only 2-3%, whereas a typical day of pedaling for me increases my energetic expenditure by about 400%.

What's impressive about the Danes, then, is not how far they pedal but that so many of them take short leisurely trips daily. Collectively, they're world beaters.

Individually, they're kinda lazy. Their typical 6-minute commute roughly doubles their metabolic rate, so it requires only about as much energy as a 12-minute nap.

Clearly, commuting Danes tooling along in their business suits and stilettos and such aren't happy because they're starting each day with a great athletic workout. It's not like they're aerobic freaks getting high on endorphins on their way to work. No wonder they don't *look* all that happy. No wonder they seem reserved and not especially smiley or joyous. Heck, they're barely awake. And no wonder they don't attribute their own happiness to pedaling per se!

The Danes are quick to celebrate their global superiority in happiness and their bicycle culture. It's all right there, a great repository of celebratory details, on the Official Website of Denmark. Yet they seem reluctant to connect the two as if causally linked. It seems as though Danes see their cycling culture as an essential feature of mainstream society, whereas they see their world-famous happiness as a byproduct of a complex array of interacting factors. They seem to attribute their happiness to Danish traits such as realistic expectations, trust in others, universal health care, and gender equity, and not primarily to their cycling habit. That's not very parsimonious, but maybe they're right.

Naturally, my intimation that cycling was the root cause of the Danes' happiness was just a joke. And yet I'd bet dollars to donuts (Euros to croissants) that we could find evidence for a partially causal linkage. As a thought experiment, imagine eliminating bicycle-commuting in Copenhagen for one year. My hunch is cortisol levels would spike and contentment would plummet. (Of course, we'd reinstate bicycle-commuting and watch the Copenhagers' happiness rebound.)

On a personal note, I feel mildly euphoric nearly every time I throw my leg over the crossbar. But why? Is it an anticipatory reaction, like an addict preparing to self-medicate? Is it nostalgia, a longing for the days of childhood freedom and baseball cards in the spokes and streamers dangling from the handlebars and banana seats? Is it the thrill of speed? Is it the permanent magic of balancing on two wheels? Is it the intrinsic danger? I don't know, but something triggers the pleasures centers in my noggin.

Obviously, I'm inclined to believe happiness in Denmark has *something* to do with cycling. Perhaps Danes are happy not because they pedal per se but because so many of them avoid driving a car in rush-hour traffic.

Imagine never again starting or ending the day in bumper-to-bumper traffic, cursing like a pirate and lapsing into road rage, especially when you can't seem to find a freakin' parking space anywhere in the whole goddamn city. Imagine never again snapping at your precious cargo in the backseat. And imagine routinely arriving at your destination on time because you've opted for a bike, perhaps a Danish cargo bike with plenty of kid capacity.

Whatever the underlying mechanism, I insist on holding onto the belief that Danes really are happier for the little pedaling they do.

I can't guarantee substituting a bike addiction for your car addiction will make you happy too. But, hey, it's worth a try. What do you have to lose, aside from that spare tire around your middle?

Like the Danes, I choose to believe we're all endowed with the unalienable rights of Life, Liberty, and the Pursuit of Cycling. Happy pedaling!

🚲 🚲 🚲 🚲 🚲

Chapter 4

Bon Voyage

My Abrupt Transition from Hardcore Lifestyle Cyclist to Rookie Road Warrior

Those famously happy Danes got nuthin' on me. Seriously, I know a bunch of Danes and let me tell ya, I'm happier than all of 'em. My pedaling-induced happiness is almost off the proverbial charts. On a 10-point scale, the average Dane scores an 8.3. Me: I'm at 9.9. And that's on a bad day. Of course, I do have an unfair advantage: now that I'm retired and free to roam far and wide, I pedal farther each day than the average Dane pedals in a month. I'm a critical mass of one, on a long strange trip, a tour that never ends.

And yet, I was perfectly content for decades as a hardcore lifestyle cyclist who never toured. Even then, though, I pedaled farther each day than the average Dane pedals in a week or two. And I really was content. I didn't long to tour. I didn't feel like I was missing anything, probably because I was already pedaling every day. I was living on my bike, taking daily micro-tours, always with rear panniers attached. Life as I knew it was good.

But because I was so devoted to pedaling, my friends said it was a foregone conclusion that I'd start touring in the conventional way someday. They were right, of course.

It would have happened sooner except for the fact that I was a full-fledged workaholic. I was immersed in an academic career and worked 365 days per year on my research. (I joked with my agnostic/atheist colleagues that I took Christmas day off, but they caught me working on that day year after year.)

Finally, a few days after completing my 44th passive trip around the sun, in July of 2004, I granted myself a couple days off to take my first-ever bicycle tour. I decided to pedal from Sault Ste. Marie, Ontario to my 88 acres (36 hectares) of forestland with a hike-in log cabin, where I'd spend a few weeks in writing retreat. It would be a mini-tour, only 397 miles (639 km), hardly a tour at all. And then, a few weeks later, I'd pedal back to Columbus, Ohio, which would be another 575 miles (926 km). Easy as pie.

I made the mistake of mentioning my plan to one of my PhD students, Siri. That's right, long before iPhone's quasi-intelligent personal assistant and knowledge navigator came onto the scene, I had a real-life version with the same name at my disposal. My mistake triggered the real Siri — she of Basque separatist, Guatemalan revolutionary, and Norse colonist heritage — to make the mistake of offering me unsolicited advice. In her defense, she could see I was about to repeat mistakes she'd made on her own rookie touring attempt after having spent years commuting by bike in Los Angeles. She ended up injured and off her bike for months. Her advice was perfectly sensible and well-intentioned. But I didn't want to hear it. And she should have known that.

We'd been close friends for a few years — she and her hubby, Bo, even stayed with me at my land during their honeymoon — and so she knew all too well about my #1 personality defect. She knew about my being homozygous for the gene RECALCITRANT. She knew if she told me to do X, I would see that as a challenge and would almost inevitably choose to do the opposite of X.

Undeterred, Siri started by saying I should seriously consider *training* for the trip, even if it was to be just a modest little shakedown tour.

I argued all too confidently that touring is basically like commuting, only more so. The fundamental difference, it seemed to me, was that instead of returning to Point A each night, I would end up at Point B. So why would I train? Wasn't that what I'd been doing all those years while pedaling everywhere daily? Fine, I said, "I'll 'train' while doing my regular commuting trips around town." (Siri claims I used air quotes. Cringe.)

Siri countered by arguing that sprinting around town each day wasn't going to prepare me for the third and fourth and fifth and sixth and seventh hour on the bike each day during the tour. She told me my body would scream at me after a few hours on the bike. She said chronic use injuries would flare up if I tried to do big miles. She said she hoped I didn't end up flat on my back popping pain meds.

I scoffed (subvocally).

She went on to advise me to buy a touring bike, to use proper cycling gloves and shorts and shoes, to limit my daily mileage during the trip, to take electrolytes and stay hydrated, to do this and that.

I argued that I was happy with my mountain bike, cycling gear was silly and decorative, moderation was for suckers, my pain threshold was super high, and I was camel-like in my ability to go without water.

Regrettably, I went on to disobey all of her sage advice.

~~~

On Day 1, in mid-afternoon, I passed through Customs and Immigration, into Canada, at Sault Ste. Marie, Ontario. This was a couple years before I started to worry about whether my digital footprint would raise red flags at international borders — recall the bike-bag fiasco — so I wasn't surprised when they practically waved me through. I pedaled through town, heading east along the north shore of Lake Huron.

Beyond the edge of town, the traffic thinned and the pedaling was nice and easy. I sailed along, spinning at 90 revolutions per minute, and found myself daydreaming about Terry Fox, Canada's all-time greatest superhero and cancer survivor, who ran along this very road — on one leg! That was in 1980, two dozen years before my little bike ride.

> I thought about the parallels. Terry and I had a lot in common. We were the same age. We'd both spent time at Simon Fraser University near Vancouver. And then we both went on to pursue ultra-marathon adventure travel while surviving with awful diseases.

I imagined Terry running toward me, with admirers cheering him on every hop-skip of the way.

Terry's epic goal was to run the equivalent of a marathon a day across the continent. He set out to raise awareness and cash for cancer. Along the way, he galvanized the country, inspired us all, and eventually succumbed to the cancer. I felt honored to share *his* road, otherwise known as the TransCanada Highway — even if I was flagrantly cheating by: 1) using a bicycle, 2) not having a prosthetic, and 3) being cancer-free.

I also found myself wondering about John Muir, the famous Scottish-born conservationist who spent a stint, 1864-1865, in this part of the world — when he otherwise might have been fighting for the Yanks against the Confederate States of America. Muir would atone for his absenteeism and go on to become an endurance athlete of the hiking variety, found the Sierra Club, sire the National Parks system, and become the patron saint of environmental preservation. I felt honored to overlap with him in this place, even if he was just biding time on the way to becoming a hero south of the 49th parallel.

I also conjured up images of the legendary French voyageurs who long ago passed through hauling furs in their massive canoes along the North Channel of Lake Huron. They were endurance athletes extraordinaire. They paddled 14 hours a day, maintaining a cadence of 55 strokes per minute, all the while singing their hearts out. Great nations of Europe coming through!

And last but not least, I wondered about the First Nations folks who preceded Fox and Muir and the French paddlers, and whose descendants still live in villages scattered throughout the region. I wondered if I'd encounter anybody from the nearby First Nation community of Thessalon, when suddenly there they were: four pre-teen lads diving, like Acapulco cliff divers, from a train trestle.

In one of those carpe diem moments where discretion is *not* the better part of valor, I decided to join them. They took turns doing double flips. They "encouraged" me to dive. They laughed as I stood on the edge not quite daring to take the plunge — still wearing my helmet. Finally, to save face, I counted to three and stepped off, accelerating feet first toward the water at 9.8 meters per second per second. The trestle was about 10 m (33 feet) high, so I was going 50 kilometers per hour (32 miles per hour) when I hit the water. That would have been fine except for the fact that I panicked and tried to break my fail by landing with my arms fully spread. Instead of knifing into the water, I did an arm-flop and sustained my first minor self-inflicted injury of the trip. When I resurfaced, screaming, with my helmet all askew, they were hysterical.

I swam back to my bike, hopped on, and pedaled down the road. I stopped a half mile down the road, dug out my binoculars, and spied on them briefly. I could see they were taking turns reenacting my majestic feet-first "dive."

A few hours later, I rolled into the village of Iron Bridge (pop. 614), 73 miles down the road, just after dark. Iron Bridge is one of those quintessential don't-blink-or-you'll-miss-it places. Once considered a bona fide Village, it's been demoted to the category of Designated Place by the folks at Statistics Canada who count human heads in their decennial censuses. More telling, this designated place is big enough to boast an indoor skating/curling rink, though evidently not quite big enough to support its own Tim Horton's. (For a Tim's fix, I'd need to wait till the metropolis of Blind River [pop. 3700], 14 miles to the east.) It also has a motel. I decided to splurge and get a room. Hey, I had cause to celebrate: I'd completed the first partial day on my debut tour. And I hadn't even injured myself, unless you count the arm-flop bruising. So, I pulled into the (dirt) parking lot. The vacancy sign was lit but the office seemed to be closed. I was about to pedal down the road and stealth camp under the stars, when I noticed a hand-written note on the office door. It read,

We're at the pub.
Vacant rooms are unlocked. Help yourself.
Remember to pay in the morning.

I ask you, is that a slice of Canadiana or what?!

On Day 2, I paid my bill and headed to the one and only diner for an *omelette de fromage*. Belly full of ova and *pommes de terre* and feeling fine, with just a hint of soreness in my quadriceps, I started pedaling around 10 AM. Feeling strong, I pedaled almost nonstop for hours, aided by a strong tailwind. I flew. I even passed a train.

> From the moment I realized I was gaining on the train, how could I resist? Eventually, I caught up to the caboose. And then I inched along, gradually passing one car after another. Finally, with one last show of nonchalant awesomeness, I pulled even with the front of the train. The engineer shook his fist at me as I pulled ahead, triumphantly.

By the end of the day, I'd done a fairly big distance. In fact, thanks to Canada's quasi-adoption of the metric system, I'd done my first-ever *double* century: 201 kilometers. Even under the imperial system, that's a solid century: 125 miles.

No wonder I was injured!

Having exceeded my pain threshold for the last hour or two of pedaling, I finally had sense enough to get off the bike. I stopped a few miles south of Sudbury (pop. 160,000), in a rocky and barren landscape. I pitched my tent out of view, on a carpet of blueberries, popped some vitamin I (a.k.a., ibuprofen) and took inventory of my symptoms.

My body had been a bundle of compromises for decades and so I expected to suffer a few flare-ups of dormant injuries on this trip. Sure enough, the mangled vertebrae in my neck had started to bother me. And I'd aggravated an old hamstring injury. No big deal.

What worried me a little were the new cycling-related neurological symptoms:

All of my fingers were tingly and numb, indicating both carpal tunnel syndrome (which affects the thumb and first two fingers) and ulnar neuropathy (which affects the last two fingers). Apparently, refusing to buy a pair of those fingerless padded cycling gloves was a mistake. Whatever.

My genitals were tingly and numb, indicating so-called bicycle-seat neuropathy. Apparently, refusing to buy a pair of padded cycling shorts was another mistake. Whatever.

Ever the optimist, I figured I could do without feeling in my fingers and genitals and still lead a happy life. No big deal.

But what really worried me was my right Achilles tendon. It was not tingly and numb. It was excruciatingly painful, indicating acute tendinitis and possible tearing. Could I manage the pain with ibuprofen and keep on pedaling? Or would I completely rupture the tendon and end up needing reconstructive surgery, with a long rehab to follow?

Apparently, refusing to buy a pair of cycling shoes — in favor of wearing spongy Tevas® — was the biggest mistake of all. Not whatever.

On Day 3, I popped vitamin I, hobbled around and somehow managed to pack up, and then started pedaling onward. I figured with any luck I'd be able to do another big day. If I could match Day 2's distance, I'd arrive at my cabin, where I could convalesce and get to work writing geeky science stuff.

Besides, the late great Terry Fox had *run* along this road, all the way from Newfoundland, on *one* good leg. He didn't whine about pain in his right Achilles tendon. He didn't even have a right Achilles tendon. He didn't even have a right leg distal to the point of amputation.

Inspired by Terry, I pedaled along the eastern shore of Georgian Bay, up and down, over the Canadian Shield topography. I climbed each hill in pain and coasted to the next beaver flowage passing under the road. I did this dozens of times. Not surprisingly, I gradually realized my left Achilles tendon was injured too. Eventually, I "limped" into Parry Sound, Bobby Orr's hometown. (He was not there to greet me. Whatever.) I'd traveled just 150 kilometers (93 miles) in about 15 hours. In my injured state, I'd barely outpaced Terry. I checked into a motel, popped some vitamin I, and hoped for the best.

On Day 4, I popped vitamin I, phoned the front desk and re-upped for another night. I alternated between working on a manuscript and icing my tendons throughout the day. I hobbled to the candy machine for dinner.

On Day 5, I popped vitamin I, phoned the front desk and re-upped for another night. I alternated between working on a manuscript and icing my tendons throughout the day. I hobbled to the candy machine for dinner.

On Day 6, I popped vitamin I, phoned the front desk and re-upped for another night. I alternated between working on a manuscript and icing my tendons throughout the day. I hobbled to the candy machine for dinner.

On Day 7, I should have been redundant. I should have done as on Days 4-6. Instead, with enough vitamin I in my system to kill a moose, I headed east over hill and dale toward my land, 42 miles away. The pain was excruciating and yet, after 12 hours, I finally made it. I locked the bike to a tree and hobbled through the boreal forest to my cabin. I spent the next week off the bike, sitting on the screened-in porch, with ruby-throated hummingbirds entertaining me throughout the day.

A week later, I needed supplies and so decided to pedal to town, 14 miles away. But first I had to replace both tubes because the local bear had once again done what the local bear does: punctured my tires. Somehow, I made it to town and back — with a new supply of vitamin I.

A year later, I still had some residual daily pain in both Achilles tendons. But now, a decade later, they bother me only occasionally, when I've done big miles. And I've become better at listening to my body and doing the right thing. When I tweak a tendon these days, I use the pain as an excuse to camp for the night or to hole up and enjoy live music for a day or two.

Overall, I'm happy to say I've undergone a successful transformation from foolish rookie to savvy veteran touring cyclist. In a latent sense, I eventually took Siri's advice. With a proper bike and all the right gear, not to mention a highly trained and remodeled body, I now span continents unscathed.

And yet I still think of myself as a lifestyle cyclist, a commuter whose commutes have become quasi-epic. I've fallen into the habit of commuting between the Pacific and Atlantic coasts, between California and Maine. These annual round-trips include side trips, forays to Alaska and Mexico and Ontario. Even so, it feels like I'm simply commuting with the space and time scales expanded.

I do these rides with nary an injury. Of course, I still experience tingling, here and there, now and then. Whatever.

~

May your transition from commuting to touring cyclist be smoother than mine. May you take helpful advice. May your Achilles tendons remain intact. May your extremities remain tingle-free. May you commune with semi-feral indigenous lads. May you be blessed by steady tailwinds.

And may you pass a train.

🚲 🚲 🚲 🚲 🚲

Chapter 5

Velo Voyageurs

Encounters with Kindred Spirits of the Cyclonomadic Variety

Ever since 1884 when Tom Stevens climbed aboard his 50-inch penny-farthing in San Francisco and pedaled east to Boston, ultimately to Yokohama, folks have been doing epic rides. And while I'm on my never-ending tour, I keep an eye out for these intrepid souls. They're rare and automatically fascinating. I can't let them slip by. I must meet them.

Bike-touring can be quite solitary, especially the way I do it. I insist on doing my own thing, venturing into unpaved remoteness, not following a designated route. I sometimes go thousands of miles — especially during winter — without seeing a fellow touring cyclist of any sort, never mind an extremist who is doing something truly awe inspiring.

> To put this in perspective, if you do a thru-hike on, say, the Appalachian Trail (as I did in '09), you're guaranteed to have daily encounters with a whole array of fellow thru-hikers. It's like a revolving door with a steadily replenishing supply of interesting Car People who've separated from their car for a few months.

Come to think of it, I haven't encountered a bona fide cyclonomad in months. But I know eventually, when I least expect it, an apparition will appear on the horizon. And it won't be a decoy; it'll be the Real McCoy, an extreme pedalista. I'll flag or shout or chase down the fellow traveler, whatever it takes. And I won't be disappointed.

Here's a little sampler of vignettes about extreme cyclists I've had the privilege of intercepting along the way:

On an ideal day in September 2011, I crossed the border from the Yukon Territory, Canada, into Alaska, USA. As I started the first real climb, inching my way up in grampy gear, I suddenly noticed a fellow touring cyclist, the first since Bellingham, Washington. He was flying down the hill, with a bulky trailer in tow. I could sense he wasn't going to stop, so I frantically flagged him down. His brakes screeched as he eventually came to an awkward stop by turning into the guardrail. Pedaling over to greet him I could tell his trailer was supporting a heavy load.

I shouted, "What the HELL are you doing?!"

He didn't greet me in any conventional way. Instead, he threw back his head and sang — like a French voyageur might have done, except in English — "North to Alaska, we go north the rush is on." I sang the next line. It was a spontaneous duet and a celebratory rendezvous between complete-strangers/instant-friends. In other words, we hit it off *tout suite*.

I demanded Klaus tell his story, which he was glad to do. His bike, he bragged, was a 30-year-old "Dutch ladies bike," the Gazelle model. Sure enough, I could see it was designed for urban commuting, perhaps while wearing a skirt. Klaus married his "blue lady" — that's what he calls her — at age 22 and he'd been riding her on mostly short day trips ever since. He'd ridden her thousands of times across town and now once across much of a continent.

But his choice of trailer was even more improbable. It was a cheapo contraption from Walmart designed for hauling around tiny tyrants, otherwise known as tikes or toddlers or tots. It was *not* designed for touring. It was basically a stroller, complete with weather-proof canopy. But his trailer contained no babies, allegedly. He claimed it was filled with thousands of carnival medals (*karnevalsorden*), tokens traditionally awarded annually in Germany to contributing members of the carnival association, local celebrities, and other deserving individuals. They'd been his father's medals, part of a massive collection. And Klaus was doing this epic ride through British Columbia, Yukon, Northwest Territories, and Alaska as a tribute to his dad, who'd died recently and from whom Klaus had been estranged for years.

The medals were Klaus's currency. He'd been doling them out to "road angels" along the way. If someone put him up for the night, that angel would get a medal along with a verbal "Sank you for your friendly." If someone gave him water or food, that angel would get a medal and a "Sank you for your friendly." But if someone flagged him down on a steep descent and implicitly offered lifelong friendship, that person wouldn't get a sniff of a medal. I didn't even get to *see* the medals.

Klaus, I'm ready to be thanked for my friendly, so please send me a medal as soon as humanly possible. It needn't be a medal symbolizing merit. I'll gladly accept the "Golden Fleece" medal. Honestly, I don't care whether it's meant to ridicule or pay homage, just send me a flippin' medal already! Send it to:

Tom Waite
c/o General Delivery
Somewhere, North America
Earth

Better yet, I'll pick it up in person when I pedal through Germany next summer. *Danke* for your friendly.

Last I heard, Klaus was walking through Poland and Germany, retracing his mother's steps from her days as a refugee. As he was traveling on his two little feet rather than his ladies conveyance sublime, he was not carrying medals.

~

A year later, I encountered another extreme cyclist who also happened to be from Germany. It was midafternoon and I was in the middle of nowhere, Kansas, USA. Curious about when I'd reach the far side of the seemingly infinite wheat field I'd been pedaling through for hours, I stopped for a moment to study my GPS. Suddenly, this guy went flying by, without so much as a nod, a grunt in my general direction, or a one-finger wave. I hadn't seen a fellow touring cyclist since California, so I shouted him down. He slowed down, grudgingly it seemed. I caught up and started pumping him for information. He was slow to warm up but did tell me he'd been traveling every day for 15 months and had covered 47,000 kilometers through 19 countries and that he'd be finishing up his round-the-world trip in a few weeks. All that remained was to pedal to New York, fly to Lisbon, and pedal home to Germany. Nothing to it.

I tried to coax a juicy story or two, but he was tip-lipped. He said the whole trip had been "easy" and he simply didn't have any "stories."

No stories? Utter horse bleep, I thought. I tried to convince him that he had lots of stories but he didn't see life that way. He challenged me to get a story out of him, so I said, "Okay, I bet you've been robbed at least once?"

"Of course," he said flatly.

"Fantastic, tell me what happened. This could be a story!"

He was in Timor, Indonesia. Having pedaled the length of the island, he was scheduled to fly to Australia the next day when he discovered his bank account had been emptied. Someone apparently had used a video camera at an ATM to get his card number. His life savings were gone, his tourist visa was set to expire the next morning, and he hadn't yet paid for his flight to Australia. And yet he seemed to have been unfazed.

"So what happened next?" I asked. "Presumably, Germany doesn't have an embassy in Timor? Did you get detained by the authorities? Did they put you in jail?"

"No, I went to a cybercafe."

"And then what?"

"I got on Skype with my bank and they put the money back into my account. It took 10 minutes. It was easy. That's not a story."

We were pedaling together while I extracted that initial non-story. I thought it was pretty good, as non-stories go, so I decided to keep pedaling with him to see if I could extract another tale or two. We flew, taking turns working in front and really punishing each other. He said as a Bavarian he couldn't stop till he got to a town with beer, so we kept pedaling for hours. Eventually, having surpassed the century mark by a wide margin, we arrived at a town big enough to have a family-style restaurant with a bar.

Along the way, I asked him lots of questions, teasing him about his hidden stories. I asked about his budget, which he was all too happy to brag about. Like me, he'd sold his house and divorced his car, and his only regular bill was for a cell phone. He was totally into the budget-traveler mindset and claimed he'd been spending only about $15 a day, not including air fare. But I suspected he was grossly underestimating his true costs, so I fished for more info. I asked about bike parts and he owned up to having spent a few hundred dollars along the way. I asked whether he had other incidental costs, things I might not ordinarily consider. Finally, he admitted his budget had a major line item that he'd been withholding. He said the overlooked line item actually accounted for nearly half of his total budget for the trip.

> I thought, of course, he has some guilty pleasure, like he loves the opera and buys the most expensive ticket every chance he gets. Or he stays at a 5-star hotel once a week. Or he takes sight-seeing tours in helicopters.

So, I was completely caught off guard when he blurted out "**_hookers_**."

I'm still shocked.

Naturally, I asked lots of follow-up questions. I'll spare you the unsavory details. Suffice it to say, this guy *did* have stories to tell. After all, he'd easily spent the equivalent of 20,000 carnival medals on sexual services.

I would have reciprocated with tales of my own illicit sexploits, except for the fact that my total lifetime hooker budget is and will remain forever fixed at ZERO! My discretionary budget is mostly earmarked for gourmet chocolate, espresso, and other non-prurient vices, not for employing sex workers, underage or otherwise.

Ready for a feast, we locked our bikes, lugged our eight panniers into the restaurant, and got situated at the bar. Without even glancing at the menu, he ordered "a large *bier*, Nachos Grande, and a *wommen*."

The bartender asked, "And a what?"

He repeated the third item. The bartender still didn't get it, so I translated.

She looked at the world cyclist/scoundrel and said, "Oh honey, you gotta go to St. Louis for that."

He turned to me and asked, "How far is St. Louis?"

~

Speaking of extreme pedaling combined with extreme frugality, I met a young guy from Japan last year near Monterrey, California. I was heading south to Mexico, enjoying a strong tailwind. He was easy to intercept because he was battling the wind, barely making headway, and glad for an excuse to take a break. He was heading north to Alaska, to climb Mt. McKinley, just one of the little peaks he was bagging in his version of the Seven Summit odyssey.

> To date, only about 300 people have achieved this ultimate mountaineering feat. They've distinguished themselves by being unique in various ways: first woman, first openly gay man, first married couple, first to use no supplemental oxygen, first to ski down all seven mountains, et cetera.

Naturally, I was less impressed by his attempt to climb the highest peak on each continent than by his attempt to be the first person to propel himself across vast expanses separating those points.

I asked him my standard question about getting robbed. Sure enough, he'd been mugged (in Colombia). Having lost everything, he chose an unusual tact. He simply stopped carrying debit/credit cards, traveler's checks, carnival medals, and even cash. Impressively, he'd resorted to relying on the generosity of strangers, impromptu road angels. He wouldn't accept anything from me, presumably because taking handouts from a fellow traveler would have been be a violation of his moral code. But he had every intention of rolling into the next town and pitching his tent on the grounds of a church within plain view of a taco truck and hoping a few tacos would somehow materialize. He'd been traveling like this for several weeks and was going strong.

~

Last year, I met another savvy budget pedaler upon rolling into Silver City, New Mexico. I arrived just in time to hear the last two songs of a 3-day blues fest and to be welcomed by a perfect-stranger/instant-friend. My new friend for life, aged 63, had pedaled 3000+ miles from Connecticut to this town nestled next to the Gila Wilderness with one purpose in mind — to enjoy the blues fest.

While in town, he needed no carnival medals or currency of any kind because he was being amply rewarded for his volunteerism. He was volunteering at the festival and so getting fed dinner, volunteering at the homeless shelter and so getting fed lunch, volunteering at a campground and so getting a free tent site and shower privileges, and volunteering at a co-op bike shop and so getting free replacement parts for the circuitous route, via California, he would take to return home.

Upon arriving in Connecticut, he'd celebrate the completion of his third lap around the conterminous 48 states. And then he'd visit friends for a few weeks before pedaling again into the prevailing winds, back to his home away from home in New Mexico, the self-proclaimed Land of Enchantment.

~

Another example of the sort of extreme traveler I encounter comes from my trip to Alaska. As I approached Anchorage on a dedicated bike path, I noticed two cyclists in my rear-view mirror. Eventually, I stopped so they could catch up and maybe even join me. We hit it off instantly. They were just out for a 60-mile training ride that day, but they've done all sorts of truly extreme trips.

Here's my favorite example:

The fellow, now in his early 60s and retired, used to be the regional supervisor for the National Wildlife Refuges in northern Alaska. And when it came time to move from one refuge to another, he and his wife chose not to move the conventional way (i.e., by bush plane). Instead, they chose to move by dogsled. That's right, they mushed to their new home. Traveling through the wilderness of the Brooks Range and staying in Native villages along the way, the woman was 7 months pregnant when they started and 8 months pregnant when they finished, as it took either 28 days (his account) or 29 days (her account) to complete the journey.

An hour after meeting them, we three spontaneous pedaling pals arrived at a Mexican restaurant and I had the pleasure of meeting the former fetus. Two decades after his sloshing across the Brooks Range *in utero*, I got to meet him *in situ*. A thriving undergraduate at the University of Alaska, he seemed none the worse for wear. In fact, he seemed robust, thanks surely to his prenatal adventure.

~

Speaking of moving by unconventional means, I met a guy last year near San Luis Obispo, California who blew me away, in more ways than one. He *zoomed* by me on a recumbent trike on a 9% grade. In tow was a big homemade wooden trailer. I was more than mildly humbled.

And then he stopped, just long enough to gloat and tell me his story. He commutes twice a year between his pedaler's paradise home in Portland, Oregon, and his surfer's paradise home in Huntington Beach, California.

(That's 5200 miles, total.) He claimed to have been in training for the Olympic Team years ago, for which event I have no idea. And he claimed to have been, in his words, the "token disabled guy" in last year's edition of the ultra-fast Race Across America. He also claimed he'd relearned to walk — twice.

And then he zoomed off, blowing me away yet again, hightailing it for Huntington Beach. It was then I realized his trike had an electric-assist motor. Vroom vroom. Of course, he also blew me away by his dedication to a lifestyle of uberfitness and epic adventure.

~~~

I'll be pedaling from San Francisco to Boston yet again soon. This time I'll retrace the route Tom Stevens took on his penny-farthing. Unlike that Tom, I'll have no chance of encountering French voyageurs hauling furs in that other conveyance sublime, the canoe. They're long gone. But I hope to encounter at least one wild voyageur of the velo variety during my commute. If I do, I'll offer him or her one carnival medal per juicy anecdote. And I'll be sure to thank all road angels for their friendly as I do my small part to help keep Earth weird.

🚲 🚲 🚲 🚲 🚲

SAFETY LAST!

Chapter 6

Truck Always Wins

And Other Astute Observations by a Road-rage Victim

Afunny thing happened on my way to do a thru-hike on the 2650-mile Pacific Crest Trail: *I got hit by a truck*! There I was minding my own business while pedaling through Modesto, California, when I suddenly saw how I would die. A truck careened around a parked car, into my lane, and accelerated right at me. A split second later, I became the disadvantaged party in a truck versus bicycle head-on collision. It hurt in that blunt-force trauma way, like a baseball bat to the cranium and ribs and hip. As I lay there in agony, I couldn't help wonder whether this was my cosmic comeuppance.

But that's when things got funny:

With the overconfidence of a typical Car Person, I'd been implicitly assuming my chances of making it through the rest of the day were damn near 100%. Upon finding myself sprawled facedown with crunched helmet and shattered skeleton, I updated my expectations. I kept it simple and divided by two, thereby downgrading my survival prospects from forgone conclusion to coin toss.

With my eyes closed, I could see myself writhing and screaming. It felt like an out-of-body experience, like I was hovering over my body observing the last few precious moments of my demise. It wasn't a pretty picture.

A crowd of gawkers and well-wishers hovered over me too. The first few to arrive included several eye witnesses, a woman who would later call herself an "ear witness" and say she'd "heard a crunch like a yeti stepping on a giant cockroach," and the man who'd stomped on the gas pedal. He apologized profusely. He admitted his culpability. Nobody had called 9-1-1 yet and he was already frantically trying to salvage his reputation. He'd gone from being sky high on road rage in one instant to hungover with deep remorse in the next. He seemed desperate to be heard and seen, presumably by the eye in the sky.

Meanwhile, a wave of vigilantism swept through the herd. At least two guys thought they'd emulate Bernard Getz, the infamous subway shooter in NYC. They wanted to dole out some harsh altruistic punishment. They yelled at the driver. They threatened him. They wanted to put their fist through his skull.

I felt no righteous indignation. That would come later. In that moment, I pitied the poor bastard and wanted to intervene on his behalf. But all I could do was wail.

I did manage to say one intelligible thing to the "first responders." They kept asking what they could do for me. I wanted to say they could check my major long bones or take chest x-rays and do a whole-body CT scan, but all I managed to gasp was, "call 9-1-1." Apparently, I continued to say this even after an ambulance, two police cruisers, and a fire truck had arrived.

And then I expanded my repertoire by saying "blanket." I wasn't deliriously referring to Michael Jackson's child of that name. I was asking to be covered, for warmth and security.

Even the driver, who would narrowly escape the charge of vehicular manslaughter, offered to help. When he wasn't fending off wannabe vigilantes, he repeatedly knelt beside me and let me know he was ready, willing, and able to make amends. At one point, he even said, "I'd trade places with you if I could."

I was speechless, but not because I felt honored to be in the presence of such a magnanimous Car Person. I wasn't figure-of-speech speechless. I was actually speechless because the excruciating pain wouldn't let me carry on a conversation. So, while wailing away, I lay there imaging what I would surely want to say to him, eventually.

In retrospect, if I could have spoken coherently, I might have said something like:

> *If you really want to trade places, you should start by lifting my mangled bicycle over your head and throwing it at your truck. I suspect you love that truck more than your wife and you're its only driver and you just came from buying a special spray to make her tires look shiny. And I know you're blissfully unaware of what that truck signals. We snicker as you drive by. We can't help but think you're bluffing, that your signal isn't an honest advertisement. Sometimes when we're unkind, we see you in your oversized truck and we sing a corrupted version of a Randy Newman lyric, 'big truck, big belly / no weenis, no heart.'*

> *All kidding aside, if you're really going to empathize, you'll throw my bike at your precious baby not once but 172 times. Since your truck outweighs my bike by*

about that much, it seems only fair that my bike should crash into your truck that many times to compensate. And then you could smash your windows, one for each of my broken ribs.

Finally, I suggest asking one of these guys to help you re-enact the scene. He would like nothing more than to beat you with a tire iron, so I bet he'd be glad to help you out. You could get on a bicycle and start pedaling. He could lurk in your truck, hiding behind a parked vehicle. And then he could punch the pedal to the floor and try to kill you with your own truck.

But I'm not interested in the kind of petty retribution that routinely passes for justice in our society. I don't want to conflate justice and revenge. What I'd like is ideal justice, not vindictiveness. I'm talking about seeking resolution through a kind process. I envision face-to-face meetings over cups of tea. We'd communicate openly and patiently. We'd seek empathy and forgiveness, not incarceration and ruination. You'd insist on making it up to me. We'd hit upon that most Seinfeldian solution: You'd offer to be my butler. *It wouldn't be anything like a life sentence, but it would be long enough for us to talk things through. We'd explore at leisure a suite of cognitive biases plaguing the driver's mind. You'd be offended at first. But I'd persuade you. I'd argue that Car People hardly have the market cornered when it comes to cognitive biases. These biases, in fact, are universal among humans and even extend throughout the Animalia portion of the tree of life. If you have a central nervous system, you're prone. And thinking you're immune is the ultimate delusion of awesomeness.*

~

This fantasy was rudely interrupted by a barrage of questions I couldn't adequately answer:

"Where are you hurt?"

"Modesto," I said with stunning lucidity.

"No, I mean what hurts on your body."

"Oh, everything above my waist."

"Does this hurt?"

"Aaaaaaaaaarrrrhhhhhh."

"How 'bout this?"

"Aaaaaaaaaarrrrrrrhhhhhhhh."

"Did you lose consciousness?"

"Am I conscious now?"

"Where do you live?"

"Earth."

"Do you have a local address?"

"Not exactly."

"Are you homeless, sir?"

"Not in the conventional sense."

"Is there someone we should contact?"

"Why?"

"O.K. if we cut off your clothes?"

"Yeah, but what will I wear?"

"We're going to put you in the ambulance now."

"Are you going to put me on a Guernsey?"

"No, sir, we're going to put you on a *gurney*. A Guernsey is a type of dairy cow."

"I know. That was a yoke."

"The police will take your bike, O.K. sir?"

Adding insult to injury, I thought, I'm not only being forced to rejoin the car culture for a dozen blocks or so — don't mention my carbon footprint — but now they're trying to impound my bike? "What do you mean by 'take my bike'? Where? Why? No, my bike goes with me."

"I'm sorry, sir, but we can't take your bike in the ambulance."

"Can someone else bring it to the hospital?"

"I'll ask the guys to lash it to the back of the fire truck and bring it over."

"That's not green."

"What do you mean, sir? You're sounding incoherent again."

"Never mind, that sounds good, put my bike on the fire truck."

On the way to the ER my new EMT pals want to talk about Lance. They seem to think I must know him. After all, I'm wearing neon yellow, I'm a cyclist, and he was here a few days ago for Stage 4 of the Tour of California. "Did you see Lance the other day?" one of them asks.

"I did," I say, "for about 2 seconds as he whizzed by at the finish line."

"He had a crash too, you know."

"I know, I saw him after the crash. He was okay."

"Yeah, we know. When we heard he'd crashed, we were hoping he'd be all mangled like you. Then we would have saved his life and become his friends."

"That's a shame. Better luck next year. Maybe *I* could be your friend. I'm an inferior substitute, but I'm available."

"You're probably superior to Lance in *some* way."

"In many ways," I say.

"Like what, sir? It sounds like you've given this some thought."

"Well, for starters, Lance's resting heart rate is a reptilian 32 beats per minute. Mine's vastly superior at about 52 beats per minute."

"Very funny, sir."

"And his percent body fat is inferior too. Must be about 3%. I hate to brag, but mine is easily in double digits."

"That's impressive, sir."

"And I've never dumped Cheryl Crow or competed with an abnormally high hematocrit."

"Or survived cancer, sir."

"Which reminds me: he's down to a single testicle. Again, I hate to brag, but I have twice as many."

Lance and I proved to be more similar than you might imagine. The next day he crashed again. This time he wasn't so lucky. Off he went in an ambulance, for stitches under his eye and a vial of Vicodin.

~

In the ER with an IV in my arm and oxygen tubes up my nose, I allocated some of my divided attention to eavesdropping on the attending nurse whose divided attention was mostly focused on fielding phone calls from friends who wanted to know about her *nuevo novio* (translation: the guy she slept with on Saturday night and hasn't heard from since). But I allocated most of my attention to rehearsing the conversation I'd later have with my assailant. I'd begin by asking whether he considers himself a good driver.

"Oh, yes, definitely," he'd say and then go on to assure me that my evidence to the contrary was an anomaly.

"Would you say you're a much better than average driver?"

"Yes, absolutely!"

"Would you call yourself an excellent driver?"

"Yes, I'm definitely an excellent driver."

"Definitely an excellent driver," I say laughing.

"What's so funny?"

"You don't know? The phrase 'definitely an excellent driver' doesn't ring a bell?"

"No, should it?"

"Well, it's funny because I've baited you into reciting a movie line. It's from *Rain Man*. Dustin Hoffman plays the main character, an autistic adult with savant syndrome. At one point, he claims repeatedly that he's 'definitely an excellent driver.' It's the scene where he's a passenger in his brother's convertible and his brother, played by Tom Cruise, throws underwear on the road."

"Yeah, I remember that scene."

"In that case, you may recall that Dustin Hoffman's character wasn't even eligible to have a driver's license."

"Yeah, I remember."

"Well, that line struck me funny when you repeated it because, like you and Rain Man, practically everyone thinks he or she is an excellent driver. In fact, I've surveyed people for years and it's almost impossible to find a licensed driver, especially a man, who doesn't think he's way above average. Meanwhile, it's mathematically impossible for everyone to be above average. This colossal mismatch between perception and reality is sometimes called the Lake Woebegone Effect, but let's call your particular case of illusory superiority the **Rain Man bias**. And confronting your self-professed awesomeness with my empirical evidence, I infer you're one of the multitudes of drivers operating under a delusion of awesomeness. But don't feel bad. It's no excuse, but you *are* a boy and boys tend to be especially prone to the Lake Woebegone Effect."

"But I've always been sure I'm an excellent driver. That's why I drive with so much confidence."

"I think you mean overconfidence or arrogance or total disregard. If you really were an excellent driver, you wouldn't have committed the whole chain of criminal acts that almost ended with my cremation and your incarceration. You would have driven with caution and concern for others. You would have driven as if your own daughter or son was on that bicycle. Excellent drivers don't have road rage issues. Excellent drivers don't come within an eyelash of going to prison for vehicular homicide."

"You sound like my wife."

"I'm glad you mentioned your wife. I wanted to ask you who drives when the two of you travel together."

"I do."

"Always?"

"Yes."

"Because you're the better driver?"

"Yes, I'm better than she is."

"That's classic," I say, laughing again. "Has it ever occurred to you that your married buddies think the same way and yet an enormous mountain of accident data shows that women are safer drivers? Let's call this delusion the **being-a-boy bias**."

"But I really am a safer driver than my wife is."

"Really?!"

"Yes, really."

"But if your wife had been driving the other night, would she have flown into a rage at the driver of a parked car? Would she have circled around the parking lot with the intent of teaching that driver a lesson? Would she have gotten herself worked up into a righteously indignant lather? Would she have returned to the scene with evil intent? Would she have made a big show of veering around the car, punching the gas pedal to the floor, and roaring into oncoming traffic? Would she have come within an eyelash of killing someone on a bicycle?"

"No," he allows, "I guess maybe she is a safer driver."

"And yet you insist on doing 100% of the driving when you travel together?"

"Yeah, I feel more comfortable when I'm driving. I *hate* being a passenger. I get nervous."

"That's because you suffer from the **illusion of control**. This illusion is pervasive. One famous example is that we value a lottery ticket more highly if we've been allowed to pick it, like a playing card from a deck. And this is despite the fact that handling the ticket has no impact whatsoever on the odds of winning. The case of men insisting on driving is more dramatic because handling the steering wheel does matter. Paradoxically, men insist on driving and when they do the chances of crashing go up.

"But never mind your recklessness and overconfidence and anger-management issues and how all that conspired to threaten my life, what I really want to know is *why* you hit me with your truck?"

"I didn't see you," he says sheepishly.

"Perfect, I was hoping you'd say that."

"You were?"

"Yeah, you've expressed another fascinating cognitive illusion. My contention is that you did see me, but I wasn't relevant."

"But I really didn't see you."

"Of course you did. You just don't realize it. I was perfectly visible, with four flashing lights and a neon yellow vest and neon yellow panniers with reflectors. You saw me. Bazillions of photons hit your retina."

"But I don't have any recollection of seeing you?"

"You don't think you saw me because you weren't looking for me in the first place. There's a fantastic video illustrating this phenomenon. The video shows several people passing two basketballs. The passes are really simple. There's no Harlem Globetrotteresque sleight of hand. The viewer's task is to count the passes. It's easy. Most viewers get it right. But then the viewer's asked to report on anything unusual she or he might have noticed. Most viewers claim they saw nothing unusual. But then they watch the video again, this time ignoring the basketballs and just watching for something unusual. What do they see? A person in a gorilla outfit walks into view, stands facing the camera, beats its hairy chest, and then slowly walks out of view."

"That's crazy. I think I see your point. You were the gorilla, right? And I saw you and yet I didn't. But why does this happen? How can you see something so obvious and not know it's there?"

"It's because our brains have been shaped by natural selection to filter evolutionarily irrelevant stimuli, like dragonflies, butterflies, and bicyclists. This is sometimes called attentional 'blindness.' I call it the **My Safety First Effect**. The notion is that we glance to make sure nothing big and lethal is coming. This is adaptive vigilance. It makes no evolutionary sense to waste time scanning exhaustively for innocuous stimuli that have no bearing on our survival prospects. But it makes perfect sense to rely on a fast-and-frugal recognition heuristic that keeps us alive. We glance in search of big fierce surrogate predators otherwise known as cars and trucks. Neurons fire like crazy when we see these stimuli. But when we don't see something that could kill us, these neurons don't fire like crazy. In effect, bicyclists and motorcyclists get filtered by our Paleolithic brain as irrelevant, nonthreatening stimuli."

"That's interesting. I've had that experience many times, where you suddenly say to yourself, 'where the hell did that motorcycle come from?'"

"Right, that's why I fully expect every last driver to filter me as a nonthreatening stimulus and then pull out in front of me. You were no exception, but I couldn't avoid you because you gunned it and took up the whole lane and mowed me down. But don't beat yourself up for that. Every driver glances for something big and deadly. They use a very simple decision rule: if no, then go. This bias is extremely widespread. It's not limited to selfish creeps, to people who are ruthlessly self-interested and shouldn't be out in public. It's not even limited to humans. This is a fundamental feature of evolved animal vigilance systems."

"I still wish I hadn't hit you."

"You wouldn't have hit me, except you were drunk on road rage. And if you continue to drive like that, your probability of mowing down a child in a cross walk will asymptotically approach 1.0. That's geekspeak for: it's only a matter of time before you hit someone else and go to prison."

~

A month later I was still sleeping in a chair. I felt lucky to be alive and even pedaling — feebly, on flat terrain — thanks to a potent cocktail of performance-enhancing drugs: Vicodin, Ibuprofen, caffeine, and stool softener. And my bent frame was mending bit by bit. But I still suffered from fluid buildup in my lung caused by jagged ribs 5th-8th rubbing on the pleura (lung lining). I was still suffering from pain from costachondral separations in my chest. And I felt like Fred Sanford about to have "the big one," thanks to a buildup of air in my pericardial cavity.

The best way to inflict these particular wounds is to shoot or stab people in the chest, but hitting them with your truck works fine too. The blunt-force trauma breaks ribs and they puncture the pleura, almost as effectively as lead projectiles and knife blades. Of course, those methods will get you into big trouble. It's better to use your truck because our societal addiction to gasoline is sanctioned, like our addictions to tobacco and alcohol. It's okay to hit someone with your lethal truck-weapon and cause subcutaneous emphysema just as it's okay to smoke cigarettes and cause your own demise with that other kind of emphysema.

Meanwhile, my new doctor and I have great rapport. He has that rare quality you like to see in a fellow Earthling, especially if she or he happens to be your physician. You guessed it, he's genuinely empathic. My one nagging concern about him is that he's human and thus prone *ipso facto* to a panoply of mistakes of reason that could rule his mind. Was he vastly exaggerating my prospects for recovery? Was he vastly underestimating the timeline and the catastrophic expense of all this treatment? Have I entrusted my wellness to someone as delusional as the typical Car Person?

Addendum

I wasn't being hyperbolic. My assailant really did weaponize his vehicle. And I still can't help but wonder: if he'd done the same damage with a baseball bat or a handgun, would the police have refused to do the paperwork?

My ribs eventually did remodel. And my chronic bronchitis and pneumonia gradually became less problematic.

Meanwhile, I never did receive adequate compensation. From my perspective, he was underinsured. In the legal sense, he was in compliance as his policy met the minimum requirement of $15,000. But in the real sense, he was underinsured because my medical bills vastly exceeded his limit. Of course, it was my fault for getting crushed in a part of the world that lags in developing progressive policies for bicycle safety. If only I'd been clobbered in the Netherlands, where the driver is routinely held fully liable for all medical expenses, regardless of culpability.

Chapter 7

Of Course the Danes are Safe: They Pedal!

How They Keep the Rubber Side Down

The Danes must be paying dearly for all of that pedaling. Sure they're happy, but at what price? Each morning, they finish breakfast (*spise morgenmad*) or just grab a quick coffee (*kaffe*) and then hop on their bicycle (*cykel*), risking life and limb all the way to work or school. And then they run the same risk in the evening. Surely, they're vulnerable, especially at intersections. Surely, they get picked off by drivers of four-wheeled deathmobiles on a regular basis.

Are the streets of Copenhagen strewn with besplattered cyclists? Is it really wreckage and carnage during morning rush hour and total mayhem during evening rush hour? Nope, turns out Danish drivers kill Danish cyclists only about twice per month. To put this into perspective, in the USA where bicycle commuting is a barely extant phenomenon, drivers turn bicyclists into roadkill about twice per *day*. At first glance, then, Danes on *cykels* seem to be much safer than Yanks on bicycles.

But this only begins to tell the story. We haven't accounted for the facts that Yanks vastly outnumber Danes and Danes vastly outpedal Yanks. We really need to compare per capita risk per unit distance cycled.

Let's take a look at the gory details, starting by revisiting the original question: don't Danes pay a price for all that excessive cycling? They must put themselves at greater risk per capita. After all, as you increase your cumulative lifetime cycling distance, your probability of a fatal crash must increase, asymptotically approaching 1.0. That's geekspeak for: if you pedal far enough, eventually you'll get clobbered.

But does this really mean Danes are trading-off happiness versus safety? Of course not, they're Danes! Just have a look at the *negative* relationship between per capita daily cycling distance and the rate of fatal crashes across several European countries. This reveals that in countries where folks pedal *more*, they face *lower* mortality risk.

Leave it to the Danes and their neighbors, especially those in the Netherlands. These folks pedal farther and yet they're safer.

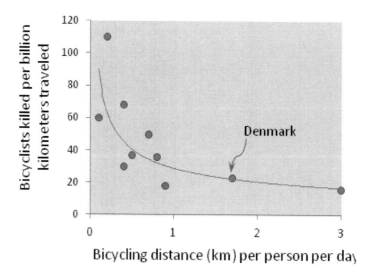

Why is cycling so safe in Denmark? What's their secret?

One obvious possibility: Maybe Danes are really safe in general. Maybe they're especially cautious while driving. If so, we might expect their roads to be safe for everyone — drivers, passengers, pedestrians, and even cyclists.

Sure enough, the roads of Denmark are among the safest in the world. In fact, the Danes are strong contenders for the gold medal in road safety. In a 2010 survey of 181 countries (and sovereign republics), Denmark (with 3.1 traffic-related fatalities per 100,000 inhabitants per year) finished in a virtual tie for #2 with Sweden.

Meanwhile, the USA finished well out of medal contention. With an annual fatality rate of 12.3 per 100,000 (i.e., 4 times worse than Denmark), it found itself way down the list in 64th place, trailing India and barely edging out the likes of Bangladesh and El Salvador. (And the USA finished 179th for *total* annual traffic-related fatalities, besting only the two most populous countries on Earth, China and India.)

As an aside, you might like to know who beat out the Danes and Swedes. And if you're anything like me, you'll demand a full explanation.

> Well, the safest country in the survey — with a traffic-related fatality rate of ZERO for 2010 — isn't even a bona fide country. It's the Republic of San Marino, also known as the Most Serene Republic of San Marino (Italian: *Serenissima Repubblica di San Marino*). It's an enclaved nanostate embedded within Italy (a la Vatican City, which was excluded from the list). It's a small parcel of land (61 km²),

with just over 30,000 residents — about the same number as in Bangor, Maine, USA.

With such a small population, we might expect the annual number of traffic-related deaths to be small but not zero, especially considering that Bangorites kill each other with cars year after year without fail. So how can we account for San Marino's perfect road safety record? Here's my initial WAG (i.e., wild-ass guess): in keeping with its monastic history and self-professed sereneness, maybe cars are banned? I couldn't have been more wrong as San Marino heads the global list in per capita car ownership rate! (And unlike Vatican City, where the speed limit for cars is 30 km/h, San Marino even hosts a Grand Prix auto race and boasts a superhighway.) And yet they reported no traffic fatalities whatsoever? Clearly, something's fishy in San Marino.

Curiosity piqued, I delved deep into the archives and discovered that San Marino's traffic fatality rate is not *typically* nil. In fact, only in the year 2010 was the rate reported as zero. In prior years, 2004-2009, annual death tolls averaged: 7.6 per 100,000. That makes San Marino roads typically much more dangerous than those in Denmark and Sweden, though much safer than those in the not-so-serene portion of the Region of the Americas otherwise known as the USA.

The upshot: I stand by my claim that Denmark's **roads** are among the safest in the world.

But does this mean Denmark's **drivers** are among the safest in the world? Not necessarily. In fact, another quick glance at a graph shows they're not.

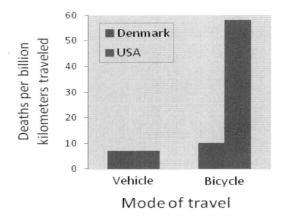

Mode of travel

Surprisingly, Danes and Yanks are virtually identical in the rate at which drivers kill people *per unit distance* traveled. This implies that the roads in Denmark are so much safer (4 times) than those in USA mainly because Danes drive so much less than Yanks (who lead the world with an astonishing 3 TRILLION kilometers driven annually).

The punchline:

Fewer cars makes for safer roads for all concerned, including motorists themselves. Danes on *cykels* seem to be safer not because drivers are better per se but largely as a byproduct of the mutual exclusivity of driving and cycling. In other words, if you're pedaling a bicycle, you're not clutching a steering wheel. The improved safety for cyclists in Denmark (and other European countries) may largely reflect the fact that there are fewer cars on the road when more people commute by bike.

By encouraging bicycle-commuting — with dedicated bike lanes and a legal system that frowns on killing cyclists — the Danes have improved road safety for everyone. They've done so seemingly not by making their drivers kinder and gentler but rather by reducing their numbers. Cyclists and drivers coexist relatively peacefully partly because it's easier to coexist with drivers when there are fewer of them. And the number of drivers is projected to keep falling, which should make cycling even safer.

How safe are Danes on their *cykels*? Check out the graph again and you'll see that Danes are already almost as safe on their *cykels* as they are in cars *per unit distance*! (In the USA, cycling a given distance is about 8 times more dangerous than driving that far.)

And according to my back-of-the-envelope calculations, traveling by bicycle is already safer than traveling by car *per unit time*.

Using fatality rates of 6.9 (car) and 9.9 (bike) deaths per billion kilometers traveled and assuming average travel speeds of 45 (car) and 15 kilometers per hour (bike) yields estimates of 3.1 x 10^{-7} car-related and 1.5 x 10^{-7} bike-related deaths per hour spent traveling. Recognizing that car-related fatalities include all victims (i.e., motorists, passengers, pedestrians, and cyclists) and bicycle-related fatalities include cyclists only, traveling by bicycle is currently about twice as safe as traveling by car per unit time.

And leave it to the Danes: it's getting safer by the minute!

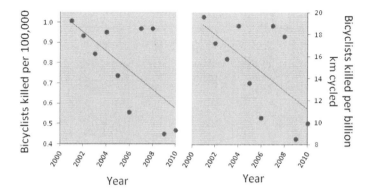

Over the past decade, cycling has become safer both per unit distance and per unit time. Pretty soon, it'll be safer to pedal a *cykel* than to sit on a *sofa*.

On top of everything else, Danes are getting safer partly because they're becoming increasingly willing to wear helmets while pedaling — and even while *walking*. The Danish Road Safety Council has launched a campaign promoting walking helmets. They've posted signs with the slogan, *en gårhelm er en go' helm* (translation: a walking helmet is a good helmet). Citing concern over the fact that pedestrians have a higher risk of head injury than do cyclists, the DRSC recommends stylish new walking helmets for pedestrians "and other good folk in high risk groups."

Not to brag, but I could be the poster boy for this long-overdue walking helmet campaign. When I get off my bike, I almost never take off my (unstylish) helmet. It instantly becomes a de facto walking helmet and then a sitting helmet and even a typing helmet. Heck, I'm wearing my typing helmet at this very moment as I hunt and peck for the right keys to finish this sentence. Sure, I look like a doofus. But, hey, I'm sitting under a grapefruit tree and that puts me in a high-risk group, so

I think it wise to obey another catchy slogan: *sikkerhed først* (safety first)!

And when I finish these final sentences, I'll pedal away more safely than the typical death-defying Dane — with six flashing lights, a neon yellow jersey and matching socks, and of course with my cycling/walking/ sitting/typing helmet snugly encasing my cranium.

May all your rides be as safe as mine.

Chapter 8

Safety First!

How to be Safer than a Dane on a *Cykel*

You're probably going to dismiss me as an apologist for all things cycling, but it's true: I've always felt safe on a bike. In fact, except for those rare moments of imminent impact with truck or pavement, I've almost always felt safer on a bike than on foot. And I think I know why: it's all about the Darwinian advantage of speed.

Here's my intuitively plausible explanation (otherwise known as arm-waving). On foot, I'm slow and vulnerable, plump and tasty. I'm easy prey. It's a primal fear. But on a bike, I'm fast and safe. The bike improves my ability to flee, to sprint to safety. Bike speed makes me *feel* safer, I think, because it potentially confers an actual survival advantage.

I can't even begin to count the number of times I've blithely pedaled through supposedly sketchy neighborhoods in the middle of the night and felt perfectly safe doing so *because* I was on my bike.

And the Speed of Car makes folks even more delusional about their safety. They feel invincible behind the wheel of their SUVs. They boldly drive through neighborhoods where they wouldn't dream of stopping and taking a stroll, and they feel safe doing it.

Most drivers also apparently feel perfectly comfortable tailgating at high speeds and yet they wouldn't dream of following someone that closely on foot.

Impeccable logic notwithstanding, I could be wrong.

I'm well aware that my addiction to traveling at the speed of bike may be perceived as an unfortunate byproduct of modernity. The bicycle after all is a very recent invention. For a quarter of a million years, modern humans were constrained to traveling at the speed of foot. Like overindulging on now-superabundant fat, sugar, and salt, my bike-addiction may represent a mismatch between historically adaptive behavior and evolutionarily irrelevant modern conditions.

My feeling safe on a bike could be illusory, so I indulge in a little faith-based superstition to help keep me safe. I carry a mojo, a good-luck charm. Specifically, I keep a St. Christopher medal stowed away in the bottom of a pannier — just in case it's kosher for a heathen/secular humanist like me to freeload, to co-opt this element of Catholic tradition. (Actually, I carry it to mollify a friend who remains a True Believer; he insists I carry Chris at all times and so I do.)

Coming from an academic field with an intellectual tradition of near-universal atheism/agnosticism, I hardly qualify as a Catholic. In fact, I recall only two occasions when someone might have momentarily mistaken me for a Catholic. The first time was when I visited the Pope, in Vatican City — along with

200,000 of my closest friends, including model Susan Anton, who towered over the throngs. Eventually, I realized she was accompanied by her then-lover, the almost-as-short-as-Danny-DeVito actor, Dudley Moore. I got distracted by this odd couple and forgot all about the Pope. Besides, my comprehension of spoken Latin was submarginal, so I really had no idea what he was saying.

And the only time I've ever done anything formal inside a Catholic church was when I served as best man in a wedding. That went sideways when I had a full-blown panic attack induced by kneeling on that carpet-covered board thingy while wearing a too-tight tux. I had to call "time out" and retreat to the apse to recover. The groom snapped at me. The priest was not amused. I've been phobic about Catholic churches ever since.

Come to think of it, a few years ago I did give an invited research seminar at the University of Notre Dame in South Bend, Indiana. During the visit, I pondered what it would be like to work there, where evolutionary biology faculty must have a high tolerance for students whose indoctrination doesn't exactly embrace the adaptationist paradigm. On the plus side, the students do seem to embrace their mandate to help the poor and homeless.

Which reminds me: when I'm touring I like to connect with members of the local homeless community. And I sometimes find myself volunteering at shelters and soup kitchens, which not surprisingly often turn out to be run by the local Catholic diocese (rather than some loose band of atheists). Maybe that has earned me a little karmic credit with the Vatican's official score-keeper.

In any case, I hope it's not too presumptuous for me to count on Chris and his placebo-effect patronage. As you undoubtedly know, Chris is the patron saint of travelers, protecting them from a vast array of threats, including lightning and pestilence. But you may not know that his powers of patronage have diversified through cultural evolution such that he now protects athletes, bachelors, soldiers, and a whole host of others from all sorts of bad luck. If only such delusions were true, I'd ask Chris to protect me daily, first and foremost, from the Car People. And each time the need arose, I'd ask for his protection against carpal tunnel syndrome, Achilles tendonitis, poison oak, athlete's foot and jock itch, bee stings, bed bugs, dehydration, dysentery, pneumonia, unleashed dogs, halitosis, and chapped lips.

Elsewhere I ask whether all of this fictional protection is worth the price I pay in increased travel time. That's right, St. Chris slows me down. The upshot: the medal (sans chain) weighs me down by 2.9 grams and that adds nearly a third of a second to each of my 5727-km transcontinental forays. (Maybe I should carry a few thousand St. Chris medals and dole them out as rewards for random acts of road kindness.) Of course, whether you wish to pay such a steep price for St. Christopher's all-encompassing protection is entirely up to you.

~~~

Magical thinking aside, I also feel safe based on formal analysis of my risk. How safe am I, realistically? You be the judge.

One way to evaluate my risk is to compare it to that of notoriously dangerous occupations. This makes sense because my retirement is like a second career where

I've assigned myself the occupation of nomadic cyclist. So where do I fall on the list? Is my risk of fatal work-related injury worse than that of a deep-sea fisher, a logger and a rancher combined? More optimistically, maybe my chronic pedaling habit is relatively benign?

To assess my risk, let's start by assuming I pedal a mere 20,000 km per year and I'm about as safe as the typical Dane per unit distance traveled (i.e., 9.9 deaths per billion kilometers cycled, which converts to the infinitesimal probability of death per kilometer cycled of 9.9×10^{-9} or a shade under one in a hundred billion). Evaluating the so-called binomial cumulative distribution function, my annual risk is 0.0002.

> In other words, I have a 99.98% chance of avoiding a fatal crash during the coming year of pedaling.

That's the equivalent of 20 fatal crashes per 100,000 hypothetical clones of me. And this means my chosen "occupation" barely cracks the Top 10 on the list of most dangerous jobs in the USA, edging out cab-driving.

My retirement gig, as reckless as it may seem to some bystanders, keeps me considerably safer than I would be spending my days overexploiting salmon fisheries or clear-cutting national forests or piloting bush planes in Alaska or collecting recyclables or scampering around on rooftops or dangling from girders on high rises. Call me Captain Caution.

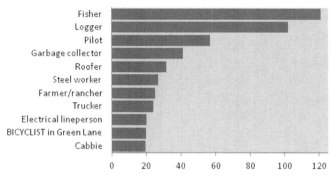

Fatal injuries per 100,000 full-time workers

On the other hand, naysayers among you will note that my self-imposed risk is on par with that of folks who install electrical lines while suspended in bucket trucks or hurtle through traffic fetching people from the airport.

And you'd be right to point out that I have every intention of taking this risk year after year. So, what's my risk of getting killed in a crash, assuming I travel 20,000 km annually for 20 years?

> It's 0.004. Framed optimistically, I have a 99.6% chance of avoiding a fatal crash. I like my chances, especially considering I have a high risk of dying from other causes during that time span and because I can presumably reduce my risk for some of them by doing so much healthy pedaling.

But let's consider a more optimistic scenario. I've already argued that I'm happier than the typical Dane, so why wouldn't I be safer as well? Let's suppose the flashing lights on my bike and my neon yellow jersey and my hypervigilance all serve to keep me considerably safer than the typical Dane on a *cykel*. Let's assume I'm twice as safe. How does this affect my annual risk? My occupation disappears from the list, as I become twice as safe as a cab-driving Yank.

And even if I were to remain only as safe as the typical Dane on a *cykel*, but reduce my annual distance traveled to 15,000 km — just under the average distance traveled by Yanks in automobiles — my risk would fall to 14.8 per 100,000 (i.e., still off the list).

But what if I follow through with my ambitious goal of pedaling the equivalent of 18 times around the world in my remaining time? My probability of avoiding a fatal crash would be 99.21%, which strikes me as acceptable.

Is this goal feasible? If I were to pedal every day for the next 20 years, how far would I need to go daily to meet my goal? It's only about 110 km (68 miles). That's perfectly doable, provided I stop squandering precious pedaling time by sitting here pecking away at this keyboard at 0.0 km/h, with grapefruits bouncing off my helmet at 10 km/h.

Turns out, it's just not feasible for me to die by cycling too much — unless of course I stage my own demise via head-on collision.

~~~

I've argued that my cycling habit is safer than it seems and yet I obviously expend a lot of mental energy pondering ways to be even safer. For years, I've tried to compensate for biases, constraints, and illusions that pervade the minds of humans, particularly while they're driving. From my perspective, all acts of driving are intrinsically dangerous, potentially lethal. And yet the typical driver doesn't see it this way. The typical driver thinks he or she is "above average" in driving ability.

Just as 95% of newlyweds claim *their* marriage will last forever — even after they've been reminded of the high divorce rate in society at large — nearly every driver I ask claims to be better than average.

These same folks readily acknowledge that they suck at doing double integrals in their head, conversing in *French*, diagramming sentences (even *en Anglais*), figure skating, playing the violin, speaking in public, remembering names, and a million other things. Yet they remain convinced they excel at driving.

This pervasive overconfidence fits with my impression that the typical driver doesn't think risks incurred by speeding, tailgating, and multi-tasking apply to him or her.

And over and above all else, the typical driver apparently has no inkling that the central nervous system filters evolutionarily irrelevant stimuli — including bicyclists, who after all are no more threatening than a gnat.

For years, I unwittingly encouraged drivers to filter me, like the quintessential invisible gorilla. I wore drab clothes and had no lights on my bike. I was as stealthy as a raccoon. But, eventually, after one too many experiences of the near-death variety, I began experimenting with ways to make myself less invisible.

And I really did perform quasi-experiments, using myself as the subject ($n=1$). The results were unambiguous: on "control days" when I didn't use neon gear or lights, I'd have one near miss after another. Drivers behaved as if I didn't exist or they grossly underestimated my speed and then darted in front of me. I was in grave danger at one intersection after another.

With empirical evidence mounting, I resorted to more and more neon gear and flashing lights, even in broad daylight. Eventually, drivers granted me the right of way more often than not. These days, I overcompensate with neon gear from head to toe and *six* flashing lights — including a retina-scorching 700-lumen flashing headlight and two 60-lumen flashing tail-lights. I'm an extremely visually conspicuous prey — like an aposematically colored venomous snake or poison frog or skunk — signaling my unprofitability to would-be predators. I've become much safer simply by making myself highly conspicuous, so much so that some drivers mistake me for a cop.

When this happens, the armor-plated varmint (APV) operating the motor vehicle sometimes stops in the middle of an intersection or where no intersection exists as if to grant me the right-of-way, which of course isn't mine. I think I've created extra risks for APVs.

Beyond making myself highly noticeable, I've also adjusted my riding style — in a gender-bending way. As my testosterone titers plummet and my lifetime tally of near-death experiences mounts, I find myself cycling with less daring and machismo. I find myself acting less like a hardcore risk-seeking young-and-male bicycle courier. I find myself emulating women, who get themselves killed at much slower rates than men in general and even while cycling.

In Denmark, two-thirds of cyclists killed in recent years (2008-2010) were men. Meanwhile, men accounted for just a shade over half (52%) of the aggregate distance cycled. Taken together, these facts indicate that Danish women are nearly twice as safe on their *cykels* as are their male counterparts.

I've been trying to copy the cycling style of several friends who happen not to carry the spindly Y-chromosome. In doing so, I find myself being more patient, deliberative even, especially at intersections. I find myself slowing down, not always showing off, not always racing against the clock or invisible competitors. And I think my slowing down is really paying off: I'm better at avoiding those suddenly opening car doors not to mention potholes and piles of GRIZZ scat. I've shifted along the speed-safety tradeoff curve in favor of safety. I really am convinced I'm getting safer. It's been *hours* since my last near-death experience.

I haven't yet resorted to female impersonation, but I may do so as it could make me even safer.

Believe it or not, a study in Great Britain found that cross-dressing paid safety dividends. Apparently tapping into chauvinistic driving tendencies, both male and female drivers gave a wider berth when a (male) cyclist wore a wig.

I think I need to do some *re*search of my own.

The next time you see me *sans* beard pedaling through your town sporting stilettos, a neon dress, and a blonde wig, you'll know why. Better safe than sorry.

~~~

Of course, the most obvious way to improve safety for cyclists would be to ban cars. If I ever get appointed to the post of Benign Dictator of Earth, I pledge to make this Job One. Until this epic change comes about, I have one humble request for Car People: please obey the 10 Commandments for Drivers, as prescribed by the Pope *et al.* (2007).

I kid you not. The Vatican really did produce such a list, which they targeted at their own bishops, priests, and other religious and pastoral workers. They produced this list to promote moral driving not so much inside Vatican City but in the world at large.

> Within the Vatican, the car ownership rate is extraordinarily high, with vehicles outnumbering residents, roughly 1000 to 800. And yet the fatal accident rate is low, presumably because the speed limit is just 30 km/h (19 mph), which happens to be the top speed of the PopeMobile. But beyond the border of the enclaved city-state, religious leaders and pastoral caregivers routinely drive at deadly speeds.

Without further ado, here's The List:

I. You shall not kill.

> Really? I hate to be snarky in this context, but isn't that plagiarism — of the *Bible*? Technically, no, the Pope *et al.* properly cited their sources, which included the *Bible*, both testaments, and of course the American Automobile Association.

> But, seriously, if bishops, priests and other pastoral caregivers need to be reminded not to *kill* people while driving around helping the needy, what hope is there for the rest of us?

Without further editorializing, here's the rest of The List:

II. The road shall be for you a means of communion between people and not of mortal harm.

III. Courtesy, uprightness and prudence will help you deal with unforeseen events.

IV. Be charitable and help your neighbor in need, especially victims of accidents.

V. Cars shall not be for you an expression of power and domination, and an occasion of sin.

VI. Charitably convince the young and not so young not to drive when they are not in a fitting condition to do so.

VII. Support the families of accident victims.

VIII. Bring guilty motorists and their victims together, at the appropriate time, so that they can undergo the liberating experience of forgiveness.

IX. On the road, protect the more vulnerable party.

X. Feel responsible towards others.

As you can readily see, the (Catholic) driver who hit me with his monster truck violated commandments II through X in that he:

II. Committed mortal harm.

III. Acted discourteously and imprudently, to put it euphemistically.

IV. Failed to help his victim.

V. Used his vehicle as an expression of power and dominance while flagrantly committing a sin.

VI. Failed to convince himself not to drive while in an unfit state of mind.

VII. "Forgot" to support his victim adequately.

VIII. Failed to meet with his victim to receive liberating forgiveness.

IX. Failed to protect the indisputably more vulnerable party.

X. Felt decidedly irresponsible toward others.

Luckily, he did manage to obey the first commandment, albeit just barely.

In light of such total disregard for the Vatican's Commandments for Drivers, isn't it high time someone developed a list tailored for the safety of cyclists? Challenge accepted. In the spirit of the 10 Commandments in the Loose Canon, the "bible" of the Church of the Flying Spaghetti Monster, I hereby offer 10 Loose Suggestions for Drivers:

I. Thou shall not use thine vehicle as a weapon, to kill, maim, or mutilate persons of the cycling variety.

> All such infractions of the moral driving code peeve thine holiness, the Great Pedaling One Above, no end. He or she who doth lose thine freakin' mind and weaponize thine vehicle will be punished severely, as the ultimate heretic infidel, with permanent loss of license and public shunning and worse.

> And thou shall always keep in mind that thine vehicle is intrinsically a weapon. Do not think for a moment that killing a cyclist "by accident" is somehow okay. Thine holiness, the Great Noodley Sky-god, has a special place in Hell for you as well.

II. Thou shall refrain from distracting thineself with the texting and the talking and the downloading of the music and videos on the phone of the cell.

Doth thou think driving is magically improved by multi-tasking, by dividing thine already too-limited attention? And doth thou not recognize that the Paleolithic brain filters evolutionarily irrelevant stimuli, including cyclists, which makes thou highly prone to committing involuntary vehicular cyclist-slaughter?

III. Thou shall refrain from all temptation to engage in the gating of the tail.

This is a pet peeve of thine holiness. Doesn't thou realize the loss of information that cascades through a peloton of drivers? The lead driver usually sees the cyclist and swerves accordingly. The first gater of the tail, whose view is blocked, overreacts and swerves even more, but the next gater of the tail has too little time to react and so hardly swerves at all, and the next gaters of the tail receive little or no timely information about the cyclist and so whizz by perilously close to elbow and knee and helmet.

Thine holiness acknowledges that the gating of the tail is a mathematical inescapability, ergo it's universal. Only an over-the-top interventionist god could magically orchestrate Car People to space maximally and then maintain a perfectly constant speed forever. Thine holiness thus really insists that thou do the best thou can, recognizing that all driving is potentially homicidal. From the cyclist's perspective, thine vehicle and thine assault rifle are indistinguishable in their deadliness.

IV. Thou shall always signal thine upcoming turn.

Doth thou think cyclists can read thine freakin' mind, that they can somehow reliably intuit thou will be making an injudicious left turn when they're going straight?

V. Thou shall refrain from all acts of rage of the road.

Failure to obey this loose suggestion will trigger the enforcement of compulsory anger-management training. And thou driving privileges shall be revoked indefinitely, until thine holiness is convinced that thou can drive without going bat-shit crazy toward cyclists.

VI. Thou shall give cyclists a wide berth.

But this does not mean thou shall totally overreact and move into the opposite lane with oncoming traffic.

VII. Thou shall pay for all medical expenses and provide support to the family members of thine cycling victims.

And thou shall do so magnanimously, without whining about the spike in the cost of thine auto insurance.

VIII. Thou shall refrain from all acts of driving while under the influence of fermented beverages or other mind-altering substances or while dozing repeatedly.

And doth thou really think the designated driver should be someone who volunteers to quit doing shots at 11 PM, such that his blood alcohol content drops to roughly twice the legal limit by the time he drives everyone home? Surely, we should emulate the Swedes, who permit each other to drive only when blood alcohol content is 0.00%. And recall, they have the safest roads in the world! (Yanks kill each other on the roads 424% faster per capita than do Swedes.) And the roads in Sweden are about to get even safer as Volvo has just launched a new vehicle that comes equipped with a special system for detecting and automatically braking for bicyclists, pedestrians, and other vehicles.

IX. Thou shall refrain from all forms of menacing, gesturing, and intimidating — including the honking of thine horn and the yelling out thine window and the showing of thine middle digit.

The honking scares the Bejesus out of cyclists, causing a spike in cortisol levels and making them madder than a hornet. The yelling makes them feel vulnerable, even though they usually can't understand your hate-filled words. And the digit-showing is pointless because they assume you're waving or giving them thumbs up.

X. Thou shall share thy road, like you really mean it, as if each cyclist is thine own child.

The eye in the sky is always watching. Always. And these days, if you go ballistic toward a cyclist — honking menacingly, nearly running the cyclist off the road, yelling thine favorite homophobic slurs out the window — thou should know that thou will be recorded by the cyclist's iDevice and thou will go viral on Spacebook. Thine reputation, such as it was, will have been shot to hell. These days, thou can't be thineself with impunity. These days, there's an app for that.

Naturally, moral driving shall be its own reward. But as an extra incentive, Heaven awaits all True Believers who obey these Loose Suggestions. In Heaven, all roads will be de facto dedicated bike lanes and there will be no horn honking, as there will be no cars. And cycling will be heavenly, with perpetual tailwinds pushing self-propelled travelers through redwood cathedrals and saguaro "forests" and across arctic tundra and along sea cliffs to vibrant towns with live music and craft beer and artisanal pizza and fresh pasta. And the wearing of thine helmet shall be optional.

Addenda

Yesterday, an old friend of mine died from complications stemming from an involuntary dismount of the worst kind. She wasn't obliterated in a car-against-bike crash. Instead, she was happily pedaling across a familiar but newly renovated bridge near her town in Massachusetts when her front wheel suddenly got stuck in a new grate catapulting her face first into the pavement. The bridge had been renovated by Car People, for Car People, and apparently with total disregard for the safety of Bicycle People. Tragically, the renovation had created a literal deathtrap for a graduate of both Harvard and Stanford and a mother of two and one fine Bike Person to boot. Be assured, thine holiness smites with great wrath all those who commit such blatant acts of criminally negligent homicide.

And today the news reports include confirmation that the driver who recently killed a man who was dribbling a soccer ball from Seattle to Brazil — in the name of charity — has been charged with vehicular homicide.

Maybe there's a crack in the amour. Maybe there's even a seismic cultural shift taking place, whereby it's becoming unsavory to kill cyclists whether through good ole fashioned malicious intent or through criminal neglect. As someone who pedaled past both of these fatal spots within the last year, I'm okay with that.

Requiescat en Pace

Flash forward a couple months:

Today, I happened upon an article in the Toronto daily newspaper. The gist: police will begin cracking down on scofflaw cyclists throughout the Province of Ontario. The rationale: this will improve safety for bicyclists and potentially lead to a veritable cycling utopia where Ontarioans will feel free to leave their cars at home and pedal to work. Priceless, I know! This is the epitome of sophistic apologia. In other words, it's business as usual as once again a bizarrely byzantine bicycle safety initiative has been dreamt up by blissfully oblivious Car People for blissfully oblivious Car People.

But it gets better. The journalist — and I use that term loosely — cited 129 deaths of cyclists throughout the province over a recent 4-year span. He conveniently failed to mention that these cyclists were killed not by other cyclists but rather in every case by Car People. Meanwhile, the death toll for Car People summed across these 129 crashes was precisely zero!

So let me get this straight, the police plan to crack down not on the killers but on the would-be victims. That should work. Just provide a disincentive for cyclists as the key feature of a cycling advocacy policy. Makes sense. Stay tuned for next week's announcement of the new minimum mandatory sentences for heinous folks brought up on jaywalking charges.

Even if you don't embrace the notion that public policy should favor the victim, surely you can support an egalitarian approach? In that spirit, here's my elegant recommendation: let's start enforcing the traffic laws for *all* people, even including the vaunted Car People. Oh wait, what am I smoking? That won't work. As far as I can tell, every Car Person violates the law virtually every time she or he gets behind the wheel.

Skeptical? Well, take a look at the data I just compiled here in Huntsville, Ontario. I arbitrarily picked 20 cars, one at a time, and followed each car for a few blocks to see whether any infractions might occur. Here's the list with the number of drivers committing each infraction given in brackets:

- Failure to stop at stop sign [6]
- Failure to stop at solid red light [7]
- Failure to stop at or before sign or line [7]
- Failure to stop at flashing red light [2]
- Failure to signal turn [4]
- Failure to signal lane change [6]
- Failure to signal pulling away from curb [4]
- Entering intersection while light is amber [3]
- Entering intersection while light is red [2]
- Straddling solid yellow line [5]
- Driving across solid white lines [6]
- Failure to yield right of way [3]
- Failure to signal merging [2]
- Tailgating [9]
- Excessive speed [13]
- Failure to allow 1 m clearance for cyclist [8]
- Distracted driving (texting) [3]
- Operating vehicle with missing headlight [1]

- Excessive acceleration [3]
- Parking in fire lane [2]
- Suspected of OUI [7]

All 20 drivers committed at least two infractions. One committed nine. On average, drivers committed a shade over five infractions. You get the point. Even in this idyllic place known as Cottage Country, where folks are notoriously polite, extralegal activities are perpetrated universally.

Even if just to pander to the Car People, I would have gladly amassed a comparable data set for cycling counterparts in the Greater Huntsville Region, but for one minor limitation: I saw no fellow cyclists, presumably thanks in part to the unwelcoming climate for such folks.

But you and I both know it would have been mayhem if any cyclists had been present. They would have pedaled like arrogant reckless fools who really shouldn't be allowed in public. I mean, you can tell just by the way they look that at least half of them are against occupying nation states for cheap gasoline and against clubbing baby seals and against maximizing one's carbon footprint.

If I were the benign dictator of Canada, I would cite all drivers for "distracted driving" every time they get behind the wheel. From the Darwinian cyclist's perspective, all driving is intrinsically distracted driving. There's no such thing as undistracted driving. That's oxymoronic because the driver is always distracted by the need to scan for cars and trucks and buses. The moment a driver gets behind the wheel, the biological imperative (i.e., survival instinct) takes over and he or she starts selfishly filtering evolutionarily irrelevant stimuli — stuff that isn't deadly, like dragonflies and cyclists. The driver starts counting basketball passes (i.e., scanning for cars and trucks and buses) and runs the risk of failing to see the invisible gorilla (i.e., the cyclist).

To remedy this distracted-driving problem I'd provide a strong disincentive — say an automatic deduction of 100 "twoonies," or $200, just for turning the ignition key — such that the typical driver would simply opt to stay home. And then, of course, I'd be forced to rescind my draconian distracted-driving law on day 2 or 3 of the ensuing mutiny.

Clearly, a genuine crackdown on drivers isn't feasible. I guess we the Bicycle People will have to brace ourselves for the flashing blue lights and harassment. Of course, you and I both know nothing will come of this. My hunch is the total number of citations issued to bicyclists throughout the province over the next 5 years will be laughably finite, perhaps something on the order of seven.

For my own edification, though, I think I'll go test this prediction right now. I'll start with a series of oxymoronic "rolling stops," which are legal maneuvers in places like Oregon that genuinely promote cycling. And I'll ad lib a few other violations. Stay tuned.

Just back from committing such acts of civil disobedience and I'm afraid to say that my lifetime total of cycling citations remains stuck on nil.

One final thought:

If Car People truly wish to improve road safety for cyclists, they could take the lead from the fine folks of Midlake, Ontario, who recently created a ball-free soccer league. Believe it or not, the kids wear uniforms and play on named teams and the teams even belong to an official league — and yet they don't use a ball. Aimed at promoting fun exercise for kids whose self-esteem could be damaged by playing the beautiful game with a ball, the league has been a great success. It's been so successful, in fact, that the inaugural season of puck-free hockey is about to get underway. You see where I'm headed, right?

What we need is a province-wide League of Car-free Drivers. They could do their car-free driving online in a massively multi-player role-playing game. They could amass points for missing digital cyclists and reducing their carbon emissions and so on. The projected outcome: with fewer Car People on the roads, bicycle safety should improve accordingly.

(Never mind that news of this ball-free soccer league proved to be a yet another spoof perpetrated by CBC Radio. And never mind the fact that I was duped yet again.)

~

An even more final thought:

I'm now back in Maine, where the 3-feet law has been in place for a couple years now, there's been a precedent-setting shift in the interpretation and enforcement of the law. Until recently, Car People who hit Bicycle People typically weren't charged for violating any motor vehicle law, not even the 3-feet law. But in a flash of brilliance and after a latency of two years, somebody has finally agreed with my vehemently held position on the matter: if you hit a bicyclist with your car, you have *ipso facto* violated the 3-feet law — by exactly 3 feet.

And so, you should be *automatically* charged for this violation, for starters.

Coincidentally, a woman backed out of her driveway 12 minutes ago, after filtering the invisible gorilla pedaling in the bike lane (i.e., me). In doing so, she violated the 3-feet law by 3 feet, knocking me off my bike and into a cortisol-fueled rage. I wasn't hurt and even managed to video-tape her as she sped away from the hit-and-run scene and then proceeded to tailgate and turn left despite an apparently inoperable turn signal. Meanwhile, the police are reluctant to charge her with violating the 3-feet rule, presumably because they have better things to do — like crack down on jaywalking.

Safety First!

🚲 🚲 🚲 🚲 🚲

GOOD MEDICINE

Chapter 9

Of Course the Danes are Healthy: They Pedal!

But How's Their Longevity?

Those pedaling Danes are annoyingly happy and safe, but are they annoyingly healthy as well? Presumably, the typical Dane arrives under her own pedal power for regular checkups with her personal physician, who gives her yet another clean bill of health. And then she celebrates her good health — plaque-free arteries and all — by pedaling across town for a savory yet healthy snack.

Leave it to the Danes to have pristine coronary arteries on top of everything else. Presumably, the typical 50-something bike-commuting Dane has cardiovascular health rivaling that of a 20-something vegan: no problems with hypertension or high blood sugar or elevated triglycerides. That's annoying, no?

LONG LIVE THE DANES

If the Danes are really so healthy, they must be among the world leaders in staying-alive. Sure enough, over the last half-century (1960-2010), the Danes and their neighbors have headed the global list in life expectancy. Only Norway (73.6 years), the Netherlands (73.4), and Sweden (73.0) harbored slightly longer-living humans than Denmark (72.2). Meanwhile, the USA ranked 16th, at 69.8 years. Long live the Danes and their happy, safe neighbors!

In the interest of full disclosure, lots of developed countries have caught up to the Danes and their long-lived Nordic neighbors in recent years. But one of these countries, USA, has started showing warning signs. The forecast is gloomy. Thanks to skyrocketing obesity, the life expectancy of Yanks is poised to fall for the first time in the modern era, plummeting by as much as 5 years over the coming decades. Meanwhile, no such downturn is forecast for the pedaling Danes.

Of course, whether cycling plays a causal role remains an open question. But to the extent that cycling makes folks less prone to obesity, we should be able to find some evidence that Danes are less vulnerable to coronary heart disease.

Let's confront this hypothesis with the cold hard empirical truth, with objectivity and skepticism. And if that doesn't work out, I'll cherry-pick a few factoids to build the case.

OF COURSE THEY'RE SKINNY

Ideally, I'd generate my own dataset. I could use calipers to pinch skin and then use a formula that converts fold size to percent body fat. Alternatively, I could weigh and then submerge each person in water, measure the displacement, and then use a formula that accounts for the fact that fat is less dense than other tissues. Better yet, I could get each person to step on one of those gizmos that looks like an ordinary bathroom scale but actually measures impedance of the electronic signal by body fat. But these methods all seem too intrusive.

As a quick-and-dirty alternative, I could simply ask each volunteer for his or her height and weight and then use a handy-dandy BMI calculator. As you probably know, BMI stands for body mass index. Calculated as body mass in kilograms divided by the square of height in meters, it's a proxy for shape, a measure of rotundity. As you may recall, if your BMI equals or exceeds 30, you're obese. (This threshold conveniently corresponds to 30% body fat.) I could easily generate a BMI dataset. But even this method feels a bit intrusive. After all, Yanks don't like to admit their true weight to anyone, including themselves.

Fortunately, I don't need to collect my own data because the kind folks at world life expectancy dot com have already compiled country-specific estimates of the percentage of adults who are obese. Let's take a look.

Rumor has it the typical Yank is less skinny than the typical human from virtually everywhere on Earth. And it's true: among the usual benchmark "industrialized" countries (including Canada, European countries, Israel, Japan, Australia, and New Zealand), Yanks blow away the competition. Nearly half of all American adults are obese (i.e., 42% of men and 49% of women, ranking 7th and 16th of 192 countries) and two-thirds of us are overweight (defined as BMI $\geq$ 25). And we're getting fatter by the year.

I figure our body fat alone would outweigh the human population in each of 96% of the countries on Earth. Collectively, our adipose tissue tips the scales at about 3 million tons, which outweighs all of our bicycles and dogs and cats combined.

How 'bout the Danes? Their classic Western diet is loaded with carbs and bad cholesterol and calories. That can't be good for their waistline. And yet they're appreciably skinnier than Yanks? Yes, compared with the typical Yank, the typical Dane is lacking by about 50 pounds of adipose tissue (or 7 dress sizes). Leave it to the Danes: despite their wealth and hence ready access to all things fattening, they remain quite lean. Only about one in six men and one in 10 women are obese (i.e., 15% of men and 10% of women, ranking 81st and 143rd). Not bad.

OF COURSE THEY HAVE GOOD HEARTS

Do the skinny Danes have better heart health than Yanks? Afraid so. While coronary heart disease (CHD) is the leading cause of death in both countries, particularly for folks in their 40s or older, the Danes at 15.4% beat the Yanks at 21.4%. On average, Yanks suffer a 44% higher risk of dying from CHD (80.5 versus 55.9 deaths per 100,000, age-standardized).

According to my back-of-the-envelope calculations, if Yanks could improve their cardiovascular prospects to match those of the Danes, we could extend about 75,000 American lives annually.

Leave it to the happy-safe-skinny Danes: They really do have lower mortality as caused by this all-important age-related disease. They really do a better job of staving off cardiovascular senescence, perhaps owing to that pedaling habit of theirs.

Just think, if you were to push your bike's pedals a few billion times, you too could conceivably slash your risk of coronary heart disease, thereby adding many thousands of seconds to your life! Seriously, though, you can potentially add decades to your life by saying no to the temptation to pursue a sloth-like lifestyle — where you push only gas, clutch, and brakes pedals and eventually experience shortness of breath while doing so.

WHAT'S SO SPECIAL ABOUT THE DANES?

If only there were another country where folks do a lot of pedaling, we could ask whether they're comparably healthy. Otherwise, we're left to wonder whether the Danes are just a statistical outlier, an anomaly. Oh wait, how 'bout those happy, safe pedaling folks in the Netherlands? They pedal at least as much as Danes. In fact, in annual per capita pedaling distance, they rank #1. If pedaling really matters, they should be healthy.

But are they comparably long-lived? Yes, indeed. Over the last half-century, they've been in a virtual tie for the longest-lived humans on Earth, with Norwegians outliving them by just a couple months, on average.

And are they skinny? Yes, in the Netherlands, only about one in six adults is obese, regardless of gender and despite their seemingly unhealthy Western diet.

And are they not too prone to coronary heart disease? Yes, when it comes to avoiding death via CHD, they're in the 97th percentile or the 6th best country in the world (i.e., they rank 187th of 192 countries in per capita risk). At a shade under 40 deaths per 100,000, the risk is 51% lower than in The States and 13% lower than in Denmark. The skinny pedaling neighbors from the Netherlands have even better cardiovascular health than the Danes. Of course they do, they outpedal the Danes.

IS IT REALLY THE CYCLING?

I'd like to think so. But enough rumor and innuendo and speculation, what does the formal literature tell us? Well, there's a mountain of evidence that contrived forms of exercise (a.k.a., "going to the gym") can improve not just indicators of cardiovascular fitness (like blood pressure) but also cardiovascular "endpoints" (like *death*).

But what's the evidence for cardiovascular benefits of *cycling*? Specifically, what's the evidence for the kind of cycling that Danes love and Yanks loathe, namely bicycle *commuting*? Well, there's a molehill of evidence. Based on eight published epidemiological studies, a formal meta-analysis of 15 measured effects of active commuting (i.e., walking and cycling) revealed robust benefits, particularly for women. Actively commuting women were less likely to develop hypertension or diabetes or incident coronary heart disease, less likely to have a stroke, and — my personal favorite outcome — less likely to kick the bucket *during the study*. That's all good news, for women.

For men, the results were equivocal. The cardiovascular benefits were still mostly positive, but weaker and less robust. And we all know why. Let's face it, men are untrustworthy. If the actively commuting men included in these studies were anything like my male friends, they commute by bicycle mostly to show off. And then, when they think nobody's looking, they reward themselves for their good behavior by overindulging on triple bacon cheeseburgers and scotch and cigars.

I now have a second compelling reason to bike like a woman: beyond keeping me safe, it may also retard the rate at which plaque clogs my coronary arteries.

Seriously, these findings provide powerful new ammo for advocates of bicycle *commuting*. We're no longer limited by wishy washy claims that it's great for staying in shape and perhaps even better than contrived leisure-time exercise.

My favorite way of framing this argument is to pit Jim the Gym Rat against Pete the Pedaler. Imagine Jim showing up at the gym on New Year's Day. He's gung-ho and has every intention of taking full advantage of his new membership. He plans to go to the gym every day for the coming year. He's resolute. He gets off to a great start, going to the gym 7 days a week in January. Little by little, though, his enthusiasm wanes. He starts skipping a day here and there. Then his schedule gets hectic and he skips several days in a row. Pretty soon, Jim succumbs to the pandemic of absenteeism at the gym. And from mid-February to the end of December, he "remembers" to go to the gym nearly once.

His excuse, of course, is that he doesn't have the time. And yet, over the course of the year he squanders 30 hours in his car commuting to and from the gym — to ride a stationary bike — and 20 times that amount commuting to and from work and doing errands. In aggregate, he spends about a month frivolously driving when he could have been spent that time pedaling. He undershoots his goal to lose 20 pounds by 30 pounds. In December, he vows to re-up at the gym.

Meanwhile, Pete the Pedaler commutes by bicycle daily, throughout the year. He gets exercise incidentally, as a byproduct of his pedaling habit. He goes a whole year without feeling guilty or stressed about exercise. He's happy, lean, and healthy.

I always found this argument to be compelling enough. I spewed it whenever someone was patient enough to listen. But now I can up the ante. Thanks to the weight of evidence, I can argue confidently that active *commuting* per se can add years to your life, particularly if you don't suffer from the Y-chromosome syndrome.

If you want to be skinny and minimize your cardiovascular risk, make like a Dane and use you pedal power. You'll be happy, safe, and lean. And as a little side bonus, you may outlive the sedentary bastards. No offense, sedentary bastards. (Nearly all of my friends are sedentary bastards extraordinaire and car addicts to boot.)

Go pedal.

🚲 🚲 🚲 🚲 🚲

Chapter 10

Pedaling to an Early Grave?

Or Delaying my Own Demise in an Evolutionary Rational Way

As an example to others, and not that I care for moderation myself, it has always been my rule never to [pedal] when asleep, and never to refrain from [pedaling] when awake.

> — Corrupted Mark Twain quote about smoking

Moderation is a fatal thing. Nothing succeeds like excess.

> — Oscar Wilde

Yo, I can't do anything in moderation. I don't know how.

> — Eminem

Yo, imagine how truly healthy those Danes could be if they weren't so half-hearted about pedaling. Let's face it, the Danes are moderation personified. If you ask me, they pedal so little that it barely qualifies as exercise. They commute a few kilometers back and forth, within their town. So I'm like a Dane on PEDs (Danish: *doping med*). I live on my bike, pedaling everywhere. I commute back and forth across continents. So, if the typical Dane enjoys an extended shelf life, I must be pedaling my way to immortality. Or not.

There's one potential problem with this self-serving prognosis: it could be dead wrong. It does fly in the face of conventional wisdom. Unlike Twain and Wilde, most sages through the ages have warned against overindulgence.

We've all heard it a million times: Moderation is a virtue. In all things moderation. Too much of a good thing is a bad thing. Don't overdo it. Are you going to drink that whole bottle of wine?

We've even uttered such clichés ourselves, haven't we? I know I have, in a pinch. And I've done so despite firmly believing this axiomatic notion stems from a macabre plot to foment complacency among petty citizenry. So I'm not proud. But forget all of that. Forget my expedient invoking of the rule. Forget its imponderable origin. What should concern us now is only that well-meaning folks insist on applying this rule to all of our favorite things, including chocolate, wine, reading, and even exercise.

For millennia, the prevailing view was: too much strenuous exercise will send you to any early grave.

Greek philosophers/physicians spread the rumors. And is it any wonder they did? The first dude to run the eponymous marathon didn't fare so well. According to legend, Pheidippides in 490 CE ran nonstop from the battlefield of Marathon to Athens — roughly 26 miles — to deliver the news that the good guys, the Greeks, had kicked the butts of the bad guys, the Persians. But then, with a flair for the melodramatic, he dropped dead right on the spot.

Apocryphal or not, strenuous exercise has been cautioned against ever since.

While this tragic version of the legend gets all of the attention, I prefer the lesser-known alternative version, wherein our guy Pheidippides ran from Athens to Sparta — 150 miles — to get help. And then he turned right around and ran back, unscathed. He didn't have a physiological meltdown. His heart didn't explode. He was apparently none the worse for wear.

If only this ultra-version of the legend were the popular one. Just think, athensers, not marathoners, would run in 300-mile races called the Boston Athens, the New York Athens, and of course the Athens Athens.

Whatever the truth about our long-gone Greek messenger, the mythology about the perils of excessive exercise persists to this day. So we can't simply dismiss it as a quaint antiquated idea, a laughable notion from the olden days. These days nearly everyone — the general public, members of the medical community, and even my mom — agrees that exercise is a good thing, *provided it's done in moderation.* And if it's done to extremes, it may take a terrible toll, supposedly.

The sports medicine literature is replete with articles about risks for ultra-endurance athletes. These risks include: oxidative stress, immunosuppression, lower-limb osteoarthritis, fibrosis, arhythmogenic remodeling of the right ventricle, and, last but not least, sudden cardiac death.

Not to be an alarmist who stoops to intellectual disingenuousness by citing anecdotes, but I suppose now's as good a time as any to acknowledge that I was pedaling my way to see Micah True a few months ago, when he had the indecency to disappear. (He was the gringo ultra-marathoner who had gone feral and was living in the Copper Canyon country in Mexico and running with the Tarahumara, the world famous indigenous people who wear guanches fashioned from truck tires and skirts on their long runs, after having carbo-loaded on vast quantities of maize beer.) Back in New Mexico for a few months, Micah went out for his daily run one morning and never came back. Friends eventually found his body in a creek bed, near Geronimo's birth place. They carried him out on a white mule in honor of his nickname, *Caballo Blanco*. My elder by a few years, he'd apparently died of sudden cardiac failure.

But, surely, sudden cardiac death and other risks faced by *ultra-endurance athletes* don't apply to folks like me. I mostly lollygag along back roads and bike paths, spinning at the optimal cadence with lightly packed panniers. Surely, I'm exempt from these concerns. Surely, they don't apply to the kind of glorified commuting I do. Surely, pedaling semi-continuously tens of thousands of kilometers annually doesn't qualify as "too much." Or does it?

You see the flaw in my logic, right? Clearly, if you were to tag along with me, you'd feel like an ultra-endurance athlete of sorts. Like me, you probably wouldn't be elite. But if you were to pump pedals at 90 revolutions per minute for 6+ hours per day for hundreds of days per year, you'd become a de facto ultra-endurance athlete.

And your friends and family — including your soon-to-be former partner — might worry. Sure, they'd ooh and aah at your remodeled body: crazily bulging quads, freakishly defined calves, glutes of steel, and, of course, BEST ABS EVER. They'd comment on these superficial signs of your uberfitness, without realizing all of the crucial invisible changes you've undergone:

- enormous aerobic capacity with VO_2 max rivaling that of Eddy Merckx in his prime
- reptilian resting heart rate rivaling that of the former cheerleader-turned-cyclist, Dubya Bush
- increased vascularization of leg muscles rivaling the intricate web of lies woven by all those cyclists desperately trying to avoid even the appearance of doping (French: *la perception du dopage*)
- maxed out hematocrit (red blood cell count) rivaling that of Lance and the boys after centrifuging their own blood

Silently, though, your friends and family would probably worry about the long-term consequences of your affliction, chronic pedalitis. They'd probably worry that you've become a card-carrying member of the lunatic fringe, that you've pedaled right round the bend.

This concern seems almost rational when I think back to my first exposure to ultra-endurance athletes. With my dad, a world-class couch potato/know-it-all/monologist, I watched the annual broadcast of the Ironman [*sic*] Triathlon from Hawaii. For the uninitiated, this race starts with a 2.4-mile swim, switches to a 112-mile bicycle ride, and ends with a standard 26.2-mile marathon run. There are no rest stops, not even between events. The elite finish in 8-9 hours.

For mere mortals like my dad, who claimed never to have run farther than a mile in his life, this seemed like a virtually impossible feat. But that was the appeal for him, I think. He seemed to enjoy the spectacle of any sanctioned form of extreme athletic masochism. He watched, as if it was a heavyweight prize fight, anticipating the moment when one of these freaks of nature would fail. He waited for the physiological knockout punch, that precise moment when they would "hit the wall," incapacitated by dehydration and fatigue. He liked to see them go down and get back up, like a nearly fatally concussed boxer.

Arguably the most iconic moment of such catastrophic failure happened in 1982. The star was Iron**wo**man Julie Moss. She was an undergrad at Cal Poly in San Luis Obispo, where every senior must complete a thesis project. Julie, a kinesiology major, was using herself as a subject in her research on the physiological effects of the triathlon. She was obviously a supreme athlete but had been training for the triathlon for just a few months. Despite her rookie status, she found herself leading the field, nearing the end of the run. She was on the verge of winning the whole damn thing, when she collapsed just a few feet from the finish line. Her closest competitor passed her for 1st place. Julie heroically crawled to the finish line and instant celebrity, besmeared by her own diarrheal discharge. It was the best 2nd place finish ever — even better than when, years later, she would win the Silver Medal in the Olympic Triathlon.

This footage did nothing but reinforce my dad's phobic attitude toward "excessive" exercise. (To be fair, he was often more superstitious than rational, as evidenced, for starters, by his triskaidekaphobia [i.e., fear of the number 13], ailuromelanophobia [fear of black cats], and mobophobia [fear of cell phones].) As far as he was concerned, these Ironfolks were "crazy" and "self-destructive" to boot. He feared for their health.

How could this be good for anyone, in the long run, he reasoned? He just knew they'd suffer the consequences eventually. Like boxers and football players suffering the latent effects of cumulative damage done by all that brain-sloshing, surely they too would suffer. At best, they could look forward to decades of osteoarthritis from the waist down. At worst, they'd succumb to sudden cardiac death. One way or another, he knew they'd pay for their addictive overtraining, for pushing themselves to the limit.

This kind of self-inflicted excess seemed to violate everything he knew about the virtue of moderation, about how too much of a good thing is bad. He figured they'd live to regret it, but they wouldn't live that long. Or so he thought.

THE PALEO PARADIGM

My dear ole dad lacked the all-important adaptationist perspective. It apparently never occurred to him that these "freaks of nature" were actually behaving in an evolutionarily relevant way. He never pontificated about how modern humans were effectively endurance athletes for a quarter of a million years, until the last few decades — when the term "sedentary lifestyle" entered the lexicon. He failed to mention that superior ultra-endurance capacity would have conferred all sorts of Darwinian advantages.

He could have offered a numerical example or two to illustrate the potentially huge advantages associated with long-distance running ability.

He could have told me to imagine two hypothetical ancestral hominids, one who walks at 3 mph and another who lopes along at the modest pace of, say,

6 mph. Imagine they travel for 10 hours daily, out and back, returning home each night. And imagine they make radiating trips, meaning they travel in varying outbound directions across days. Superficially, it seems the runner might have a two-fold advantage based simply on the difference in travel speed. But effective search area increases with the square of the one-way distance. Therefore, the runner would have a whopping four-fold advantage in search area: 2878 versus 707 square miles.

He could have told me to imagine another individual who runs a bit faster, say, at 7 mph. By running just 1 mph faster, the superior runner would be able to search an area 36% larger than the other runner. Hypothetically, this individual would be able to gather more resources. And this individual might choose to spend more time on competing activities such as mate attraction or territorial defense. In the jargon of economics, this superior runner might pay fewer lost-opportunity costs.

My dad could have argued that natural selection has favored individuals with superior long-distance traveling abilities for millennia. But he refrained. He didn't waste his breath postulating that individuals with superior endurance would have been better at foraging for food and information and would have enjoyed payoffs based on signaling their superior status. He didn't explain how his own sphericity reflected the mismatch between his ancestrally adaptive primal urges under modern conditions (i.e., superabundance of rich processed foods with a short commute between couch and fridge). He thought they, the Ironmen and Ironwomen, were the ones behaving irrationally. He never got around to acknowledging that these Ironfolks were apparently ultra-healthy and likely to outlive us all. He just judged them ungenerously, peppering his rant with his favorite word, "idiots."

EMPIRICAL EVIDENCE

What do the data tell us? If it's true that triathletes take years off their lives, they must be dropping like flies by now.

It's just anecdotal, but Julie Moss is alive and well, so well in fact that she still competes at a high level. (She must be thriving generally as she's apparently too busy to accept my friend request on Spacebook.)

Actually, it's a bit premature to do a proper survival analysis for these folks. The Ironman phenomenon didn't really get started till the late 70s. We need to be patient and wait for some of the Ironpersons to die before analyzing their survivorship.

If only there were an already-existing dataset, for some other set of endurance athletes. Luckily, there is. Thanks to the Finnish obsession with quantifying all things Finnish, the Finns have amassed a goldmine of relevant data. And luckily, it's already been analyzed.

Let's have a look.

THE FINNISH EXPERIENCE

Do *endurance* athletes live longer, despite conventional wisdom? Yes, a resounding yes!

Elite athletes (n = 2613 men) who competed between 1920 and 1965 were compared with contemporaries (n = 1712) judged to be perfectly healthy when they "volunteered" for their stint with the Finnish Defense Forces.

Glossing over arcane methodological details that only a science geek could love, life expectancies were estimated with 95% confidence limits using the stratified Kaplan-Meier product limit method and the Cox proportional hazards model.

And here are the main findings:

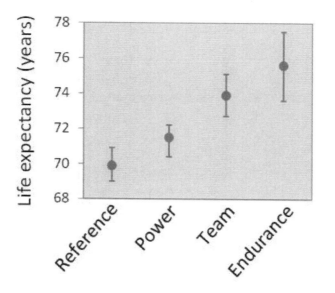

The **Gold Medal** in the all-important category of Life Expectancy goes to "Endurance" athletes (i.e., long-distance runners and cross-country skiers). They outlived the Reference cohort by an impressive 5.7 years, on average.

The **Silver Medal** goes to the next-most-aerobic group, the so-called Team guys, who participated either in a team sport (basketball, hockey, or soccer) or as jumpers/short-distance runners in track and field. They outlived the Reference guys by 4.0 years, on average.

The savvy reader will notice the broadly overlapping confidence intervals between the Gold and Silver Medalists, which means we can't confidently infer that Endurance guys truly outperformed Team guys in this all-important event.

As a former ball-hogging striker in soccer and frenetic point-guard in basketball, I'm okay with this.

As a consolation prize, the Bronze Medal goes to the Power guys, who spent their glory days hitting each other in the head, pinning each other to the mat, or lifting and throwing heavy objects. Although they outlived the Reference guys by 1.6 years, on average, these two groups were statistically indistinguishable as indicated by the overlapping confidence intervals.

To belabor the point, with 95% certainty the true underlying life expectancy could have been as low as 70.4 years for Power guys and as high as 70.9 years for Reference guys. Thus, while we can't infer that Power guys outlived Reference guys, we can infer they were outlived by both Team and Endurance guys.

As someone who could never punch my way out of a wet paper bag and could barely lift (never mind throw) a discus or hammer, I'm okay with this too.

Do these findings imply that endurance athletes outlived their counterparts due to chronic vigorous exercise per se? No, in principle, the exercise could have taken years off their lives, even though they still outlived their counterparts. Allow me to clarify.

As a card-carrying emeritus member of the loose band of experimental scientists, I offer this cautionary quibble:

We can't make any strong inference about a causal linkage between exercise and longevity because the athletes were "assigned" to their chosen specialty presumably based on interest or body type or natural ability. In a world free of ethical concerns over how we treat Finns, individuals would have been assigned randomly to treatments. Then we could have made strong inferences.

Instead, we're left to wonder whether athletes who chose to participate in endurance events were predisposed to lower risk of coronary heart disease and whether those who chose to participate in power events were predisposed to higher risk.

It remains unclear whether an individual who "chose" to participate in a power event would have typically lived longer if he'd been assigned to an endurance event. Likewise, we have no way of knowing whether an individual who participated in an endurance event would have typically died younger if he'd been assigned to a power event. Again, whether aerobic exercise directly causes greater longevity remains unclear.

Having said all of that, this much is clear: for this particular dataset, we can reject the folkloric notion that endurance athletes die young. It's conceivable that they might have lived even longer if not for overtraining, for suppressing their own immune system, for developing an "athlete's heart." But the fact remains: they outlived their counterparts.

How'd they do it? Did they do a better job of avoiding death by coronary heart disease? Yes, in fact, both Endurance and Team guys had statistically significantly lower cardiovascular mortality odds ratios than did Reference guys, which is a fancy way of saying former aerobic athletes faced a lower annual risk of coronary death.

A follow-up study revealed that these athletes enjoyed not just improved life expectancy but improved active life expectancy as well. They didn't simply live longer and thereby rack up extra years spent in a nursing home. They remained active, independent, ambulatory. They enjoyed a higher quality of life. And they did so despite a slightly increased incidence of lower-limb osteoarthritis, obviously a small price to pay.

As someone who wouldn't mind prolonging his stay on Earth while maintaining nearly full pedaling capacity, I'm okay with this.

ROBUST EVIDENCE

Assuming you're a skeptic, you must be wondering whether the Finns are a special case. You may even suspect me of withholding contradictory findings.

Well, I'm glad to report that a collection of published studies (14 as of 2010) confirm:

Elite endurance (aerobic) athletes and mixed-sport (aerobic and anaerobic) athletes tend to outlive their counterparts from the population at large, mainly thanks to better coronary health.

Meanwhile, elite power (anaerobic) athletes have provided equivocal results. (In one study, power lifters suffered a four-fold increase in mortality rate relative to the reference group.)

These findings reinforce the conclusion that vigorous exercise, especially if it's aerobic, may improve life expectancy in elite athletes.

So it may come as a surprise that several of these studies show the longevity benefit extends to professional baseball players. Former Major and Minor League Baseball Players have outlived their counterparts (i.e., old guys who couldn't hit a curveball or break a pane of glass with their fastball). Not sure what to make of this, except to suggest that scratching-and-spitting like a Neanderthal may be more aerobically demanding than it looks.

All kidding aside, playing baseball for pay is quite physically demanding. Consider the year-round dedication, extremely long seasons, behind-the-scenes strength training, and pregame rituals like batting practice and infield practice and fly-ball shagging and calisthenics and jogging in the outfield and so on.

As someone who misspent his youth crouching behind home plate and hitting weak groundballs to the second baseman, I'm okay with this. But as a middle-aged adult who lives on a bicycle, what I'd really like to know is whether extreme endurance cycling per se improves one's prospects.

VIVRE LES CYCLISTES DE LE TOUR DE FRANCE

Luckily, the first-ever paper on longevity in elite endurance cyclists just appeared. I'm glad because I thought I was going to have to do the analysis myself, which of course would have robbed me of valuable pedaling time. And I'm glad the news is good: despite repeated claims in the media that Tour de France cyclists die prematurely, the findings are very encouraging. They're myth-busting, in fact.

Based on current dead-or-alive status of 834 French, Italian, and Belgian cyclists who rode in the Tour de France between 1930 and 1964, cyclists outlived the general public by:

17%, on average!

Median longevity (i.e., age at which 50% of individuals were still alive) was a full 8 years greater for the former cyclists:

81.5 versus 73.5.

Of all studies to date (now 15), this one on Tour de France cyclists revealed the biggest survival advantage of all. That's right, the *Grand Prix* for enhanced life expectancy goes to the boys on bicycles, not to those on skis or skates or their own two feet.

As someone who pedals addictively, I'm okay with this.

I think we can bury the myth that Tour de France cyclists have been dying prematurely.

And keep in mind, these guys competed "back in the day," when they consumed red wine and cigarettes as if they were performance-enhancing drugs.

Time will tell whether participants in other extreme cycling races — Ride the Divide and Race Across America come to mind — will extend their lives as well.

~

It goes without saying (*ça va sans dire*), even if endurance cycling proves to be the best life-extending form of exercise, we still don't know the optimal dosage. I don't know about you, but I don't intend to undershoot the optimum.

~

All this jibber-jabber about life expectancy makes me wonder about my prospects. To satisfy my morbid curiosity, I applied the Cox proportional hazards model to forecast my own demise.

I'm doing all of this excessive pedaling while living with one of those awful diseases of the still-incurable variety. In my case, it's Huntington's disease. I have the defective gene. It's been sequenced and so I know the precise details, the number of CAG repeats. And I know how to interpret the literature and how to translate my repeat number into a personalized survival curve. That is, I know how to put statistical confidence limits on my expiration date. And yet, it feels too creepy to report these numbers.

Let's just say my prospects of persisting as long as the famed supercentenarian Jeanne Calment (1875-1997), like yours, are dim indeed. But there's a disturbingly high likelihood I won't last another decade, particularly if I sit here too long typing and hence squandering precious life-extending cycling time.

Even so, my pie-in-the-sky goal remains to die in pristine condition at an advanced age. I even hope to break Madame Calment's longevity record of 122 years. But to beat her, I need to know her. So, what were her secrets to success?

It seems she had several:

First and foremost, she was a cyclist. She pedaled like a Dane, here and there. And she did so until her 100th birthday! Sure, she only pedaled slowly — so as not to lose the baguettes and bouquets from her basket — and mostly on the flat streets of Paris and Arles, but she did so for eight decades. Imagine the accrual of health benefits.

Second, Jeanne had only one child, which also could have improved her longevity. Evolutionary ecologists have long been fascinated by the so-called fecundity-survival life history trade-off. We say Jeanne paid a minimal "reproductive cost," defined as the incremental increase in parental mortality risk incurred by having and raising each child. Madame Calment's death even inspired a study, which confirmed that, historically, British royals who had more children tended to die younger. Turns out, kids really will kill ya'. (My own mother used to say to her four children, "You kids will be the death of me." If she only knew.)

Third, Calment's one and only husband died in his 70s, which means she outlived him by 55 years, thanks partly no doubt to the cessation of spousal nagging.

Fourth, Jeanne attributed her longevity partly to her Paleo-style Mediterranean diet, which included copious amounts olive oil (which she also slathered on her skin), port wine, and chocolate.

Fifth, she apparently didn't want to ruin her health and so she quit smoking — at the age of 117!

Not surprisingly, I choose to believe the main reason for her success was the cycling. By pushing pedals she arguably pushed back her expiration date by nearly a half-century. Even so, if I really want to break her record, I should probably play it safe and simply mimic her whole lifestyle.

Let's see how I'm doing:

I'm in good shape regarding olive oil. It's already an essential food group in my own version of the Paleo-Mediterranean diet. I even apply it to my elbows when they look too much like a pachyderm's (okay, daily).

I consume so much chocolate — exclusively 90% or above cocoa powder — that I don't have even a single excess oxidant in my entire body, though I do get mild magnesium poisoning now and then.

I really need to rededicate myself when it comes to wine intake. Truth be told, my consumption of fermented beverages of any kind has fallen to an all-time low in recent years. I'll do better.

I have neither progeny nor husband to take years off my life.

As for smoking, I need to make up for lost time and develop a serious habit *tout suite.*

Finally, I plan to pedal more, starting as soon as I click on SAVE and power down and stick this Googley gadget in a pannier.

You should go pedal too. Pedal all night if it feels right. And may you enjoy good health, rivaling Madame Calment's, supple skin and all.

Chapter 11

Can't Stress This Enough

Reality is the Leading Cause of Stress and Cortisol Can Save Your Hide

Denigrated as the bane of our existence, cortisol is arguably the cyclist's best friend. Like a smoke detector, it jolts you into a sustained hypervigilant state when it matters most: when you find yourself amid intrinsically lethal Car People. After all, there's nothing more detrimental to future Darwinian fitness than failure to avoid a big fierce car.

> — Inspired by R. Nesse, S. Lima, and L. Dill

I f pedaling forestalls cardiovascular senescence, cures halitosis and shingles, mends broken hearts, saves Mother Earth, and solves crimes, then surely it must be the perfect way to cope with stress. This promise — that cycling is a great way to reduce stress especially during rush hour — provides a seemingly powerful rational for self-propelled, two-wheeled commuting.

There's just one teensy caveat I really must offer:

From the adaptationist's point of view, stress in the face of danger enhances one's prospects for survival. Thus, I hereby challenge the near-universal view that we should blithely reduce our stress, whether by popping pills or pushing pedals.

Here's the conventional wisdom:

As everyone "knows," stress is bad, so bad it'll kill ya. To prolong your tenure as an Earthling, then, you should begin by reducing stress. According to the medical community, stress — once adaptive as part of the flight-or-fight defense — is now undesirable because the world has become such a safe place. Supposedly, this defense, a relic from our Paleolithic past, is doing us more harm than good under modern conditions, where big fierce animals only rarely ingest human flesh. Supposedly, it's the stress that's killing us now, not the lions and tigers and bears (oh my). And supposedly cycling can counteract that stress, even though vigorous pedaling in and of itself is stressful. That's the dogma.

Of course, as a skeptic I wouldn't be worth my weight in Lycra if I were to tell such an expedient tale. (Please overlook the fact that my weight in Lycra converts to a small fortune: at $80 per 2-ounce garment, I'm worth $12,000.) Fear not, I intend to confront this conventional wisdom, this whole all-too-intuitively-plausible web of lies, with the cold hard empirical truth.

Along the way, I'll review the fascinating literature from the field of evolutionary ecology, where stress is viewed as indispensable. I'll share the all-important Darwinian medical perspective, elucidating why our flight response is only apparently paradoxical in its overreaction to scary stimuli. And I'll review some tantalizing new findings in contemporary *Homo sapiens*, showing how extreme stress can dramatically improve the accuracy of snap decisions in life-or-death scenarios.

Don't worry, it'll be a stress-free read, with a pro-cycling spin in the end.

MAINSTREAM PERSPECTIVE ON STRESS

Consider my contemporaries, those perpetual hordes of miserable Yanks, pursuing their lives of noisy desperation. They complain endlessly about being "stressed out," "under a lot of stress," and "coping with stress." They like to say the stress is killing them. They suffer through stressful commutes between dysfunctional homes and unpleasant workplaces. They're stressed about the sullen teens with whom they share the house owned for decades to come by the bank. They're stressed about rising costs, eroding "values" of the kind they hold dear, and their bulging waistline. The list goes on. They're just plain stressed.

What does all this stress do to us physiologically? Well, supposedly, it's all about the effects of cortisol. This hormone, produced by our own adrenal glands, is implicated as the smoking gun, the cause of a whole host of stress-related diseases. The mainstream medical community views this "problem" with their usual evolutionary agnosticism. They view high levels of cortisol as worrisome, pathological even, something they should fix. Lately, it's even seeped into societal consciousness that cortisol is bad, like a poison. Rumor has it chronically elevated cortisol:

- suppresses the immune system
- reduces bone density
- increases adipose tissue (in the Buddha belly region)
- atrophies the brain
- exacerbates depression

- lowers libido

By extension, if we don't mind being sickly-paunchy-miserable celibates with the brittle bones of forgetful supercentenarians, then we should keep subjecting ourselves to stress.

But it's not just members of the medical community and general public who see cortisol as problematic. Ever complicit and opportunistic, Big Pharma stands poised to make windfall profits by providing the masses with new pills designed to fix the perceived cortisol problem. And gurus in the realm of elite cycling prescribe interval training schedules designed to manage cortisol levels. Everybody, it seems, hates cortisol. Everybody but yours truly, that is.

As an evolutionary ecologist, a true believer of the adaptationist paradigm, I prefer to think of cortisol as a life-saver rather than simply a toxin. I see the complaints about cortisol as incidental costs that may be vastly offset by the all-important benefit of staying alive.

EVOLUTIONARY ECOLOGY OF FEAR

Corticosteroids, including cortisol, play a key role in an adaptive self-defense system, the so-called fight-or-flight response. Faced with the possibility of imminent death, there's the immediate adrenalin rush and the lesser-known norepinephrine rush. And then the adrenal glands start pumping out cortisol. This cortisol spike indirectly increases the availability of glucose, which fuels sustained vigilance and escapability during a period when it often makes no sense to forage.

Alternatively, the spike in cortisol may be an adaptive response to the body's internal smoke detector. If so, cortisol's main role may be as an anti-inflammatory. Even if this were true, cortisol levels could still be a reliable proxy for stress levels. Stay tuned.

As the argument goes, cortisol helps animals escape, helps them make better decisions at the most crucial moment. It helps them save their own hide or feathers or scales or moist integument. It helps them avoid passing through a carnivore's digestive track, thereby foregoing opportunities to make new copies of their own selfish DNA or to continue investing in existing copies (a.k.a., the little darlings).

To convey the scope of empirical support for this pervasive view, I'll synopsize a few recent studies.

Group-living animals often benefit from reduced predation risk, thanks partly to an early-warning system. Consider a young Belding's ground squirrel foraging in a meadow in the Sierra Nevada. It's a month old and freshly emerged from the natal burrow. It's plump and tasty, highly digestible, and highly vulnerable. Though equipped with some innate predator-avoidance abilities, it has a lot to learn. Luckily, its parents remain invested. They're vigilant and quick to give nepotistic alarms calls when they detect a predator. But they don't inflexibly utter a generic call. Instead, they use a slightly more sophisticated predator-specific system. Like Paul Revere's binary code ("one if by land, and two if by sea"), they convey whether each imminent threat is by land or air. They utter a "trill" if a terrestrial predator's afoot and a "whistle" if an aerial predator's aloft. And juveniles respond differentially, as revealed by Jill

Mateo's elegant experimental work. Mateo discovered that trills but not whistles trigger a spike in cortisol. This makes good adaptive sense because trills signal the presence of a terrestrial predator, which is likely to engage in a persistent hunt locally. An increase in glucose, facilitating sustained vigilance and escapability, may come in handy when a highly motivated terrestrial carnivore with deadly weaponry is on the prowl.

The lack of cortisol spike in response to whistles makes good sense too. Aerial threats tend to be brief as hawks typically rely on stealth and so, after the element of surprise has been lost, they tend to continue on their way looking for an unsuspecting target. Any spike in cortisol in this context would occur after the danger has already abated.

Cortisol thus seems to play a role in avoidance of terrestrial predators during the early aboveground phase of life, a period of grave danger and high mortality for pudgy juveniles.

Group-living can improve safety even in species that don't give alarm calls. In a larger group, animals have a lower per capita risk of being targeted. As predicted, individual animals tend to spend more time vigilant and hence not feeding when in smaller groups, as documented in an enormous literature over the last few decades. As a corollary, an animal's finding itself in a small group (or solitary) may be stressful in and of itself. If so, we should expect to find elevated cortisol levels in individuals in small groups. Sure enough, a recent study by Michelena Pablo *et al.* revealed that sheep in smaller flocks spent more time vigilant and had concomitantly elevated cortisol, even though no predator was present. This novel finding suggests that cortisol plays a key role in making individuals safer under social conditions corresponding to potentially elevated predation risk.

Some group-living animals bunch tightly together, in a self-protective way, when a predator arrives on the scene. This tendency, called shoaling (when fish do it), can even be "inherited" non-genetically, as mediated by exposure to mom's cortisol. Take the three-spined stickleback, a small fish native to inland coastal waters. Eric Giesing *et al.* exposed some stickleback moms to a simulated threat (a model of a northern pike, a notoriously voracious piscivore) for 30 seconds daily. These moms produced eggs with elevated cortisol (compared with control moms who weren't subjected to these scare tactics). This chemical signal had a latent impact on the offspring. As if heeding their mom's warning, offspring exposed to maternally derived cortisol during the egg stage went on to engage in tighter shoaling behavior as juveniles. That is, they clumped tightly as if a predator were lurking nearby. The moms arguably programmed their offspring hormonally such that they were better prepared to cope with a dangerous world.

The studies highlighted above combine to make my point that evolutionary ecologists view corticosteroids as a key feature of an adaptive defense system.

But the most germane study to date — for cyclists hoping to gain some insight about how best to survive in a world full of Car People — was done Maria Thaker *et al.* on Eastern fence lizards. They performed an elegant experiment to elucidate the causal role of corticosterone in mediating the escape response. They dosed some subjects with metyrapone, a drug that blocks corticosterone synthesis. Then they exposed subjects to a novel "predator," a red box on a telescopic pole. The drug impaired the subjects' escapability (i.e., they were slower to initiate flight than were control individuals). The drug also did residual damage: drugged subjects didn't learn as quickly as did control individuals who fled sooner and spent less time hiding across repeated encounters with the "predator." But fear not, these effects proved to be reversible when Thaker *et al.* restored the subjects' corticosterone levels (exogenously, with a dermal patch laced with the stuff).

I've encouraged Dr. Thaker to perform a follow-up study using red boxes in the shape and size of SUVs with cyclists as subjects. She wasn't amused. She's decided to persist in squandering her considerable talents studying lizards in urban environments in India. To each her own.

In the absence of cyclist-specific findings, I'm left to extrapolate recklessly. Here goes: as someone who lives on a bicycle, I'm not too thrilled by the prospect that physicians may soon begin doling out cortisol-blocking pills to Car People. If this catches on like the Zoloft craze, many drivers could end up operating their lethal weapon while under pharmaceutically diminished decision-making capacity. Not good.

Meanwhile, I have no intention of popping pills to down regulate my cortisol synthetic pathway. I prefer to remain hypervigilant. I want to be poised to make lightning-quick decisions, to dart or swerve or brake or accelerate, to make just the right self-preserving maneuver. And I want to retain full capacity to recognize threats and maximize flight initiation distance and minimize time spent hiding upon each repeated near-fatal encounter with one of those big boxes on four or more wheels, red or otherwise.

As an aside, I can't tell you the number of times I've unintentionally elevated corticosteroid levels by startling and nearly squishing lizards and ground squirrels and human pedestrians. It's an ethical conundrum that I have plenty of time to ponder as I pedal along playing the role of a red box. In the last year alone, I guesstimate I've triggered at least 10^6 "cort" spikes in birds (including scrub-jays, sandhill cranes, blue-winged teal, yellow-billed magpies, and great blue herons); 10^4 in mammals (including grizzly and black bears, mountain lions, wolves, coyotes, and ground squirrels galore); 10^3 in reptiles (including side-blotched lizards and horny toads and Gila monsters and sidewinder rattlesnakes and even Eastern fence lizards);10^4 in amphibians (including spring peepers and newts); and 10^3 in fish (including salmon and trout and even sticklebacks).

Meanwhile, in the last year, I've been startled to one degree or another by roughly 893,247 Car People. Not that I'm keeping score.

The interim punchline:

Throughout our evolutionary history and continuing through my ride this morning, reality has been the leading cause of stress. And the reality from where I sit, precariously perched on a bicycle — almost as if surfing on the hood of a car and fully unprotected aside from the plastic bowl strapped to my head — is that the world remains a dangerous place. Is it any wonder I have the elevated cort levels of a solitary sheep and a juvie ground squirrel combined?

THE SAFE-WORLD MYTH & THE SMOKE DETECTOR

I hereby contest the myth that the world has become a safe place and elevated cortisol represents an unfortunate relic of our evolutionary history. Nearly everyone seems to believe this dogma. Even scholars in Darwinian medicine argue, metaphorically, that our internal smoke detector keeps going off even though house fires have been all but eradicated. That is, modern-day stimuli cause frequent false alarms, triggering cortisol spikes, even though we've virtually extirpated the big fierce animals that used to consume our flesh and we no longer subdue big, intrinsically dangerous prey with spears and arrows.

On the contrary, I contend that the world remains plenty dangerous and that our elevated cortisol levels may be a good thing, when it matters most. Below, I'll attempt to bust the safe-world myth and then I'll ask whether we can dampen each other's cortisol levels with impunity.

It's fashionable to assume we live in a much safer world than our ancestors did. I think this is an illusion. Just because we almost never get ingested by big fierce predators or trampled by big prey doesn't make the world safe. We've replaced those "natural" stressors with a vast array of deadly surrogates. We kill each other with cars, bullets, and bombs at alarming rates. And this, from an evolutionary perspective, is like predation. If you get scraped off the pavement and hauled to the crematorium, your future Darwinian fitness plummets to zero precisely as if you'd been ingested by a big fierce carnivore.

To get a handle on how dangerous the modern world might be, consider these factoids:

Globally, death rates due to unintentional (6.2%) and intentional injuries (2.8%) are substantial. Excluding suicide, nearly 8% of deaths are accidental. In principle, they could be avoided by being more vigilant, by swerving to miss the oncoming car or dodging the bullets, by staying home. Clearly, it still pays to be on your toes, to flee and hide. In the parlance of evolutionary ecology, this rate of death-by-injury represents a substantial "opportunity for selection." That is to say, it's hard to imagine evolution by natural selection no longer plays a role in shaping our defense system. (There's a good reason those annual awards for hilariously stupid acts of self-inflicted death are called the Darwin Awards.) Clearly, death by fatal injury still matters.

Consider cars as surrogate predators:

Even in rich countries, where the vast majority of people die due to biological aging, the opportunity to die by accident remains impressive. At 12.3 road-related deaths per 100,000 per year, 2% of deaths in the USA are due to traffic crashes. Worldwide, the per capita death-by-car rate is even higher and motor vehicle crashes are the number one cause of death-by-injury for children. Cars kill!

> Or if you prefer the logic of the right-to-bear-arms crowd, cars don't kill people, people with cars kill people.

No wonder Yanks are stressed. They're addicted to their death machines. Driving is the single most dangerous thing a typical American does on any given day. Of course Yanks have high cortisol levels. They *should* be high. Sky high.

The Darwinian medical perspective:

The optimal rate of false positives can be arbitrarily high (i.e., even >99%) if the consequences are grave enough and if the cost of the alarm is finite. In other words, our natural defense system only apparently overreacts when someone cuts us off in traffic or tailgates or texts-while-driving or otherwise threatens our life. Because the potential cost is absolute (i.e., death), we should expect frequent cortisol spikes. We should expect lots of false alarms as any given cortisol spike could be the one that saves us and our precious cargo.

Assuming stress-induced spikes in cortisol still facilitate decision-making in dangerous situations in the modern world, suppression of cortisol could conceivably backfire and lead to bad decisions when they matter most. You may be inclined to agree, but wouldn't it be more compelling if there were some actual evidence?

CORTISOL FACILITATES SNAP DECISIONS

For decades, scientists in various fields have studied effects of cortisol on human performance. However, these studies almost universally have suffered from two major shortcomings:

First, they've set out to confirm the researchers' *a priori* belief that too much cortisol is detrimental to performance.

Second, they've quantified performance of evolutionarily irrelevant tasks such as public singing or exam taking.

161

Fortunately, at long last, a study aimed at examining the impact of cortisol level on decision-making under danger has been done. This ground-breaking work by Drs. Modupe Akinola and Wendy Berry Mendes provides compelling initial evidence that stress-induced cortisol spikes can improve an individual's decision-making in a life-or-death scenario.

Here are the gory details:

The profs recruited 81 male police officers in Boston to participate in the study. Each subject was exposed to a social stressor prior to the decision-making task. The stressor involved a confederate who claimed he'd been discriminated against based on race. Each subject's cortisol level was measured twice, once before and once after exposure to this stressor, and the difference was computed (i.e., post minus baseline). This measured cortisol reactivity was then used as a predictor of performance in the decision-making task. In this task, each subject completed a series of binary choices (i.e., shoot or don't shoot) in a video game-like format, where a potentially hostile target was either armed or unarmed (and either black or white). Each subject was instructed to respond as quickly as possible by "shooting" if the target was armed and otherwise "holstering" his imaginary gun.

The main finding:

Subjects with bigger cortisol spikes tended to perform better, especially when subjects were armed (and black).

Some remarkable details:

The subject with the single biggest cortisol spike outperformed every other subject in the study, all 80 of them.

Subjects who showed little or no cortisol spike performed much more variably. Some of them performed fairly well but others performed abysmally, as poorly as if they were guessing or using a coin toss for each choice. (Perhaps they were often too slow to react as any response exceeding a threshold lag of 0.84 seconds was scored as an error.) Whatever the explanation, those subjects who had little or no cortisol spike often failed miserably in this scenario.

Future studies should experimentally manipulate cortisol levels as Thaker *et al.* did in Eastern fence lizards. And yet, this study on police officers provides compelling novel evidence that individuals with bigger cortisol spikes made fewer errors in a highly threatening situation.

One takeaway point:

If drivers are anything like cops, I wouldn't be inclined to recommend cortisol-blocking drugs to help them cope with the stress of commuting. Au contraire, I want Car People to have elevated stress-induced cortisol levels if that's going to augment my survival prospects. I thus pledge to do my part to stress out drivers, to spike their cortisol. Cycling after all, unlike public singing, is a life-or-death proposition.

Naturally, I've encouraged Dr. Akinola to expand the scope of her work to include cyclists and drivers, to investigate the underlying relationships between stress and survival in folks who travel on two and four wheels. She's lukewarm. I think I stressed her out.

Perhaps I should start using myself as subject. I'd start by asking whether it's a good thing that I elevate my own cortisol level by pedaling. I'd ask whether it improves my snap decisions at busy intersections. I'd ask whether that makes me less prone to getting killed on my never-ending tour.

MY SPECIAL RELATIONSHIP WITH CORTISOL

Persons living with Huntington's disease have elevated levels of cortisol, so I have a special challenge. For me, any little stressor — especially any conflict with a conspecific — sends me into a full-blown snit, an all-out fight-or-flight reaction. Fortunately, I always choose flight. And man do I flee, usually at about 26 mph. And within an hour or so I've recovered. But by then I'm so far down the road that I just pause and offer a lame digital apology.

Generally, I prefer to see my supposedly pathologically elevated cortisol as a blessing in disguise. Sure, it's annoying to be consistently on edge, wired, jittery — as if my body were covered with cortisol-laced dermal patches. And it may jeopardize my chances of ever coping with social stress. But in the context of cycling, it may confer the all-important avoid-becoming-roadkill advantage. It makes me attentive, and safer for it, I believe. I'm pre-adapted for this life on two wheels. Thanks to my special status, I'm better able to avoid one of those unspeakable involuntary dismounts, where I become the new hood ornament for some momentarily scared yet permanently emotionally scarred Car Person. How's that for wishful thinking?

Seriously, when I'm away from traffic, say on a dedicated bike path or on rural roads with precious few cars, pedaling feels stress-free. I'd like to believe the pedaling really is keeping my cortisol levels down at times when I don't need to be so wary. But I really should keep cotton wads on hand so I can collect my saliva and assay my cortisol levels.

This has become standard protocol in studies aimed at showing the magical stress-relieving properties of commuting by bicycle. All such studies, by the way, implicitly assume that stress is bad. Clearly, future studies should incorporate my view that stress while commuting may be adaptive.

I also hope that being a highly trained endurance athlete gives me a plasticity advantage. Specifically, I hope my pedaling habit helps lower my baseline cortisol level and reduce the magnitude of my cortisol reactivity, especially when I'm not even on the bike. Who knows, if I get fit enough, maybe emotional crises will trigger smaller cortisol spikes. Maybe.

My perpetual pedaling is partly a way of coping with cortisol. I'm trying to keep my cortisol levels from reaching damagingly high levels and staying there. And it seems to be working. As long as I avoid roads with heavy traffic and narrow shoulders and belligerent drivers, I experience no road rage. I "commute" with little stress on most days.

If I were a conventional cycling commuter participating in a study, I'd self-report low everyday stress, good sleep patterns, good vitality, general happiness, and perfect absenteeism.

Plus, I've all but eliminated other major stressors from my life. I've opted out of high-pressure careerism and public speaking engagements and social expectations. I refrain from all opportunities to sing publicly or take exams or shoot criminal suspects. I have no deadlines. I'm a monastic cyclist. I have no expectations of myself except to pedal (and type a little now and then).

In fact, I think I'll go pedal now. At the moment, I'm at my backwoods log cabin in Ontario, Canada, and so I'll be pedaling my Pugsley, the beastly all-terrain bike with massive knobby tires. But first I need to patch the tubes because the local bear has punctured them again while ransacking my cabin, thereby causing my cort level to skyrocket for the umpteenth time.

Go pedal your own Pugsley. There's nothing more to see here.

🚲 🚲 🚲 🚲 🚲

Chapter 12

In Pursuit of Happiness

Psychoactive Effects of Pedaling
One's Ass Off

I f pedaling is a panacea for just about every physical ailment a human might conceivably endure, then surely it's an elixir for mental health issues as well. And surely, the curative power of pedaling extends well beyond alleviation of everyday stress. Surely, pedaling's also an effective way of keeping anxiety and depression at bay. Surely, pedaling even has the potential to keep one from getting sucked into the ultimate vortex, the downward spiral leading one to ingest too many prescription painkillers or otherwise cause oneself to converge on ambient temperature. I sure hope so.

Of course, any skeptic worth her weight in Lycra would contest this premise, arguing the effects of pedaling on levels of magic molecules, including serotonin, may be pharmacologically real but ephemeral. If so, perceived benefits of cycling on the psyche may be little more than shots of dopamine — like the ones your brain gets suffused with each time you receive a Facebook "like" or other such brain candy via social media.

If you're still reading, please ignore all alerts on your iDevice. Please give me your undivided attention. How can I tell my story if you're seeking hits of dopamine elsewhere?

More pessimistically, these benefits may amount to nothing more than the placebo effect, which to be fair can save your life. And to complete the hand-wringing, mental health professionals may caution that self-prescribing my drug of choice, Exercise®, could do more harm than good. I'll take my chances. So far, I've chosen to treat my own mental health problems by pushing pedals, not by popping pills.

Like any skeptic, I'm wary of the all-too-popular notion that we should simply pop pills to fix a dopamine or serotonin "imbalance" — like taking a daily dietary supplement. This notion strikes me as too good to be true, partly because it's what pharmaceutical folks would have us believe.

This is the shameless trickery drug companies use to peddle their brain candy. They pretend your problem, if you even have one, is due to a simple imbalance. If that were true, then they wouldn't get sued for making such claims and a quick fix might be advisable.

Of course, the other scurrilous thing they do these days — in the name of capitalism in its purest (most evil) form — is to advertise their products on television, even explicitly suggesting you solicit a prescription from your doctor.

The black box details underlying mental health are extraordinarily complex. And I make no pretense about my ability to unravel these neurophysiological mysteries. I'm just here to testify that pedaling seems to help me cope with chronic anxiety and depression and even get through bouts of suicidal ideation while living with Huntington's disease. And I'll tell this tale from an adaptationist point of view.

Speaking of which, the Darwinian medicine perspective on psychoactive drugs is a straightforward application of the smoke detector principle. Like symptoms of a cold or flu, symptoms of mental illness can often be safely treated with drugs. Of course, before reaching for the prescription pad, a prudent clinician would routinely rule out any true underlying conflagration, like Dengue Fever when the patient has cold/flu symptoms or like a brain tumor when the patient has psychotic symptoms.

I don't doubt that mental health problems including depression can often be safely treated with drugs. But does that mean we should rely on such drugs in the way we almost automatically self-medicate to treat cold or flu symptoms?

Picture my car-addicted contemporaries, those hordes of miserable Yanks who cope by popping pills, which they pick up at drive-thru pharmacies.

> That's right, in the country that invented drive-thru fast food "restaurants," we now have drive-thru drug stores, not to mention drive-thru banks and coffee shops and wedding chapels and even funeral homes. In some states, we even have drive-thru liquor stores, which makes good sense because carousing Car People are often way too drunk to walk to the store but not too drunk to drive.

Seriously, though, quick fixes of the drive-thru variety have become a National Pastime for car-bound Yanks. Rumor has it physicians are on the cusp of offering drive-thru diagnoses of depression in 43 of the 50 states. Finally, common sense prevails.

THESE DAYS THERE'S A PILL FOR THAT

As if it's a bona fide pandemic, diagnosis of depression has increased by 400% in the last decade. And so Americans now spend an enormous amount of money on antidepressants:

$11 billion annually (that's right, with a B)!

To put that pittance in perspective, Americans now spend as much on antidepressants as they spend on coffee ($11 billion) and bottled water ($11 billion), and a little more than they spend on bicycles (plus gear and accessories, $10.5 billion). And they spend almost as much on happy pills as they spend on chocolate ($16 billion) and guns (perhaps about $15 billion).

To take yet another gratuitous potshot at the American stereotype, Yanks have been spending 22 times as much on antidepressants as on Twinkies ($500 million). That is, until recently, when Twinkies were discontinued. Presumably this devastating news triggered a tsunami of societal depression and a spike in Zoloft sales. Or, possibly, a surge in pedaling. Time will tell.

As I write these snarky remarks about stereotypical Yanks, I sit amid a diverse crowd of countercultural hominids. Here's the inventory: 16 GBLTQers; five openly hetero hipsters, including two freegans and one permaculturist; four aspiring visual artists, including one graphic novelist; and one singer-songwriter. As I scan the patio, I can't help but notice ways in which I'm unique. Let's see, I'm the only person dressed in neon or wearing a typing helmet. I'm apparently the only person who doesn't self-identify as Latino. And as if I never got the memo, I'm the only person whose integument totally lacks tattoos. Which raises the question: if this little gaggle of tat-covered folks is at all representative, Americans must be spending a helluva lot of their disposable income on ink these days? But do they spend more on tats than antidepressants? Yes and no. Yanks currently spend only about $2.3 billion annually on body art, but a whopping $66 billion getting it removed.

But the most salient factoid I've cited already: Americans now spend a little more on antidepressants than they spend on bicycles. The problem with this, as I see it? Americans apparently love to pop pills but hate to push pedals. Which prompts the obvious tip for my fellow Americans: stop wasting all that money on bicycles (wink). Alternatively, stop wasting so much money on pills designed to boost serotonin in the brain (by targeting reuptake inhibitors) when you might accomplish the same goal by simply pedaling your bike (and leaving reuptake inhibitors to their own devices). Yes, rumor has it exercise can boost serotonin levels.

PALEO PERSPECTIVE ON PEDALING PLAIN PEOPLE

This pandemic of depression arguably arose as a byproduct a sedentary lifestyle with ubiquitous stressors. If so, we might gain some support by looking at the old order Amish and Mennonites, the self-described plain people. The children commute by bicycle, racing home from each one-room school house in four directions, with older kids breaking away and younger kids riding in loose pelotons. The adults too have an active lifestyle, burning about 6000 calories per day, as they work the land by hand, on foot and with horses, and run their households the old-fashioned way. Coincidentally, the incidence of depression is negligible.

To put this in perspective, imagine your acquaintances who drive to the gym three times per week and spend an hour or so engaging in some kind of contrived workout. They do so under the impression that their regimen is optimal, that more frequent or longer sessions at the gym would provide diminishing returns and perhaps even amount to counterproductive overtraining. (They even feel judgmental toward those few individuals known as gym rats who apparently have addictive personalities and spend hours daily at the gym.) Workout completed, they hit the shower and then drive back to spend the rest of the day desk-bound.

Meanwhile, the Amish and Mennonites do the equivalent of a week's worth of such workouts each day — by noon! Day after day, their energetic expenditure exceeds two weeks' worth of contrived workouts. And the benefits seem to include vastly reduced risks of obesity, coronary disease, diabetes, and even depression.

As for me, I choose to emulate the Amish kids by pedaling daily.

In fact, whenever I get a chance, I love to pedal *with* them. They think I'm ridiculous, what with the wrong kind of beard and shamelessly flamboyant clothing and flashing lights.

A few months ago, I even had the privilege of pedaling briefly with a young Amish couple who were honeymooning on their bicycle built for two. The bike had been built for two in the last century and it looked like all of the original parts remained. When they went into a general store to buy Gatorade and whoopee pies, I furtively lubed their rusty chain.

They noticed. I now have a standing invitation to stay at their farm.

But I prefer "commutes" so long that my daily energetic expenditure rivals that of a typical Amish farmer, whose lifetime intake of Zoloft is nil. And even though I'll never get into their heaven, at least I get to eat like I'm Amish, while staying semi-lean and approximately happy.

MY SPECIAL IMBALANCE

Unlike 99.999999% of Amish and Mennonite folk, I have that pesky Huntington's gene. And that's problematic for happiness.

Here's a bit of the jibber jabber (a.k.a., the abstract, the authors' own summary) from a hot-off-the-press article by Chen *et al.* (2013):

Dopamine (DA) plays an essential role in the control of coordinated movements. Alterations in DA balance in the striatum lead to pathological conditions such as Parkinson's and Huntington's diseases (HD). HD is a progressive, invariably fatal neurodegenerative disease caused by a genetic mutation producing an expansion of glutamine repeats and is characterized by abnormal dance-like movements (chorea). The principal pathology is the loss of striatal and cortical projection neurons. Changes in brain DA content and receptor number contribute to abnormal movements and cognitive deficits in HD. In particular, during the early hyperkinetic stage of HD, DA levels are increased whereas expression of DA receptors is reduced. In contrast, in the late akinetic stage, DA levels are significantly decreased and resemble those of a

Parkinsonian state. Time-dependent changes in DA transmission parallel biphasic changes in glutamate synaptic transmission and may enhance alterations in glutamate receptor-mediated synaptic activity. In this review, we focus on neuronal electrophysiological mechanisms that may lead to some of the motor and cognitive symptoms of HD and how they relate to dysfunction in DA neurotransmission. Based on clinical and experimental findings, we propose that some of the behavioral alterations in HD, including reduced behavioral flexibility, may be caused by altered DA modulatory function. Thus, restoring DA balance alone or in conjunction with glutamate receptor antagonists could be a viable therapeutic approach.

Here's my personalized takeaway message:

To compensate for declining titers of dopamine percolating through my brain, I may need to up my daily dosage of pedaling over time to remain happy adjacent. Can do!

As for my behavioral inflexibility (namely, addictive pedaling), I choose not to fret about it. I don't wish to purge this behavior from my vast repertoire of inflexible behaviors because my pedaling habit obviates any concern about dopamine "imbalance." At least I hope so.

Disclaimer

I'm not a physician. I don't even play one on smellevision. So, in the interest of my not getting sued, I suggest you consult a physician. Having said that, I'm all for psychotherapy and pharmaceuticals where necessary, but not as a substitute for an active lifestyle.

As everyone knows, exercise is routinely "prescribed" for those of us with an ovoidal *bauplan*, for those of us in need of a morphological make-over, of a smaller surface area-to-volume ratio. That is, physicians routinely recommend exercise for patients at risk of obesity-related conditions including coronary artery disease. Less frequently, they recommend exercise as an antidote to despair. I think exercise is woefully underprescribed in this context. So, in a totally laic way, I hereby prescribe the bike-as-drug in the hope that it will help keep you mentally healthy.

Here I provide a blank script. Use it at your own discretion.

WAITE DARWINIAN MEDICAL GROUP
Tom Waite, PhD
[Pedaled Healthy Distance]
555 Downhill Lane,
Somewhere, EARTH

Prescription

to Pedal !

Refills: 1 2 3 4 5 PRN NR

If I can pedal back the years, maybe I can also recapture that elusive state of mind called happiness. And maybe you can too. Maybe pedaling will be part of a holistic antidote to despair.

Go pedal. Pedal like it's the first day of summer vacation. Pedal your way to a clean bill of mental health. Pedal your way to bliss. It could make you as happy as a Dane.

Don't be afraid to smile and laugh while pedaling. Laugh like you're the teacher's pet in a laugh yoga class. (Never mind the fact that laugh yoga has been made illegal in India.)

Keep on keeping on.

And one final sales pitch: If you push pedals rather than pop pills, you won't risk all of those nasty side-effects, including but not limited to sleepiness and insomnia (complete with somnolence), nervousness, nausea, headache, tremor, dry mouth, dizziness, diarrhea, skin rash, loss of appetite, and suicide — not to mention my personal favorite, *abnormal* ejaculation.

GOING
GOING
GREEN

Chapter 13

Of Course the Danes Aren't Green: They're Rich!

Busting the Green Cycling Myth

The Danes are world beaters. When it comes to global comparisons, these modest pedaling descendants of Vikings blow away the competition. It seems like there aren't enough superlatives to go around. They're among the happiest, healthiest, safest, and even tallest people on Earth. But are they unimpeachable? Nope, turns out they're very close to the bottom of the global list in the only category that our descendants will ultimately care about: overconsumption and waste production.

HOW BAD IS THE NEWS?

Well, you might want to sit down for this, especially if you happen to be in Denmark. Among 153 countries ranked from smallest to largest by per capita ecological footprint, the Danes finished 150th. Denmark managed to best only the United Arab Emirates, Qatar, and Bahrain — oil-rich countries with lots of sand and precious little ecologically productive land who make no pretense about green initiatives. Ouch.

HOW UNSUSTAINABLE IS THE DANISH LIFESTYLE?

The typical Dane has an ecological footprint of 8.2 global hectares (gha), about the size of 11 soccer fields. There's just one problem with effectively sequestering this much ecologically productive land to meet one's resource-consuming and waste-producing demands: it vastly exceeds the 1.8 gha available per person. The typical Dane thus lives as if there are 4.5 planet Earths available. By extension, the typical Dane appropriates natural ecosystems worldwide which inexorably contributes to the global extinction crisis.

The *aggregate* ecological footprint of Denmark doesn't seem so obscene thanks to the fact there are only a few million of the tall happy pedalers. To put this in perspective, the aggregate footprint of Yanklandia exceeds that of Denmark by 50 fold. But that should be no consolation for the Danes, who would lose their status as world leaders in all areas, including happiness, if adjusted for population size.

I should apologize for the bait-and-switch. You see, I've known for a long time that the Danes are about as egregious as anyone in this all-important way. When it comes to failure to live within Earth's means, they're downright abysmal. They even eked out the Yanks, who tied the Belgians for 149th place in the Global Sustainability Sweepstakes, at 8.0 gha. Cringe.

At this juncture, I'd like to say a few encouraging words to the fine folks of Denmark, where footprint denial has become part of the national psyche. With the hubris of a typical Yank, I hereby offer a totally unprofessional psychoanalysis of your entire nation state's mental state.

I suspect you're inclined to rationalize about how none of your pedal-happy neighbors are anywhere near the sustainable ecofootprint of 1.8 gha — not even the Netherlands, which at 6.2 gha ranks 142nd worldwide. I suspect, like rich folks everywhere, you thought you could have your *kage* (cake) and eat it too. And I suspect you were duped by your outstanding performance in those other global lists, including happiness and cycling and longevity.

In coming to terms with your footprint reality, I think it's important to recognize you're not evil or even intrinsically unsustainable. The problem is that there are now 7 billion of us. And we can't all live like you. We're already overshooting global carrying capacity. We're spending down on the natural capital, not living on the interest income.

Isn't it time to get real, to go through a catharsis? I'm not saying you should hang your collective head in shame. I'd hate to see you to plummet down the global happiness ranks. But you really must move past the denial stage. The oblivion that worked so well for so long won't work anymore. It's time to wake up and do the right thing.

For starters, I suggest you be more circumspect about presenting yourselves as model citizens of the Earth, when after all we only have one of them. Only by coming to terms with the truth can you realistically expect to become world leaders in the movement toward global sustainability.

We need you to lead the way.

ARE DANES SIMPLY TOO RICH TO BE GREEN?

Across countries, per capita wealth (PPP) is a remarkably reliable predictor of per capita ecological footprint. (Otherwise, I wouldn't bring it up.) With some inevitable scatter, people in richer countries tend to have bigger footprints (slope of fitted regression line = 0.72, r^2 = 0.75, P < 0.0001, n = 149 countries). So much for the sophistic apologia that wealth enables richer countries to do a better job at conservation.

With this in mind, it should have come as no surprise that the Danes have such big footprints. At 15th among 180 countries, their PPP ($42K) is in the 92nd percentile, which suggests a correspondingly massive footprint. And sure enough, with the 4th largest footprint among 153 countries, they're in the 98th percentile. The Danes are rich and, unsurprisingly, they have very big footprints.

To belabor the point, there's nothing special about the typical Dane's footprint. It was a bit bigger than predicted, but 55 countries had a bigger deviation between observed and predicted footprint. It was hardly an outlier.

The Danes may be exceptional in other ways, but they're not exempt from the generality that rich countries are way over the so-called global fair Earthshare (1.8 gha). Indeed, none of the 48 richest countries in the world have a per capita footprint below that sustainability threshold. Denmark happens to be among the richest of those rich countries and, not surprisingly, trails 98% of countries in the sustainability competition. Even for the Danes, it's not easy being green.

But how do we reconcile the fact that the Danes lead the world in pedaling with the fact that they also lead the world in environmental impact? Is the notion that pedaling helps make us green nothing but a cruel hoax?

WHAT GOOD IS ALL THAT CYCLING?

Let's not be too hasty in declaring the green cycling myth busted. Let's pause at least long enough to ask whether other countries with a strong cycling culture have smallish footprints. Unfortunately, of the Top 10 countries ranked by bicycles owned per capita, only China at #10 has a per capita footprint (2.2 gha) approaching the sustainability threshold (1.8 gha).

And China is doing everything in its power to crash the lavish party rich countries have been throwing for themselves. China wants to be a nation of Car People too. China wants to be rich.

Other countries in the Top 10 make it look, spuriously (that's geekspeak for misleadingly), as though cycling somehow drives countries toward rampant overconsumption. Here's the list, with per capita footprint (gha) given in parentheses:

1) Netherlands: 0.99 (6.2)
2) Denmark: 0.80 (8.3)
3) Germany: 0.76 (5.1)
4) Sweden: 0.64 (5.9)
5) Norway: 0.61 (5.6)
6) Finland: 0.60 (6.2)
7) Japan: 0.57 (4.7)
8) Switzerland: 0.49 (5.0)
9) Belgium: 0.48 (8.0)
10) China: 0.37 (2.2)

At the risk of stating the obvious, I offer three interim punch lines of the Gorean inconvenient-truth variety:

First, the top nine countries have footprints vastly exceeding the global fair Earthshare. They all behave as if we have extra planet Earths at our disposal. They're all unsustainable by a wide margin.

Second, a high rate of bicycle ownership — a standard bragging point for bicycle advocacy folks — could be taken as a warning sign. Owning lots of bicycles is apparently just another symptom of affluenza, that highly contagious and virulent disease afflicting rich people.

> If so, bicycle-ownership rate should covary with car-ownership rate. And it does: the nine countries atop the bicycle-ownership list are among the top countries on the car-ownership list as well. Indeed, the Finns, Japanese, Swiss, and Belgians own more cars than bicycles. And even the Danes have a car-ownership rate of 48 per 100.

Third, the bicycle, as even the most diehard velophiliac must admit, is no panacea. It may make you fit and happy and healthy and even single, but it will not make you automatically green. Far from it. Unless you take special measures, a bicycling habit may even expand your already bloated footprint.

DOES CYCLING HELP ANY COUNTRY STAY GREEN?

One thing is abundantly clear: having lots of bicycles does anything but assure rich countries of genuine sustainability. But if you're sufficiently optimistic, you might find hope in China's combination of rampant utilitarian cycling and relatively small, albeit rapidly growing, footprints.

Which begs the question: is the second most populace country, India — with now over a billion inhabitants and cyclists galore — still below the sustainability threshold and if so can we attribute that to cycling?

Yes and a qualified no. India's per capita footprint, at 0.9 gha, remains well below the sustainability threshold. Meanwhile, nearly half of all households in India own a bicycle. But this doesn't imply that cycling drives sustainability, that there's a causal linkage. I'd argue cycling isn't the real cause of small footprints in India and other developing countries. People in poor countries with multitudes of cyclists aren't "green" because they pedal. Rather, they're green *and* they pedal because they're poor. Poverty is the real cause of small footprints and cycling is largely a byproduct of necessity. And yet the possibility remains that cycling could help poor countries maintain their small per capita footprints.

CAN CYCLING MAKE EVEN RICH INDIVIDUALS GREEN?

Whether cycling can facilitate appreciable shrinkage of already-bloated footprints in rich countries remains an open question. To be skeptical, it seems to be an intractable problem. To see why, we must begin by acknowledging that cycling doesn't intrinsically make an individual's lifestyle sustainable. Indeed, it can easily exacerbate matters, particularly if you're from a rich country. It can easily lead to a net increase in the size of your personal ecological footprint.

To see how insidious this effect might be, consider these hypothetical case studies:

Scenario A —
A colleague of yours suddenly develops a recreational cycling habit. This doesn't come as a surprise because he's recently moved to Silicon Valley, where cycling is the new golf and he's expected to pedal with his boss. In any case, he buys a new high-end road bike and an array of accessories including a skintight MAMIL suit and a bike rack for his SUV. Several days each week he transports his car ornament/bicycle to meet the right folks who pedal in the right places. He's hooked. By the end of the first year, an honest accounting reveals that the cycling-related component of his footprint vastly exceeds the sustainability threshold (1.8 gha) and the per capita footprint of 100+ countries. From the footprint-minimizing perspective, your colleague would have been better off staying home on his couch.

Scenario B —
Another colleague of yours fancies herself quite the eco-saint. She divorces her car and commutes by cycling only. She saves $10K per year by not owning, insuring, maintaining, and operating an automobile. But then she splurges during her holidays. Unfortunately, an honest accounting reveals that she spends her savings on trophy vacations and hence on jet fuel and other highly consumptive goods and services. From the footprint-minimizing perspective, your colleague might have been better off not even owning a bicycle.

I suspect failure to reduce one's footprint via cycling is a general outcome in rich countries. Fortunately, this is easy to fix: simply invest your cycling-related savings in a genuinely green way. (Hint: Your portfolio should not include petrochemical companies.)

CAN WE PEDAL OUR WAY TO SUSTAINABILITY?

Pedaling alone just won't get us there. But before answering this question more thoughtfully, we need to specify the goal. So, to be crystal clear, I'm talking about strict ecological sustainability whereby our collective footprint would no longer exceed global carrying capacity. I'm *not* talking about *faux* greenness whereby rich folks live in blissful ignorance about their own impact while often grandstanding over some bogus green initiative. These affectations reach great heights of absurdity.

Here's my new favorite example:

In 2011, Justin Timberlake — a non-Dane — received something called the Futures Award from the oxymoronically named Environmental Media Association. The haircut who presented the award cited JT's oxymoronic eco-friendly golf course. Priceless, I know.

Never mind that golf is anathema to conservation. Never mind that tax credits going to private country clubs for pretending to give a rat about environmental impact have been widely condemned as perverse subsidies. Never mind that putting up bluebird boxes — an innocuous activity in and of itself — is an expedient way of assuaging green guilt. Never mind that improving golf course management within the USA doesn't make it onto the list of the top million conservation needs worldwide. Never mind that we're in the midst of a global biotic holocaust and that the real hotspots of massive extinction risk are found elsewhere, mostly in the tropics. Never mind that JT might have received a proper ecological education if only his life hadn't been hijacked by the Mickey Mouse Club and pop stardom. Never mind that JT was celebrated for worrying about mice when there are tigers afoot. Never mind all of that.

My big gripe is this:

JT's personal ecological footprint is gargantuan and hence obscene. What message is he unwittingly sending? Allow me to translate. Paraphrasing his acceptance speech, I think — while floating face down in his own hypocrisy — he was really trying to say:

Sure, we'd need thousands of planet Earths if everyone lived like I do, but hey thanks to my self-aggrandizing green initiatives, I can scam all of you totally unsuspecting fools. Am I awesome or what?!

If my lampoon is misplaced and he really does care, then he'll probably do something legitimately helpful any day now. He'll probably start by "anonymously" bequeathing, say, 98% of his wealth to buy up biodiversity hotspots, with the proviso that these critical areas be set aside in perpetuity. Or he could mimic Ted Turner and spend the $98 million restoring huge tracts of degraded land. Either way, he'd be left with $2 million. Paying himself a salary based on interest income alone, he'd still be wealthy. And I'd be the first person to praise him for doing the right thing.

CAN THE DANES LEAD A GREEN MOVEMENT?

If Danes genuinely wish to shrink their footprints, they'll need to make wholesale changes to their lifestyle. They could start by mimicking India. To do so, Danes would need to shrink their footprints 89% (from 8.2 to 0.9), which would be accompanied by a nearly identical

90% cut in PPP (from $42K to $4K) and a 96% cut in car ownership rate (from 480 to 18 per 1000 inhabitants). This degree of voluntary belt-tightening seems highly improbable, but if anyone can do it, it's the Danes, *er det ikke* (*n'est-ce pas*)?

Besides, I'm only calling for wholesale retrenchment with car-free roads and meat-free diets — not a shutting of the Lego factories. I'm not a complete and total killjoy, at least according to my (car- and meat-addicted) mom.

As for pedaling, the already happy-to-pedal Danes should strive to become hardcore green pedalers.

THE GREEN PEDALING CHALLENGE

Assuming you don't aspire to be like the typical contemporary Dane, you're probably wondering what it would take to become a legitimately green cyclist. How big a challenge would it be?

Clearly, I'm not talking about some feel-good ploy like the CLIF Bar 2 Mile Challenge, whereby folks were "challenged" to pedal for a few minutes — to help solve the global warming crisis. Puhleez!

I know I've already picked on a country and a pop star and now I'm picking on a corporation, but I call this the CLIF Bar 2 Mile Delusion. My quibble (wink) is that if every able-bodied Yank accepted this so-called challenge, the impact on climate would be infinitesimal. I'll concede that this "challenge" makes sense if the real unspoken goal, the hidden agenda, is to instigate a highly contagious fad that sweeps through the culture becoming an all-out cycling pandemic. But that hasn't exactly transpired. Yanks, on average, continue to pedal only a few bicycle lengths daily. Meanwhile, some participants in the 2 Mile Challenge no doubt have been tricked into thinking they've done the right thing, that they've done enough.

Here's my modest suggestion: scrap the 2 Mile Challenge, an embarrassingly trivial goal to begin with — like asking someone to give a penny to charity or operate a Segway for 20 minutes while chewing gum. I say be bold and take the X Mile Challenge, where X equals all of the mileage remaining in your life. Divorce your car. Marry your bike. Pedal everywhere. You'll save $10K per year and if you're truly green, you'll refrain from spending that wad of cash on jet fuel and such. You'll donate every penny to a truly green initiative.

Go ahead, make my day: accept my Green Cycling Challenge. You'll thank me later. In fact, if you see fit, feel free to donate your windfall savings to my sustainability fund (offshore account number available upon request). Alternatively, send your billions of bitcoins to a Nigerian Prince of your choosing. Either way, may you pedal happily, safely, sanely, and even greenly.

$$$$$$

Chapter 14

Pedaling in Muir's Footsteps

To a Warmer Yosemite

May 31, 2011

Re: Inconvenient news from a still-protected but warmer Yosemite

Dear Mr. Muir,

You don't know me from Adam or Eve, but I feel compelled to write you this letter (96 years after your death) as I just returned from your old stomping grounds, Yosemite, Earth. I have good news and bad news. The good news, in a nutshell: your park, Yosemite National Park, still exists and, superficially, it's every bit as spectacular as it was in your heyday. The bad news: our activities have created a global biotic holocaust and even Yosemite is under siege due to anthropogenic global warming. On behalf of my now 7 billion fellow Earthlings of the naked ape variety, I must apologize.

I'd like to update you on the harsh realities of our times. Along the way, I'll share a few observations that will make you roll over in your grave, which FYI happens to be situated a short walk — short by your standards — from the "Big House," your manse in Martinez, California. Hardly anybody walks anywhere in the USA these days. Most of us are much too busy appropriating natural ecosystems worldwide and burning fossil fuels to waste time walking. And the climate change we've caused globally has impacted the ecology of your beloved Yosemite. I'll return to this grave matter after I catch you up to speed.

But first allow me to introduce myself. Like you, I was always nuts about the natural world and spent as much time as I could exploring wild places. Unlike you, I completed one degree after another, spent over a decade doing ecological field work in northern Alaska, and eventually settled into a cushy "profship" (as you called it after turning down Emerson's offer to work at Harvard). I loved my academic career. I worked in the field of evolutionary ecology, which may prompt you to infer that Darwinian logic has completely supplanted your world view of creationism. An enormous amount of empirical support for evolution by natural selection has emerged since your death and no credible scientific debate remains. I'm sure you'd be thrilled by this revolutionary intellectual advancement, the greatest in human history.

In any case, I loved almost every aspect of my career, but then along came my diagnosis. These days we know with exquisite detail the underlying mechanisms of inheritance and we can even unravel the precise make-up of each of us. In my case, I inherited a mutant "gene," which foretells a specific unfavorable fate. Never mind the grisly details. Suffice it to say that I immediately converted this bad news into an opportunity. I gave myself permission to defect.

Like you, I went adventuring. Like you, I walked. Unlike you, I also cycled. You walked to Florida, covering roughly 1000 miles. I emulated you by first cycling from

Ohio to Ontario, Canada, revisiting your stomping grounds from your conveniently timed self-imposed exile (when you otherwise might have served in the military). I then cycled east to Maine. Upon arrival, I mailed my bicycle to Georgia and then did a quintessentially Muirian thing: I walked roughly 5,000,000 steps — to get my bike, so I could ride it back to Maine. But unlike you, I didn't do any bushwhacking because these days there's a 2200-mile footpath, the Appalachian Trail, which runs all the way from Maine to Georgia. You'd love it. The trail was conceived a few years after your death, and it's been growing in popularity ever since. Notwithstanding my claim above that hardly anyone walks anymore, about 3000 adventurous humans annually attempt a continuous end-to-end hike. And most of them idolize and even fetishize you — for your ethics, your commitment to conservation, your image, your beardedness, your reputation.

After cycling back to Maine *in winter*, I headed out to California to do a similar trip on the Pacific Crest Trail. As the name suggests, this is the western analog to the Appalachian Trail. It runs 2650 miles from the border of Mexico to the border of Canada. And you'll be thrilled to learn, I think, that there's a section called The John Muir Trail. Fittingly, it's in the High Sierra (The Range of Light, as you called it).

Unfortunately, a funny thing happened on my way to the PCT: I got hit by a motorcar, a truck, while pedaling through Modesto, California. You remember Modesto, the town in the San Joaquin Valley named for its modesty. Well, Modesto is still *muy modesto*, but you wouldn't recognize the place. In your day, it was a little unincorporated burgh of about a thousand hominids. These days it's bigger (>200,000) than was San

Francisco (~58,000) in 1869. Anyway, I got crushed in the accident and haven't been able to return to hiking. My ribcage was mangled so badly that I couldn't carry a pack. Other injuries made it hard to use trekking poles (i.e., new-fangled walking sticks).

Fortunately, even though I effectively lost use of one lung, I can pedal on flat ground with little pain. While rehabbing for the PCT thru-hike, I've been hanging out in Modesto writing and spending lots of time pondering you and your legacy. Your footprints are everywhere on this part of Earth. As the young folks would say, "Dude, you're totally famous."

Your fame is reflected in ubiquitous namesakes. The region is littered with them. I'm writing to you from a bohemian cybercafé situated just a few hundred feet from John Muir Elementary School. And nearby there's a John Muir Court, a John Muir Park, and so on.

You were famous in your own lifetime, I know. You hobnobbed with the Great T.R. (President Teddy Roosevelt to you), tycoons of industry, and even Ralph Waldo Emerson (Waldo to you). But you've become überfamous in your afterlife. Like your esteemed contemporaries, your name yields a whopping number of Google hits (3.1 million versus 5.1 million for Hank Thoreau, 10.3 million for Waldo, and 11.1 million for Teddy). (Mr. Muir: Remind me to explain Google hits?)

As further evidence of your superstardom, you're one of only three people who has an official day in the State of California. April 21st is John Muir Day. If I had the authority to do so, I'd declare every day to be John Muir Day, in perpetuity, for the whole planet. Heck, we'd celebrate John Muir Day, John Muir Month, John Muir

Year, John Muir Decade, John Muir Century, and John Muir Millennium. Just so you know.

So here I am squatting in California, surrounded by constant reminders of you and your stellar legacy. And wherever I pedal, I inevitably encounter new reminders, places where you've left your metaphorical footprints. This happened during my recent jaunt retracing your footprints to Yosemite. As I climbed out of Coulterville pedaling east, I saw a sign indicating that I was traveling the recently dedicated John Muir Highway, a 19-mile stretch of pavement. If that isn't incongruous enough, I learned that a shindig in your honor, the John Muir Festival, was scheduled for the next weekend in LaGrange, Coulterville, Greeley Hill, and Lake Don Pedro. One of the featured activities was to be a caravan of "vintage" cars traveling in your footsteps, from Coulterville to Smith Station. Never mind the cringeworthy facts that you refused to own a car and our addiction to cars underlies the threat to biodiversity in Yosemite.

Presumably, you'd like to know why I was tracing your steps from the Central Valley to Yosemite. Well, I had two reasons. First, I was on my way to the Strawberry Music Festival, held biannually near the Hetch Hetchy Dam.

Yes, I'm sorry to report that the dam, anathema to you, is still in place. And while on that unsavory topic, I really must commiserate with you regarding the bad stuff that was going down toward the end of your days. I don't know how you coped. It must have been exhausting. Hetch Hetchy was a losing battle for you. The cultural addiction to the automobile was just starting to take hold. And right across town from your manse in

Martinez, that monstrosity of an oil refinery was under construction.

Second, I was traveling your route from Modesto to the Hetch Hetchy area to reimagine your trip and to experience first-hand the current biodiversity along your pathway to the High Sierra.

You set out on June 3, 1869. You walked from San Francisco to Yosemite. You used your "two little feet," to borrow from Greg Brown's lyric about you. (FYI, you've inspired a couple dozen songs so far.) I set out 142 years later. I used my two little feet too. But I used them to push pedals. I cheated. You couldn't have done so as your trip predated the commercial availability of bicycles by a decade. I suppose you could have pedaled a prototype of one of those wacky penny-farthings, the precursor to the modern bike with the absurdly massive front wheel and tiny rear wheel. (Heck, considering your acumen as an inventor, I suspect you could have made your own pedal bike.) Alternatively, if you'd just waited till 1880, when you turned my age (52), you could have traveled at bike-speed (circa 15 mph).

As I pedal hither and yon in California, I often imagine you on a bike. I imagine your terminal-length white beard flapping in the breeze. And I imagine you wearing that itchy wool overcoat and that less-than-ideally aerodynamic top hat. But sometimes I picture you modernized, wearing skintight Lycra, using a stream-lined helmet, and sporting shaved bulgy legs.

I hope the fanciful description above doesn't offend you. But, hey, at least I didn't say anything about your apocryphal mid-life crisis. I didn't describe your buying a car, a Lamborghini no less (as did an irreverent student at the John Muir College at the University of California at San Diego).

Okay, back to reality:

Despite the lasting impression that you walked solo with a crust of bread in your overcoat pocket, you actually went marching through with a great herd of grazing herbivores (2050 sheep), plus two pack horses, one Saint Bernard (your faithful companion, Carlo), several shepherding dogs, and a quartet of humans (including a Native American man, a Chinese man, the owner of the sheep, and a shepherd). That's ~8238 feet marching through, with ~2062 mouths to feed. I must say, this is not the sort of leave-no-trace camping that folks these days imagine you did.

In any case, you traveled at the speed of sheep and so it took you roughly 10 days to go from Modesto to Hetch Hetchy. As for me, I went rolling through on two wheels, at bike speed. No entourage. No sheep for my succor or supper. Of course, my little trek took one day and I had access to taco trucks, Chili Huts, Pizza Palaces, fast-food joints, and convenience stores along the way.

Speeding through the San Joaquin valley, I tried to imagine the landscape as it looked in your day as I passed through almond and walnut groves and cherry plantations. You see, long ago the valley was converted wholesale to an agro-industrial complex. Imagine your fruit trees in Martinez extending in monocultural blocks all the way to the Sierra foothills.

Along the way, I tried to ignore pelotons of pukers (i.e., fellow citizens who nauseate me) roaring by my elbow. They were in SUVs and extended-cab trucks, many of them with trailers in tow. On the trailers were big motor boats or ATVs. And when I wasn't being buzzed by these four-wheeled menaces, I was being buzzed by pelotons of attorneys and dentists and other disreputable types on the noisiest motorcycles money can buy (i.e., Harley-Davidsons, which just so happen to be made in your first adopted state, Wisconsin). They were all on their way to "enjoy" Yosemite, believe it or not.

I crossed the Tuolumne River, pausing briefly to admire a massive colony of cliff swallows. I imagined you might have admired a precursor of this very colony. Minutes later, I arrived in LaGrange. You wouldn't recognize the place. It's still situated at 249 feet above sea level and still on the edge of the foothills, of course, but its days as a gold-mining boom town ended long ago. No longer does it boast a population in the thousands, complete with a "China Town." These days it's a mostly tame little bust town. It harbors a meager population of 345 and that may include the free-roaming pit bulls and goats. I stopped at the general store to buy Gatorade for the climbing ahead, but I had to wait for the storekeeper to return from fetching one of the town's AWOL goats.

Next stop, after the first real climb of the day: Coulterville (elevation: 1699 feet a.s.l.; population: 250). Despite its serious shrinkage since you passed through, you might still recognize this place, thanks to one distinctive landmark, the Hotel Jefferey (1851). It still had that new-hotel smell in your day. According to an historical plaque, the Jefferey accommodated the Mexican Community and included a cantina and a fandango hall. These days it accommodates nobody as it's boarded up. No fandango for me, so I continued on my way.

I climbed through chaparral habitat. Within an hour, I entered yet another floristic province, with manzanita and gray pines and interior live oaks. Along the way, I was either going too fast or working too hard to botanize the way you did while traveling at sheep speed. You were able to appreciate the subtleties of the ecological transitions along the elevational gradient. At bike speed, I mostly just noticed the rapid turnover of the avifauna. In the valley, it was all mockingbirds and western kingbirds and black phoebes and yellow-billed magpies and red-winged blackbirds and mourning doves and crows and western scrub-jays and acorn woodpeckers and common flickers. Valley birds. But by the end of the day, at a stealth campsite perched on the cliff overlooking Hetch Hetchy canyon, I encountered none of these species. The whole community had turned over as I climbed the old railroad grade. At the end of the day, I was a mile above the San Joaquin Valley and surrounded by Nashville warblers, Cassin's and warbling vireos, red-breasted nuthatches, dark-eyed juncos, olive-sided flycatchers (singing "quick, three beers"), Stellar's jays, and common ravens. Yosemite birds.

Over the next three beautiful sunny days, I attended the nearby Strawberry Music Festival, mysteriously arriving by bicycle each morning to join the mob of Car People who pushed gas pedals to get to the outdoor venue. I think you would have enjoyed the scene. Much of the music was old timey or bluegrass or newgrass, much of it with roots in Scotland, your homeland. With fiddles and mandolins and guitars and banjos twanging in the background, I spent lots of time contemplating the ecological changes that are underway, thanks to global warming.

I thought about whether I could do some quick-and-dirty comparison between an already-existing historical dataset and a new dataset I'd generate on my way back down to Modesto. But because I'd be descending at speeds reaching 43 mph, I wouldn't be generating any data. And so I thought I'd be left arm-waving if I ever got around to writing this letter. Luckily, when I arrived back in Modesto and did a quick literature search, I discovered a wonderful paper, published 3 years ago.

Here's a little background:

You may recall toward the end of your life Grinnell and Alexander, from the natural history museum at UC Berkeley, were gearing up for an ambitious survey of the small-mammal communities along the "Yosemite Transect." Well, they pulled it off. Starting the year of your death, 1914, and running through 1920, they trapped small mammals along a transect starting at LaGrange in the Lower Sonoran Life Zone and extending up the elevational gradient to Lyell Canyon in the Hudsonian-Alpine Life Zone.

You may recall crossing paths with Grinnell in Sitka, Alaska. As you know, he championed the now old-fashioned concept of ecological niche and he also recognized a relationship between climate and geographic range of species. This was prescient, in light of the warming trend in recent decades. Believe it or not, Yosemite has warmed by about 6 degrees since your death.

As I said above, your legacy, including Yosemite National Park, remains intact. Unfortunately, you and your contemporaries never anticipated that global warming would threaten the ecology of protected areas like Yosemite. But we contemporary conservation ecologists collectively fret that setting aside parks like Yosemite, in retrospect, was like building sandcastles below the rising tide. We predict the geographic ranges of species in montane parks like Yosemite to shift upward, contracting along the trailing lower-elevation limit.

To test this prediction, Craig Moritz and colleagues replicated the original Yosemite Transect study. The punchline: half of the small-mammal species have undergone an upward range shift, by about 1500 feet, on average.

I know you spent much of your Yosemite time botanizing and ruminating about geology, and yet you were a versatile naturalist with a good familiarity of small mammals along *your* transect. You could identify everything from shrews to mice to voles to ground squirrels and tree squirrels to pikas and marmots and even woodrats. I recall your writing about the Douglas tree squirrel, in particular, so you may be pleased to learn that its elevational range has remained stable.

Unfortunately, 10 species have experienced a range contraction. For all of these species, there's been an upslope shift in the lower limit, consistent with the predicted response to warming. In none of these species has the *upper* limit of the range shifted upslope, so there's been a contraction of the elevational range, along the trailing lower limit.

Four of these 10 species — bushy-tailed woodrat (*Neotoma cinerea*), Belding's ground squirrel (*Spermophilus beldingi*), alpine chipmunk (*Tamias alpines*), and American pika (*Ochotona princeps*) — occur in the Hudsonian-Alpine Life Zone, at the highest elevations, so they have no place to go. They're trapped on shrinking islands in the sky, surrounded by unsuitably warm habitat.

My hunch is three of these species may be especially vulnerable to future warming because they rely on hoarded food. The woodrat, sometimes called a packrat, is a legendary hoarder. The alpine chipmunk, a hoarder extraordinaire, is of special conservation concern because it's indigenous; its entire geographic range is restricted to the Sierra of California. And the pika makes hay, which it stores. (Belding's ground squirrel, famous for its kin recognition and nepotistic alarm-calling, doesn't hoard food to survive the winter. Instead, it stores energy in the form of enormous wads of body fat.) To the extent that the woodrat, chipmunk, and pika rely on cold storage to preserve their hoards, they may be extinction prone considering forecasts of continued warming.

Sorry to be the bearer of such bad news. Although your contributions remain as important today as ever, we now know that we can't simply set aside additional protected areas around Earth and assume a laissez-fair approach will yield the desired outcome. We need to incorporate forecasts of how climate change will shift species ranges.

If we could reincarnate you, we'd encourage you to use your influence to help curtail global warming. And I'd be glad to teach you how to ride a bicycle so you could make a symbolic statement about the importance of minimizing one's personal carbon footprint. You could divorce your Lamborghini and live like the pedestrian you were, 'cept you could use your two little feet to push pedals. I think you'd enjoy the speed.

Thank you for your enormous and lasting contributions. And thank you for taking the time to read this letter.

Yours very greenly,

Thomas A. Waite
Associate Professor [retired]
Dept. of Evolution, Ecology, and Organismal Biology
Ohio State University
Columbus, Ohio, Earth

P.S. Over the past three years, whenever I find myself pedaling through California, I'm drawn to your place in Martinez. It's become a ritual for me. I go to the Big House, sit quietly in the tower as you once did, and then I strike off in one direction or another. And it seems wherever I go, there you are.

On the first such foray, I set out from your place and pedaled to Point Reyes, now a protected area and a birding hotspot. And along the way, I'm glad to report I visited a National Historic Site that bears your name and happens to harbor an awe-inspiring old growth forest of majestic redwoods.

On the next such foray, I set out from your place and pedaled north to Alaska, your favorite destination on Earth, aside from Yosemite.

A year later, I set out from your place and pedaled the Anza Trail to Nogales, Mexico, retracing the route traveled by the Anza Expedition, which aimed to settle/Catholicize the San Francisco Bay Area. (That worked.)

And when I make my biannual transcontinental forays between the Pacific and Atlantic Coasts, I always pass through Martinez. It's a rule. In fact, I'll be leaving your old stomping grounds near Lake Huron in Ontario, Canada soon and pedaling in a meandering way back to Martinez.

Your place has become my mecca and ground zero. It's our nexus. All roads lead to and from Martinez, Earth.

🚲 🚲 🚲 🚲 🚲

Tom Waite

CONVEYANCE SUBLIME

Chapter 15

The Conveyance Sublime

The Most Efficient Mode of Transportation Ever Devised

I read a study that measured the efficiency of locomotion for various species. The condor used the least energy per unit mass to move a given distance. Humans came in with a rather unimpressive showing about a third of the way down the list. That didn't look so good, but then someone had the insight to test the efficiency of locomotion for a person on a bicycle. The bicyclist blew the condor away. That's what a computer is to me: it's the most remarkable tool that we've ever come up with. It's the equivalent of a bicycle for our minds.

— Steve Jobs (paraphrased liberally)

The bicycle is the most remarkable tool we've ever come up with. It's the equivalent of a personal computer for our mobility, general health, and overall betterment.

— Tom Waite

Aren't bicycles great? You can travel anywhere on those things!

— Some guy in a bike shop

How am I able to commute transcontinentally? How can I be bicoastal, summering along the Atlantic coast, wintering along the Pacific coast, and roaming everywhere in between? Is it because I'm awesome? Nope, it's because, despite what nearly everyone I meet seems to believe, cycling is easy.

Even if the conveyance sublime fails to make you fit, healthy, sane, happy, or green, it's guaranteed to make you instantaneously efficient and freakishly so. In fact, it costs less energetically to move your body a given distance by pedaling than by using any other means of transport. Pedaling a bicycle — sitting on a padded seat and making your feet move in circles — is orders of magnitude more efficient than sitting still on a jet or luxuriating on a luxury liner, dozens of times more efficient than driving a car, and several times more efficient than riding on a train or driving a moped. And when the long-awaited personal jetpack — a real energy hog — becomes commercially available in 2014, the bicycle will remain the most efficient means of transportation ever devised. Bar none.

But I've really downplayed the sales pitch:

Beyond being the most efficient means of human transportation, bicycling is also more efficient than any mode of locomotion in nonhuman animals ever studied by physiologists. To date, these studies have been limited to a few dozen species. But if we could feasibly measure the energetics of locomotion in all extant animal species, we might conclude bicycling is more efficient than any form of locomotion shaped by natural selection.

Unsurprisingly, a pedaling human is more efficient than a galumphing elephant or a swimming-through-soil naked mole rat or a hopping kangaroo or a knuckle-walking gorilla or a frolicking dolphin or a peristaltically wriggling earthworm or a flapping goose or a waddling penguin or a sliding slug or a slithering salamander or a sprinting sloth.

What's truly remarkable, though, is that a pedaling human is more efficient than its closest known rivals in nature because they — big broad-winged birds — use a seemingly energy-free mode. They ride thermals, spiraling upward without flapping; then they glide toward their destination, losing altitude as they go. Then they soar on another thermal till they glide again. They store gravitational potential energy as they soar, and expend it as kinetic energy as they glide. Repeating this cycle throughout the day, some birds can travel hundreds of miles without flapping their wings.

It's a sight to see. And you needn't pay an admission fee. Just look up.

Of course, this soar-and-glide mode isn't completely passive and so isn't energetically free. Though it looks effortless because the birds don't flap their wings, they do make thousands of fine adjustments of feather orientation and posture on each ascent and each descent, all involving muscular contractions. And so, while it's much cheaper than flapping flight, birds using this mode have a metabolic rate about double their rate at rest. And that's about as efficient as locomotion gets.

This mode is so efficient that engineers working in the area of biomimicry are trying to emulate it for unmanned aerial vehicles, commonly known as drones. By mathematically mimicking the best byproduct of natural selection, they hope to optimize the performance of drones — in the name of ever increasingly efficient killing and spying and such. (Still in the R&D phase, Amazon may someday deliver your packages using a fleet of drones.)

And yet, birds that travel using this ultra-efficient mode (with a cadence of zero flaps per minute) aren't as efficient as a pedaling human (with a cadence of 90 revolutions per minute).

And this isn't even a fair comparison in the first place because the soar-and-glide mode can only be used on favorable days, when columns of warm air rising from the ground to cumulus clouds aid the bird's ascent — like vertical tailwinds — for each bout of gliding. Meanwhile, a pedaling human is rarely aided by a tailwind so strong that she doesn't even need to pedal, except in cycling heaven (or if eastbound in Arizona).

This eclipsing of nature's best by the bicycle is remarkable partly because human-engineered designs, even when they intentionally mimic nature, are usually poor imitations of the real thing.

As an evolutionary ecologist who collaborated with engineers on biomimicry research, I can't help but ask which byproducts of natural selection were mimicked in the designing of the bicycle. What on Earth was the biological inspiration? At first glance, it's hard to construe the bicycle as a case of biomimicry — a reinventing of nature's wheel — because nature doesn't do wheels. Or does it?

At best, a few organisms turn themselves into a ball or a crude approximation of the Flintstone wheel and move in a self-propelled way, somersaulting to safety:

Some caterpillars, when attacked, morph into a crude replica of a spokeless wheel and then do a few backwards somersaults, which allows them to sprint to safety at 40 times their normal speed.

Mantis shrimp can do many spectacular things. They can kick an octopus's butt, strike faster than a bullet, and break open clams. They can also do backwards somersaults to avoid being stranded during low tide. At 72 revolutions per minute, they approximate the suboptimal pedaling cadence used by so many casual cyclists.

Mangolins (a.k.a., spiny anteaters) — those armored critters that look almost as reptilian as mammalian — have been reported anecdotally to escape from lions by rolling into a tight motionless ball and then intermittently somersaulting to eventual safety.

These exemplars have provided biological inspiration for the now-familiar somersaulting robots, but it seems highly improbable that folks who "discovered" the bicycle were inspired by somersaulting escape artists from the Animal Kingdom.

Besides, somersaulting in nature can get you killed. Some male spiders selfishly trade their life for sex by doing a somersault during copulation, thereby offering their soft underbelly as food to their gravid partner of the moment. Hypothetically, the well-fed female then uses that male's sperm preferentially, over those donated by non-suicidal males, to fertilize her eggs. (Don't try this at home.)

Dismissing the absurd possibility of somersaulting backwards across the continent — perhaps no more absurd than riding backwards on a BMX bicycle as a guy did legendarily a few years ago — I plan to keep pedaling in the manner in which I've grown accustomed. And in doing so, I'll continue to travel with nonpareil efficiency.

I'm able to migrate transcontinentally with bird-like efficiency because cycling represents a quantum leap in efficiency vis-à-vis walking. Despite many generations of natural selection favoring individuals with heritable walking superiority, walking remains only about 65% efficient. That is, about 35% of the work done by your legs while repeatedly falling forward on two inverted pendula and braking to catch your balance gets lost as heat. By contrast, 99% of the force applied to your pedals gets realized where the rubber meets the road. And that's where Newton of the Sir Isaac variety comes in, but I'm getting ahead of myself again.

This extraordinary efficiency enables me to commute easily between the two Portlandias, the big one in Oregon and the little one in Maine. If I were feeling truly lazy, I could match the power (30 watts) of a typical pedestrian who creeps along at a Paleolithically relevant 3 mph and yet I'd travel at thrice that speed. But I almost never feel *that* lazy. In fact, I routinely maintain a modest 100 watts, which means I cruise at about 14 mph under ideal conditions (i.e., flat and calm). Working only about as hard as a soaring-and-gliding bird, I can travel 100 miles daily in less than 7 hours. And so I could routinely make the 3000-mile one-way trip in about a month, if only I didn't get waylaid along the way — bedazzled by pornographic landscapes, intriguing Car People, and live music.

DARWINIAN CAVEATS

There's one little problem with bragging about how cycling is more efficient than any mode of locomotion: efficiency maximization may be the "wrong" optimization criterion. Sparing you the esoteric (algebraic) details, animals in nature should be so lazy only under special conditions.

To clarify, imagine your favorite wild animal gathering resources and delivering them to a central place such as a nest full of babies. The optimal strategy (i.e., best travel speed) would maximize the rate of delivery subject to the constraint that your favorite animal must balance its own energy budget. If its net self-feeding rate is very high, then the optimal speed approaches rate maximizing. That is, if it's extremely easy to feed itself, it can afford to go very fast, which isn't efficient. But at the other end of the continuum, if your favorite animal's net self-feeding rate is very slow, then its provisioning trips should be efficient. It should travel at a slower speed.

So while efficiency is a standard bragging point used by bicycle advocates, it's really just an endpoint of a continuum. And unless you're barely able to meet your own needs, the optimal travel speed is faster than the efficiency-maximizing speed. Which means even though you're more efficient than virtually any other creature on Earth, you could be even more efficient if you just slowed down.

But, presumably, you don't truly want to minimize the work you do to transport yourself a given distance. For mathematical reasons that will soon become clear, that would require slowing to a shade above 0 mph. Clearly, that would be maladaptive, unless you magically have infinite time to accomplish your goals.

I don't know about you, but I prefer a cruising speed that vastly exceeds efficiency-maximizing, which makes sense given my extraordinarily high self-feeding rate.

With a superabundance of taco trucks and clam shacks along my favorite roads, I really have no interest in touring at the speed of sloth. Sure, I may joke about how my time constraint has been relaxed, how I have nowhere to be, how I don't care when I get to Point B and don't even know where point B is. And yet, with a cruising speed of 14 mph, I exceed the efficiency-maximizing speed by nearly 14 mph. What's my hurry?

I see two obvious advantages to my excessive speed:

First, I'm highly motivated to treat each day as an opportunity to exercise. I want the health benefits that accrue when I sit on a padded seat and work moderately hard for several hours. Besides, I can't bear the thought of traveling at a speed slower than that maintained by elite marathon runners (i.e., 12 mph).

Second, I prefer to travel at a fairly high speed because when I'm pedaling I'm foraging — for opportunities, views, adventures, entertainment, bike shops, stealth camping spots, Wi-Fi hotspots, birds, and even food. I'm not specifically trying to maximize such payoffs, but I'm not trying to minimize them either. I'd like to think I travel at or near my own idiosyncratically optimal pace, subject to the constraint of not wanting to get clobbered by a well-armored Car Person.

WHY IS THE BICYCLE SO EFFICIENT?

To get some insight, let's consult the Father of Bicycle Physics, Sir Isaac Newton. Let's call him "Ike" as in "bike like Ike." Ike died in 1727, a century-and-a-half before the bicycle came into existence and yet — prescient fellow that he was — taught us almost everything we need to know to explore the fundamentals of the physics of cycling.

First and foremost, he provided us with the Laws of Bicycle Motion.

As you undoubtedly already know, he also developed the eponymous method used to approximate the first root of polynomial expressions (see next chapter). And it goes without saying that such expressions can be evaluated using *his* infinitesimal calculus. And of course, the forces involved in cycling can be measured in newtons (1 N $\equiv$ 1 kg·m/s^2). And the calories burned while pedaling can be converted to Fig Newtons, which works out to about 19.8 per typical cycling day for me. (Let me save you some Googling time: The Fig Newton is named after Newton, Massachusetts, which in turn was not named after Ike.)

All joking aside, let's have a quick look at Newton's Laws.

First law: If there is no net force on a bicycle, then its velocity is constant. The bicycle is either at rest (if its velocity is equal to zero [duh]), or it moves with constant speed in a single direction.

To maintain a desired cruising speed, all you need to do — once you've put the bicycle and its passenger in motion, overcoming inertia and accelerating to the cruising speed — is counteract the forces conspiring to slow you down. These forces include: gravity, which has a minimized impact where the road is flat (duh); aerodynamic drag, which increases faster than linearly with bike speed as you generate your own headwind; and friction of the drive train, which is a minor concern provided you remember to lube your chain every few hundred miles.

All of which means it takes so little work to keep a bike rolling along at a moderate cruising speed that you could lollygag (provide your own operational definition) and still cover great distances. Once in motion, you stay in motion, rolling along and pedaling only hard enough to maintain momentum. You cruise.

By contrast, when walking you effectively hit your brakes with each stride — to keep from falling on your face. Plus, there's no coasting when you're on your two feet. Cyclists happily escape these intrinsic inefficiencies to bipedalism.

Third law: When a bicycle exerts a force $F_{bicycle}$ on Earth, Earth simultaneously exerts a force $F_{earth} = -F_{bicycle}$ on the bicycle. This means the forces are equal in magnitude and opposite in direction.

This law has two key implications for Bicycle People:

First, the bicycle moves forward because — as your high school physics teacher mysteriously claimed — Earth pushes back against the tire. It does so with a force equal and opposite to the one you indirectly apply against Earth via pedaling. And fortunately the force you apply to the pedals is *extremely* efficient (99%) at generating the force against Earth.

Second, the gravitational force applied by you and your bicycle and your loaded panniers is offset by Earth in a perfectly counterbalancing, equal-and-opposite way. This means you can pedal in a smooth and steady way, without bouncing up and down like a pedestrian who must flex her muscles to compensate.

This helps explain why really big guys can pedal effectively and why it's easy to carry a very heavy load attached to the frame of a bicycle.

While doling out kudos to Ike, it strikes me as curious that Einstein achieved capital-eff fame by exposing the limits of Newtonian logic and yet he was a Newtonian through and through, at least when it came to cycling. Daily, he pedaled his way around Princeton, the town and the campus, all the while obeying the laws of Newtonian physics. Presumably, he powered his bike at about 30 watts, or 30 newtons per meter per second, which gives you some idea of what a weakling Newton must have been. According to legend, Einstein even had the inspiration for his General Theory of Relativity while perched on his bicycle, obeying Newton's Laws and yet musing about traveling at the speed of light in an unearthly strong gravitational field.

As for me, I strongly prefer to travel under Newtonian conditions, roughly 671 million mph slower than the speed of light — maxing out at 43 mph — while enjoying Earth's gravitational field on every descent.

Chapter 16

There's Always a Headwind

And Other Cycling Myths

Bipedalism was a major evolutionary innovation in humans, the only obligately bipedal primate. By walking upright our ancestors could travel while carrying loads of chocolate and wine and other essentials. And then along came the bicycle. Talk about a major innovation!

Cycling represents a quantum leap in Darwinian fitness-related advantages. It allows the pedalista to triple travel speed while expending only as much energy as a pedestrian. It allows a vast increase in effective range, with concomitant increases in access to resources and information. And it allows the pedalista to carry extra-heavy loads. Is it any wonder roughly half of all people on Earth own a bicycle even today?

But why is the bicycle so sublimely efficient? To answer this question, let's explore the physics of cycling with special emphasis on my ongoing transcontinental commutes. And let's confront evolutionarily uninspired dogma along the way. Shall we?

The Bicycle Equation

Let's keep it simple and use the familiar Newton-inspired expression for the power required to propel a bicycle and its motor/passenger and panniers in a straight line at a steady cruising speed,

$$P = gmV_b(c_f + s) + c_d V_a^2 V_b,$$

where I'm sure I needn't remind you:

P is pedal power (in watts), g is Earth's gravity (9.8 in meters per second per second), m is the combined mass of the bicycle and motor/passenger and "luggage" (in kilograms), V_b is the velocity of the bicycle plus the animate and inanimate stuff on it relative to Earth's surface (in meters per second), c_f is a dimensionless constant (= 0.0053) for the combined friction of the drive train and tires, s is the slope (grade) of the road (defined as the dimensionless ratio of rise over run, not in degrees), c_d is a constant for aerodynamic drag (= 0.185 kilograms per meter), and V_a is the effective (realized) velocity of the pedaler relative to air molecules.

If you haven't dozed off, you've surely gathered that the first term on the right-hand side (RHS) represents the power required to overcome friction and gravity, and the second term on the RHS represents the power required to overcome drag (the resistance put up by those pesky air molecules).

We could use Newton's infinitesimal calculus to gain insights, but let's confine ourselves to a few Waite-specific numerical examples. To estimate V_b (or m) we'll use Newton's method of solving iteratively for the first root of a polynomial expression (using the What-If Analysis option in Excel). And to estimate P we'll simply plug and chug.

Let's start by considering "ideal" conditions, which is to say flat ($s = 0$) and calm ($V_a = V_b$). Coincidentally, when I started pedaling this morning, I "climbed" from 85 to 88 feet above sea level in the first 2 miles. That's pretty flat ($s = 0.0003$). And when I stopped to hold a licked forefinger in the air, I couldn't detect directionality. That's pretty calm. (Later, I'll inject a bit of realism and explore impacts of hilliness and windiness.)

THERE'S ALWAYS A HEADWIND?

If you've ever pedaled a bicycle while not totally oblivious and especially if you've done so while nude (as a friend of mine once did through the state of Nevada), you've surely noticed a cooling sensation on exposed skin on the front of your body. It seems like there's a headwind. Indeed, for cyclists, it almost *always* seems like there's a headwind. But is this an illusion, perhaps an example of pervasive pessimism bias in *Homo sapiens pedalus*? Or is it a real phenomenon?

The savvy among you are way ahead of me. You've already recognized that the component of power required to overcome friction and gravity (i.e., the 1st term on the RHS) increases slowly as a linear function of cruising speed (V_b); whereas, the component required to overcome drag (i.e., the second term) increases as a cubic function of V_b. You've reasoned that the power required to overcome drag increases dramatically with cruising speed. This means when you increase your pedaling effort by just a little, you waste a lot more energy and do a lot more work pushing against the intensified self-imposed headwind. (Now that you've seen the algebra and peeked at the graph below, you have no one to blame but yourself.)

You can readily convince yourself of this phenomenon by generating your own empirical evidence. Here's my report. If I cruise at walking speed (3 mph), I can't really feel the air on my skin. Not surprisingly, solving for P reveals that only 5% of the power required to propel the 118-kg combination of myself+bike+panniers is used to overcome drag. But this component skyrockets as I speed up. At my typical cruising speed, 15 mph, nearly 60% of the power is used to overcome drag. And when I get rambunctious and speed up to 25 mph, nearly 80% of the power is used to overcome drag. At this speed, I can really feel the self-generated headwind holding me back.

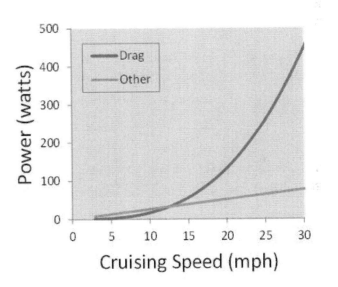

Imagine what it's like for elite cyclists who routinely travel faster than 25 mph. For them, cycling really is a matter of pushing through the wind. They pedal in a truly wasteful way, which may seem counterproductive, but keep in mind they're not the least bit interested in efficiency. They're racing. (Even when they're on a solo training ride, they're racing against the clock, against invisible competitors.) Implicitly, they're trying to minimize time to completion, not maximize efficiency. It's as if they've been commissioned to deliver an all-important message or a vaccine and only the winner gets rewarded. And in the process, they're signaling superiority. It's as if they're showing off, ultimately for improved prospects in the areas of sex and survival.

As for me, I prefer not to beat myself against an extra-strength, self-imposed headwind all the livelong day. So I usually maintain a decidedly noncompetitive speed. Sure, by pedaling at a snail's pace, I delay my arrival at point B each day. But that's okay because as a solo touring cyclist I finish both first and last every day, irrespective of speed. And time minimization is a nonsensical optimization criterion for me because point B is usually unspecified. In other words, I usually don't care where I finish each day. Plus, by slowing down and pedaling more efficiently I save precious internal fat reserves. How's that for adaptive?

~~~

Virtually omnipresent headwinds are simultaneously illusory and real. Sometimes we're facing our own self-generated headwind compounded by an actual externally imposed headwind. And sometimes we're benefiting from a tailwind, but even then we may feel like a headwind is slowing us down.

This tendency not to appreciate a tailwind is all the more remarkable because the tailwind actually helps our speed *more* than an equivalent headwind hurts it. I kid you not.

Here's an example:

Routinely, I supply about 100 watts of power. On a calm day, my cruising speed is 15 mph. If "cursed" with a 15-mph headwind, my speed decreases by just 5 mph; but if "blessed" with a 15-mph tailwind, my speed increases by a full 9 mph. (Algebraically, this makes sense: a tailwind reduces V_a, which dramatically reduces drag because drag is a function of V_a squared.) And yet, I tend not to appreciate, or even notice, the tailwind. But why?

Presumably, my tendency to take for granted a tailwind is partly attributable to the fact that I *feel* a headwind. Pedaling with a 15-mph tailwind at 24 mph is equivalent to facing a 9 mph headwind (while at a standstill). The *realized* headwind is weaker when there's a tailwind, but its effect is still real. I'm not inclined to celebrate the tailwind because I feel a headwind in my face. No wonder we cyclists think there's almost always a headwind.

Of course, sometimes I'm blessed with a tailwind so strong that V_a falls below the detectability threshold. Then it feels as though there's no wind. And I feel like I'm having a great day. Naturally, I attribute my awesome speed to my extraordinary fitness, not to a tailwind I conveniently ignore.

Sometimes when I have a very strong tailwind, I reduce my power output and slow down enough not to feel a headwind. But I don't slow down enough to feel the tailwind. Instead, I pedal along in that "comfort zone" where the effective wind (V_a) is so weak as to be undetectable. Again, I celebrate my speed by attributing it to my fitness, a synergistic byproduct of my training regimen and true underlying genetic superiority.

Because I only occasionally enjoy such strong tailwinds, pedaling for me is routinely a matter of pushing through the wind. Under the vast majority of conditions, as I "power" along at 100 watts it feels like there's a headwind because *effectively* there is. And it's all right there in the algebra. As Ze Frank would say, that's how science dooo.

~~~

But wait, that's just a proximate explanation of the phenomenon. The compelling ultimate, or evolutionary, question is why? In other words, what's the adaptive value of being oblivious to a big benefit associated with a tailwind and yet being very sensitive to a smaller cost associated with a headwind?

Superficially, this bias seems irrational and yet it could be *ecologically* rational. It's easy to dream up plausible scenarios where this bias could translate into improved survival prospects. For instance, imagine it's critical to get home before dark. If the cyclist has a strong expectation of getting home before dark with no wind, then a sudden tailwind wouldn't change the expected (positive) outcome. But a sudden headwind could doom the cyclist to returning late. Under ancestral conditions and even today, this could cause an individual's future Darwinian fitness to plummet to zero.

In this scenario, if my goal is to arrive at a warm safe refuge before dark, I might need to maintain a speed of, say, 15 mph. This could be very demanding, perhaps not even feasible. Recall, as I tool along at 15 mph under calm conditions, my power requirement is 100 watts. If I were cursed with a 15-mph headwind, my power requirement would increase by a whopping 175 watts; whereas, if I were blessed with a 15-mph tailwind, my power requirement would decrease by 58 watts. The effect of the wind in this example is *three* times greater for the headwind than the tailwind.

Pedaling into a headwind entails a spike in energetic costs. So a headwind is potentially *very* bad news and an equivalent tailwind is good or neutral news. No wonder we pedalers are obsessed with headwinds.

From an adaptationist perspective, it pays to be attuned to vagaries of weather that increase time and energy costs. To devote more attention to a headwind than a tailwind, to give it greater valence, to be stressed out by it, to have elevated cortisol levels — these seem like adaptive responses. Under ancestral conditions, any change in environmental conditions that suddenly tripled energetic demands and jeopardized the completion of a goal (like returning to a safe shelter or delivering essential resources) must have been a real attention-grabber.

To convince yourself, take advantage of the fact that the conveyance sublime allows you to travel such great distances that you can get into trouble. Do this in Alaska, in winter, during a blizzard. Go too far. And then cope with a headwind that threatens to triple your time of arrival at the next building with a woodstove. Trust me, you'll feel the adaptive stress response.

Even under benign conditions, I like to indulge my primal urge to avoid any fitness decrement associated with headwinds. I conveniently take days off when facing strong headwinds. Or I use a nifty trick for turning a headwind to my advantage: I simply change my direction — by precisely 180 degrees. It helps to be nomadic in this context. Free of the constraint of returning nightly to a central place, I can avoid headwind-induced stress, elevated cortisol, and a negative energy budget. Of course there's a downside to this tendency: I spend an inordinate amount of time bouncing off the east coast of North America, as dictated by the prevailing winds.

WEIGHTY MATTERS

Beyond allowing us to travel so fast that we experience a self-imposed headwind while pedaling downwind, the bicycle allows us to do so almost independently of mass *on flat roads*. In this context, Newton doesn't really care how heavy our bike is, how fat we are, or how much stuff we have in our panniers.

Skeptical? A quick look at the equation might help. You'll see that mass cannot impact the power required to overcome drag as m doesn't even appear in the second term on the right-hand side. You'll also see that the remaining component of power is a linear function of mass.

Still unconvinced? Well, check out the graph showing how traveling with loaded panniers only minimally impacts my cruising speed. With empty panniers, I would travel at 15.6 mph. With full panniers, I travel at 15.2 mph.

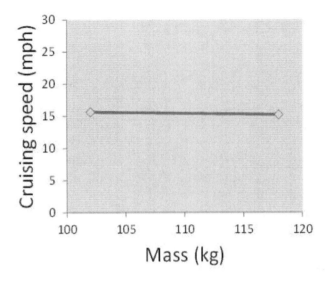

Mass (kg)

How does this affect my transcontinental commuting time? With empty panniers, I could do the trip between the Portlandias, assuming flat roads, in 227 hours. With loaded panniers, it would take me 233 hours. If I were to pedal 8 hours per day, I'd reach my destination in about 29 days. So it costs me a fraction of a day in increased travel time to carry my stuff. This strikes me as a perfectly acceptable trade-off. After all, what are bicycles for if not to carry your sleeping bag and other survival gear?

Speaking of which, the bicycle allows its pedaler to carry remarkably heavy loads. When it isn't being underutilized as a child's toy or a piece of recreational equipment, it can be extremely efficient in this context. With a bicycle you can transport loads that no pedestrian could manage. For instance, while supplying 100 watts of power, I could carry a metric ton (1000 kg) and do so while outpacing a pedestrian, at 3.9 mph. To put this in perspective, I could transport almost a dozen clones of myself. On foot, I could give one such clone a piggyback ride, for a few hundred feet. Maybe.

Alternatively, I could carry the same load and maintain my preferred cruising speed of 15 mph by increasing power to 464 watts. Fortunately, I'm fit enough to pull this off — not all the livelong day, but for good stretch. So, if I wanted to do so, I could deliver a few pianos per day while traveling at my usual touring speed. I'm not saying I will, but I could. Alternatively, I could carry tens of thousands of carnival medals and dole them out to kind strangers. Or I could add 357,141 St. Christopher medals to my current load of one — for extra protection against halitosis and chapped lips and such.

~

All of the examples above assume the world is devoid of hills. And that's not quite true. The real world is hilly and so I should apologize for focusing till now on the simplified version of the equation, where $s = 0$. Obviously, the power required to overcome gravity depends on mass (duh). To compensate you might consider getting lean, squandering lots of money on an ultralight bike, and minimizing your pannier contents. Alternatively, you could restrict yourself to pedaling within those vast interstitial spaces on the Earth's surface where $s \approx 0$.

Admittedly, I'm too heavy to climb 9% grades while supplying my preferred 100 watts of power. At that power, my hypothetical speed is 2.0 mph. I say hypothetical because it's hard (for me) to balance a bike while climbing such a steep grade at walking speed. Besides, what's the purpose of the bicycle if not to travel faster than a pedestrian?

Of course, I could climb faster if only I lightened my load. Let's suppose I were to drop 30 pounds of surplus adipose tissue, much of which protects my hypothetical "six pack." How fast would I climb at my preferred 100 watts? Just 2.3 mph and that's not quite good enough.

At my current weight, I manage to climb at walking speed or faster by working harder, not by dieting or jettisoning my gear. I don't mind doing the extra work. In fact, I want the exercise. I crave the challenge. By increasing my power output by 50%, I can climb 9% grades with a fully loaded bike at 3 mph. Doubling my power output increases my speed to 4 mph, which is plenty fast. And when I eventually reach the pass, I reap the reward for getting my extra mass to the top as I fly down the other side, passing scrawny cyclists without even pedaling, pushing effortlessly through a 43 mph gravity-generated headwind. And that's sublime.

~

May your conveyance be as sublime as mine. May your sweet ride carry you far and wide. May you experience nothing but self-imposed headwinds. May you cruise at an ideal near-invariant speed that shall remain virtually independent of your waistline or the contents of your panniers, at least while rolling along flat roads. May you remain lean enough to climb with ease. May your conveyance and you stay happily married, forever or till crash do you part.

Go pedal. As for me, I'm off to help a friend move her piano. And then I'll be dancing on pedals across Eurasia. Don't miss me too much.

INQUIRING
MINDS

Chapter 17

Inquiring Minds

As I roam far and wide, I get asked tons of questions. Inquisitive folks want to know about my safety, sanity, expenses, itinerary, purpose, solitude, encounters, contingencies, and stuff. In no particular order, here's a litany of some of the most frequently annoying questions along with my glib, snarky, bumbling, and yet sometimes marginally thoughtful answers.

Nice day for a ride, isn't it?

This one stumps me. I know it's rhetorical and I should just take it in stride, but it's so damned annoying. For me, it's not an innocuous bromide. It's certainly not an effective conversation starter. It's a thought-terminating platitude, an insult to cognizing humans everywhere. There ought to be a law. Or a special place in Hell. Or both.

Okay, that's hyperbolic, even for me. But if I had my druthers, I'd ban it. All Earthlings would kindly cease and desist. So please stop saying this to me. I'm not amused. It doesn't make me want to chat. And it's not because I'm a misanthropic troglodyte. Meeting people along the way is a huge part of the appeal. I just don't want to exchange platitudes. Deal?

But what *really* bothers me is this: the question expresses a **vacuous self-evident truism**! And the person asking the question apparently doesn't realize this. From where I sit high on my plastic saddle, every day, by definition, is a nice day for a ride, an ideal day, the best day yet. So the question is fatally flawed; it presupposes that some days — strictly speaking, at least one day since the invention of the bicycle — are exceptions. I decry this preposterous notion. And yet the question leaves me tongue-tied.

What I really want to do, obviously, is launch into a rant. I want to say, for starters: "Yes, like every other day in history without exception, today is a perfect day for a ride!" And to bolster my position, I want to dig out my jacket and show the slogan written across the butt-flap. It reads, "NEVER A BAD TIME TO RIDE." No better words have even been written across one's butt and that includes "JUICY" and "PINK."

How do I actually react? Well, usually I freeze. It's all I can do not to look annoyed. Sometimes, I manage to blurt out, "Every day!" And sometimes I shout "NEVER A BAD TIME TO RIDE," as if the questioner can somehow visualize the butt-flap. This outburst usually truncates the conversation, which is to say the questioner fakes some reason for hurrying off. As someone who didn't wish to be accosted in the first place, I'm okay with that.

~

Why saying "it's a nice day for a bike ride" is *especially* annoying here in California: the weather is extremely and consistently pleasant, warm and sunny day after day, week after week. It's monotonously ideal.

To get a sense of what I've had to endure during the last month while pushing pedals and hunting-and-pecking at the keyboard, check out the daily records for rainfall

(May 13 to June 13, 2013): 0, 0, 0, 0, 0, 0, 0, 0, 0, 0, 0, 0, 0, 0, 0, 0, 0, 0, 0, 0, 0, 0, 0, 0, 0, 0, 0, 0, 0, and 0 nanometers. To belabor the point, some of you geeks will surely enjoy these summary stats:

- Mean = 0
- Median = 0
- Mode = 0
- Minimum = 0
- Maximum = 0
- Range = 0
- Variance = 0
- Serial autocorrelation: 0
- Slope of trend: 0
- Percent days with rain: 0
- Total accumulation = 0

Despite the appearance of irrefutable constancy, there were three days this past month when it was overcast in the afternoon. On those days people were apparently bound by convention to comfort each other by saying, "Well, it started out a pretty day."

As for temperature, the daily high averaged 85°F (29°C), and the coldest day maxed out at room temperature, 73°F (23°C). I spent the last month luxuriating under the grapefruit tree at the outdoor café, all the while basking within my thermal neutral zone.

And yet the locals found it fitting to comment on the exceptional favorability of specific days, as if commiserating with me over my having been unable to pedal on days when conditions were downright hostile. I tried to grin and bear it. I didn't slam anyone for uttering the platitude. But my patience is wearing thin.

Maybe I should start retaliating with platitudes of my own. You know the ones that pass as thoughtful conversation these days. I could say, "It is what it is," or "Everything happens for a reason," "There's no 'I' in team," or "I know, right?"

Oh crap, here's comes a curious fellow now. He's made eye contact. I pity him already. Please, sir, don't say it. Please. Stay tuned.

Okay, I fended him off and, thankfully, he didn't say it after all. Instead, he asked, "Dude, where'd you get those saddlebags?" And I said, "EVERY DAY!"

My response was a non sequitur, but at least I didn't launch into the whole zero thing. And to my credit, I did go on to give him a sensible answer: "They're made by Ortlieb and you can buy them online." I also refrained from telling him what I was writing as he approached me. We had a "nice" platitude-free chat. I know, I need to lighten up. Well, that's not going to happen.

Maybe I should take a different tact altogether. Maybe I should be a true contrarian and say, "No, so sorry, but I'm afraid I'm going to have to call you on that. Today is most decidedly not a nice day for a ride. Now yesterday, that was a nice day for a ride. Tomorrow's supposed to be even better. Today, not so much, but thanks for asking."

~

On top of all this, consider it from the Paleo perspective. The offensive question clearly reflects our modern disconnect from the natural environment. Our ancestors must be rolling over in the grave, giving us the big collective eye-roll. They faced real challenges. They had to get food without becoming food, and they couldn't sit around waiting for ideal conditions. They had to cope with bad weather and forecast life-threatening vagaries, or else die from exposure.

This could account for our lingering fascination with weather, even though rich people are insulated from these concerns. Most of the Petroleum People I observe leave their climate-controlled home in the morning, get immediately into a climate-controlled car (with pre-heated seats), and drive to their climate-controlled workplace or the climate-controlled mall. They live within their thermal neutral zone, free of thermal stress. And yet, they retain a hypertrophied ability to discern even slight variation in local climatic conditions.

How was your ride?

This one stumps me too. It's often asked by a has-been competitive cyclist who fancies himself quite the fading star and really wants to kick-start the conversation so he can brag about his own unverifiable exploits of epic proportion, his glory days in Lycra. So that puts me on-guard.

And then there's the inappropriateness of the question. The question would be appropriate if I were a fellow roadie who just spent the last few hours in a training session, sprinting around some local route. But I'm a nomad. I don't think of my never-ending tour as a series of daily rides. I don't think of the days as discrete units. I don't usually think of what I've done in a day with any real sense of accomplishment. Instead, I see my pedaling efforts as part of a single semi-continuous ride, one that I've only just begun.

So, as if to jerk the conversation in the right direction, I often say something like, "I've been on a tour that never ends for a few years now, sort of like Bob Dylan's never-ending tour." Whenever someone asks Dylan how his tour *was* he gets testy too. It's the wrong tense because the tour is ongoing.

Or I sometimes say, "The ride from Mexico was great, but then I bounced off the coast in Maine and I've been going into the wind ever since. But that's been great too."

Or I say, "Well, I've had no near-fatal involuntary dismounts lately, so that's good."

But usually I goof and say, "Great!" And then the guy launches into his spiel about how truly awesome he used to be. (For my I own perverse amusement, I usually trick him into admitting that he got cut from his high school's basketball team.)

Where did you start?

Another deceptively straightforward question, you'd think, and yet it throws me for a loop. I usually try to convey that *where* I started is the wrong question because *when* I started is so much more interesting. And so I usually blurt out something like, "I've been touring since 2009, semi-continuously, taking a few weeks off here and there, so a better question is when I started rather than where."

I tried this approach earlier this afternoon. It elicited the typical response, "But *where* did you start?"

Ever the smartass, I said, "Well, my mother will never confirm it, but I believe I was conceived in Orono, Maine."

"Oh, down south," was the response. (I'm in Canada at the moment.)

Where are you from?

"Earth," I always say, usually in my booming outdoor voice.

WARNING: I've learned the hard way that this is *not* an acceptable answer when the question is posed by a Customs & Immigration officer. To admit you have no fixed address and haven't had one for years can be problematic when you're asking in effect, "May I, a disreputable character, a probable lunatic on the lam, enter your country to commit crimes, work illegally, parasitize your social safety net, and ultimately beg for asylum?"

Last year I bungled this question worse than ever. Arriving at the Canadian side of the border in Niagara Falls, I blurted out "Earth," which got me sent to the special room for smartasses. When questioned further, I almost rose to the occasion by mentioning Maine and California as places where I sometimes visit for a few weeks at a time. Unfortunately, I couldn't provide a street address for either place. That didn't go over well. But then I made matters worse by saying that I was heading to my "cottage in Muskoka." This backfired when the interrogator asked for the address of my cottage and I couldn't give him one. I had to admit my place isn't really a cottage, that it's actually a backwoods log cabin with no road access and hence no address. He then asked me to provide proof of ownership, like a deed or a property tax statement. "Sorry," I said.

This year I was prepared. I stopped just shy of the border to memorize my sister's street address in Maine (even though she'd recently moved to India), dig out my passport and a copy of a property tax statement, and otherwise psych myself up for the interview. Wouldn't you know it, the guy at the booth waved me right on through?!

But where do you live?

"On my bike," I almost always say, when not at a border crossing. And then I usually describe ever so briefly my habit of pedaling everywhere every day. What I really mean to say: "I'm peripatetic. I live briefly at many points scattered across the Earth's surface."

Where are you headed?

"Alaska" or "Mexico" or "Maine" or "Denmark" or "India," I usually say, depending on which is currently most distant. If I say the name of some nearby town, this usually tricks the person into thinking I'm just out for the day or for a little weekend jaunt. And I'm not interested in having *that* conversation.

The routine response: "I could never do that!"

I always scoff and point out that it's just sitting on a padded seat and making your legs move. (And these days, on a high-performance trike with an electric-assist motor and hand pedals, you can travel the world even if you don't have functioning legs. And with an Electrical

Muscle Stimulation device onboard, in principle, quadriplegics could tour as I do.)

Where are you going today?

"Don't know yet because I haven't checked the wind," I often say. And it's often true. If I don't have a timetable, I really do let the wind dictate my travel plans.

And even when I am trying to connect points A and B where A is San Francisco and B is Boston, if the wind changes abruptly to a strong easterly one, I've been known to backtrack for a day or two.

Last year, once in New Mexico and once in Kansas, I spent the day traveling the "wrong" way, heading west because the wind had changed. Both times local folks approached me and said things like, "You should have been here yesterday. There was a guy doing the same thing you're doing, but he was going east, so you'll never meet him."

"You mean *me. I* was here yesterday."

"No, this guy was going east."

"Oh, too bad. It would have been fun to meet him."

If the questioner persists, demanding to know where I'm headed that day I usually acquiesce and offer up a familiar place name about 100 miles away. But I sometimes point out the obvious: if the wind changes, I may reverse direction, in which case it would be well over 27,000 miles to that destination.

How far do you go each day?

"That depends. Usually about 90 miles." But sometimes I get ambitious and sail downwind overnight. On those days, I might go twice that far.

My most frequent net distance traveled is zero nanometers. In other words, I take lots of days off. But they're not true zeroes. They're "nearoes" because even on those days I always do some pedaling. On other days, I might get distracted after an hour or two and decide to spend the day birding. And if I reverse direction because the wind has changed, my net distance traveled is about -90 miles.

How fast do you go?

"Usually, much too fast, but anywhere from 3 to 43 mph."

On a steep climb, I slow to walking speed, in grampy gear. Then I max out at 43 mph on the descent. That's the speed at which I consistently touch the brakes, at which self-preservation trumps thrill-seeking. But I usually cruise at about 15 mph, when it's flat and calm. I can do that sustainably for hours on end, pedaling at 90 rpm. Late in the day I sometimes taper off to 12 mph. And if I have a strong tailwind, my average cruising speed might be about 24 mph.

But sometimes I prefer to cruise at a slower speed and do a lot of coasting, especially if I'm birding. Last evening, I pedaled slowly because I was trying to enjoy yellow-billed magpies arriving at their nocturnal roost. And I didn't want to run over any of the California ground squirrels who were making their last kamikaze dashes of the day across the bike path. And I didn't want to misidentify black phoebes as Western kingbirds and vice versa along the way.

My permanent complaints about cycling are that it's too fast and it's on a road. On any given day, I'd prefer to be walking or paddling in a remote wilderness, not whizzing along disconnected from the natural world and trying not to crash or get yelled at. And yet, I love it.

Where do you sleep?

"In my sleeping bag. Why, where do *you* sleep?"

I usually stealth-camp, often near the road. I hide in plain sight. One of my favorite places to sleep is on top of high banks, where the road cuts through the bedrock. Nobody but yours truly ever goes up there, so these are very stealthy spots. But even more fun is to hang my hammock in someone's apple tree or to sleep on the deck of a sailboat. My favorite spot, though, is the yard of any old friend. My M.O. is to show up after dark or when nobody is home and simply pitch my tent on their front lawn or front porch or even in their living room. Usually, I get discovered in the morning, just in time for a wonderful reunion, complete with breakfast and a shower.

There's always a place to stealth-camp. If you can't be seen when you lay on the ground, you've found a home for the night. But it's a good idea to sleep in an area where you don't expect early-morning dog-walking. It can be startling to be awakened by a panting-and-drooling pit bull.

It's also good to allow plenty of distance between yourself and the nearest homeless folks. They don't want you encroaching on their turf.

Last year, I met a fellow touring cyclist who was "wrapping up" his round-the-world tour. In the 450+ days he'd been on the road, he'd stealth-camped all but two nights. On those two occasions he forked over some cash to stay at a commercial campground, where he could take a much-needed shower and do some laundry. But every other night, even in all of the countries with names ending in "istan," he'd simply camped wherever he pleased. Sometimes, like the night I met him, he camped not so stealthily, pitching his tent across from the local police station. He figured that made it easier for the local authorities to roust him in the morning. They served as his alarm clock. And if they tried to hassle him, he would plead foreigner's ignorance and pedal away.

A few weeks later, I met the stealthiest of all the stealth-camping cyclists on Earth. He sidled up to me at a free outdoor concert at L.L. Bean's in Freeport, Maine. He had all the right stuff, including a Long-haul Trucker loaded with four yellow Ortlieb panniers. He said he wanted to chat but first he had to go "check in." A few minutes later, he reappeared. His brown Hennessy hammock had been hung with care in a tiny island of trees in the middle of the parking lot within a stone's throw from the stage. With 6000 onlookers, he'd set up camp for the night, in plain sight. That's stealthy.

Of course, when I feel like luxuriating, I get a room. I'm no purist. I don't feel the need to hide *every* night.

~

But the more interesting question is: "When do you sleep?"

When I'm camping I often sleep at "biker midnight," getting into my sleeping bag at sundown and falling asleep almost immediately, just as Venus appears — in a most evolutionarily relevant way. This is how the diurnal birds do it. The oak titmice and ladderback woodpeckers and phainopeplas and others minimize their risk of getting bumped off by bigger critters that go bump in the night by going motionless and silent when darkness falls. They also minimize energetic expenditure during the long nocturnal fast. Which speaks to the functional significance of sleep: it's all about maximizing future Darwinian fitness by not getting killed or too malnourished during the night.

Where are you staying tonight?

"Don't know yet, but I suppose I could stay at your place, if you insist."

This shameless ploy works about 12.7% of the time. But it's really just a joke as I almost always decline any invitation, solicited or not.

What if it rains?

This is when I sometimes make a big production and dig out my jacket and show the slogan on the butt-flap, "Never a bad time to ride." If the person seems gullible, I might mention my special waterproof tires. If pressed, I usually acknowledge the only real downside of biking in the rain: drivers are more likely to kill me.

But what do you do in winter?

This one never stumps me. "I keep pedaling," I always say.

In 2009-2010, I pedaled back to Maine from Georgia in sandals (covered with neoprene booties), arriving in January. And a couple years ago, I pedaled through Alaska, the Yukon Territory, and British Columbia under wintry conditions. And for decades, I've pedaled virtually every day of the year, no matter where I happen to be, including Alaska, Maine, Ontario, Oregon, or California.

Are you heading south for the winter?

"Actually, I think I'll head north like I did last year, when I pedaled to Alaska."

But you can't pedal when it snows, right?

"Wrong!"

Cycling in the snow is no more interesting than cross-country skiing or ice-skating or ice-fishing or ice-sculpting or anything else humans do in the snow. Let's not forget that indigenous people have lived in the high arctic for millennia. With this in mind, cycling in the snow doesn't make me intrepid or anything out of the ordinary.

Even so, inquiring minds want to know how I do it, so here's a little info:

For starters, I use wide tires with an aggressive tread during winter and so I'm usually able to keep on pedaling when it snows. And if the accumulation reaches, say, 3-4 inches, I wait for the plow to go by once. As soon as the road is passable for Car People, it's passable for me.

And if it's a real blizzard, I have a big advantage over the Car People, provided I have access to my winter bike, the Pugsley. With 4-inch-wide knobby tires (available with studs), I can pedal where no car can go.

Here's one example of the Pugsley Advantage:

Several years ago, a blizzard hit the Lower Great Lakes Region. I was in Columbus, Ohio, where three feet of snow fell in 24 hours. The city was shut down. There was no gridlock, as there were no cars. The university shut down. The downtown shut down. But I didn't shut down. I hopped on my Pugsley and pedaled everywhere, passing snowplow trucks all over the city. I also passed TV crews who were out braving the elements to sensationalize the "natural disaster."

To them I was a spectacle. Not surprisingly, I got shouted down by three TV crews and subjected to an interview each time. Their main question: "What *is* that thing?!"

Two days later I got an email message from an old friend. It said, "I saw you on TV shilling for Surly bicycles. You uttered the word 'Pugsley' 17 times. I hope you're getting royalties."

The Pugsley, and various knock-offs, have become all the rage in snowy places. In Alaska, ultra-marathon races are no longer dominated by mushers and cross-country skiers. These days, the grand prize winner of such gruelathons is often a pedaler.

If only the gold prospectors who pedaled one-speed bicycles down the Yukon River had been on Pugsleys! They could have outpaced the mushers. They could have arrived first and staked the best claims.

Occasionally, I've been waylaid by a big storm when I didn't have access to my Pugsley. A prime example: I was pedaling from Georgia to Maine in midwinter, when a storm hit. I took refuge in Lynchburg, Virginia, which for the record frowns on lynchings, public or otherwise.

Lynchburg was actually named after a rich guy named Lynch and not for its history as a center of lynchings; in fact, Lynchburg is better known for its history of sterilizing the feeble-minded, epileptic, and genetically unacceptable than for lynching folks.

The total accumulation was a modest 16 inches, but that's an extreme event for the foothills of the Blue Ridge Mountains. And so it came as no surprise that the local municipal workers were unprepared and quickly overwhelmed. They got on-the-job training. It was obvious to me, based on my having lived in the snowiest place in North America, the Lynchburgians didn't have enough plows. What's more, they had no discernible contingency plan in place. They haphazardly drove around town with dump trucks loaded with snow, seemingly confused about where to deposit them. Eventually, on day three after the storm, the whole crew resorted to dumping load after load of salted snow right off the bridge into the James River. Problem solved! Never mind the environmental protection laws, including the Clean Water Act. Never mind the eco-narc with binoculars.

While spying on the snow-removal fiasco, I holed up in a dive motel for five days. You know, the kind of motel where you end up sleeping in your sleeping bag and get itchified by bed bugs anyway?

And I hung around town, in tights and cycling sandals, failing to keep a low profile. I spent long hours luxuriating in the bohemian coffee house, perusing its library of biographies of confederate army legends. (As the only major city in Virginia not overrun by the Union Army during the Civil War, this collection seems to reflect lingering civic pride.) I read several of these tomes cover to cover, including one about my supposed doppelgänger, Stonewall Jackson. I found every eatery where I could carbo load on my preferred veggie Paleo diet (e.g., piles of fresh whole-grain pasta covered with gorgonzola and pine nuts and dried cherries and sun-dried tomatoes and fresh basil, with a balsamic-reduction drizzle, of course).

And wherever I ventured, the townsfolk took turns asking me many of the FAQs in this list. I answered patiently, with nary a hint of snark, and then they almost invariably said, "Well, sorry you had to get stuck in Lynchburg." They even said this at the Chamber of Commerce Visitor Center! Intrigued by how pervasive this sentiment might be, I decided to wander into the mayor's office to see whether even he would console me in this way. Unfortunately, the mayor was unavailable, presumably because he was out assisting with the snow removal.

I guess you generate your own heat, right?

Right, but I also generate my own wind chill, which according to the ole husband's tale causes pneumonia. It can be a delicate balancing act. Under some conditions, the faster you go the colder you get. And if you work too hard, you sweat and then inevitably get cold. I tend to err on the side of underdressing, especially on long challenging climbs. And if it's cold enough, I'll pause at the height of land and put on an ultra-light down jacket for the descent.

In winter, climbs are especially welcome. Sometimes it's the best way to get warm and sometimes I intentionally choose a route with big climbs, knowing the descents may be bone-chilling.

Do you have a blog?

"No, I'm too lazy to blog."

I obviously don't mind setting aside a block of time and writing a whole book's worth of "updates," but somehow blogging seems like drudgery.

Can I follow you on Facebook or Twitter?

You're welcome to send me a friend request on Spacebook, and I may even accept it, but I don't post my status because I insist on keeping a low profile. To me, broadcasting my whereabouts would be an affront. I want to spend my time in the biosphere, not the twittersphere. It's not much of an adventure if you're being cyberstalked by your mommy.

And by keeping my latitude-and-longitude private, I'm able to stick to my modus operandi of paying surprise visits to old friends. So, if you suddenly spot a tent on your front lawn or perhaps even in your living room, don't be alarmed. That's just my way of saying, "Hey, Ed Stacey, how the hell have you been all of these years?"

What's the best place you've cycled?

"They're all tied for first place."

At least that's what I like to tell myself when I'm pedaling through a region that's especially bike unfriendly, where shoulders are narrow and drivers are hostile.

But that's not what I usually say. Most often, I say something rambling like, "Alaska, for all of the obvious reasons, the steroidal scenery, the grizzlies and caribou, the mountains beyond mountains, snow-capped peaks everywhere you look. For the 40 mph winds coming off the glaciers, for the salmon in the streams, for the mile-wide braided river beds, the best places on Earth to camp. And because long stretches of roads have a wide shoulder with a rumble strip, so it feels like you have a semi-dedicated bike lane to yourself. And in the fall, there's precious little traffic, so it feels very safe. And the main roads parallel and crisscross major rivers, so the grade is usually fairly gentle."

Or I say the Yukon Territory, for many of the same reasons.

Or I say Oregon because the mountains and the desert and the coast are all beautiful. And because the cities are about the most bike-friendly places in North America. To get waylaid in the pedaling paradise of Portlandia is a dream. To pedal with the pedicab drivers as they ferry revelers from strip joints to late-night food trucks is a blast. To ride with hipsters with their saddle 8 feet high, atop their functional velosculpture, is a blast. To ride in actual bicycle traffic is a thrill, especially after pedaling solo for thousands of miles. And to pedal through the state and experience a level of bike friendliness rivaling Portland's in town after town, especially in Eugene, is a wonderful thing.

Or I say Washington, for many of the same reasons. To sit in the food co-op in Bellingham watching cops on bicycles nab one Car Person after another for endangering Bicycle People is most gratifying. To pedal to Seattle, mostly on dedicated bike trails, makes Washington feel Oregonesque.

Or I say Arizona, for the Saguaro cactus. Need I say more?

Or I say New Mexico, for oh so many reasons. The wind. The elevation. The funky towns, like Silver City. (The town everybody knows by name, Truth or Consequences, isn't particularly funky, sorry to say.) The Gila Wilderness. Did I mention the wind?

Or I say Maine because it's covered with transitional boreal forest and there's a prime opportunity for fried clams and craft beer every 9 miles along the coast. Plus, I have beautiful friends there, people of genuine kindness and enormous talent. And until my lovely sister, Mz. Laura, moved to India, I had an oasis, a place where I could show up unannounced, sleep on the back deck and steal leftovers from the fridge, with impunity.

Or I say Ontario because the terrain is so similar to that in Maine. And because I have this sanctuary in the backwoods, where I currently sit on my screened-in porch engulfed by red spruce and balsam fir and Eastern red-cedar and paper birch, with sarsaparilla and jack-in-the-pulpit and Solomon's seal and bracken fern at my feet. And with Mavis, my "pet" porcupine, snoozing under the porch.

Or I say California because I've developed a habit of starting and ending legs of my never-ending tour near San Francisco, in Martinez, at John Muir's house. And of course California offers simultaneous views of the mountains, desert, and ocean. Not to mention the many bike-friendly spots along the coast. Not to mention the redwoods. Not to mention the High Sierra. Not to mention the countercultural stronghold in the northern coastal reaches. Not to mention tremendous climbs and descents. Not to mention the ideal weather. Despite its superabundance of Californicators, California is a pedaler's paradise.

Or I sometimes get around to mentioning New York because I've developed the habit of commuting back and forth along the Erie Canal Trail between Albany and Buffalo each time I travel between Ontario and Maine. Most of the trail is along the original tow path used by Sal and the other mules, and the canal itself remains mostly intact. As I pedal along, I thank the long-dead workers who indirectly built this dedicated bike path. (Unlike me, they got up well before the crack of dawn for the first of many shots of whiskey from their daily ration.) Thanks indirectly to their manual labor, there are free campgrounds at some of the locks. And the broken-down towns bisected by the canal remain mostly intact. It's a perfectly pleasant way to commute "all the way to Buffalo."

You must meet a lot of interesting people?

"Not yet. You could be my first."

Actually, it happens daily, this meeting of interesting people. It's inevitable. Of course, it helps that I find all of my conspecifics, those fellow naked apes, endlessly fascinating.

While fellow touring cyclists are few and far between, I do have almost daily close encounters with People of the Car and Town varieties. They're often quite curious about what I'm doing and/or they want to brag about their epic feat, like when they pedaled a few hundred miles during the summer of '77.

Or they want to rescue me or befriend me. These people I call road angels (Patri comes to mind).

Or they see me as a kindred spirit and want to confess their dastardly deeds, those that got them incarcerated. That's right, among the most fascinating people I meet along the way are the ex-cons. What can I say, I'm a magnet for felons. They apparently see me as a "fellow traveler," a kindred spirit of sorts. It's the phenotype, mostly the beard, I think. Whatever the attraction, I'm glad it's there because they love to tell me their life story.

Here are three examples of such encounters, which happened on consecutive days as I was pedaling from Mexico, the nation state, towards Mexico, the little town in Maine:

It's late in the day as I roll into a hardscrabble town in one of those big flat red states, which shall remain nameless. I pedal up to a grocery store hoping for a quick in-and-out so I can find a good stealth spot before dark. As I look for a lockup site, I get accosted by a guy. He's very scruffy, looks like he's done some hard livin'. He asks me one question about my trip, interrupts me almost immediately and starts blabbing his life story, sordid details and all.

It goes like this: He runs away from home at age 12, hitchhikes from Boston to Oklahoma, where he steals a car. A few hundred miles down the road, he runs out of gas. He has no money, so he proceeds to live in the car. A couple days later, the police start snooping around, so he needs to get resourceful. He gets hired to do grunt work at a truck stop, getting paid under the table. But it's a dead-end job, so he's on the lookout for a more lucrative way to spend his days. Thanks to his precocious entrepreneurial spirit, he develops a thriving career in unsanctioned pharmaceutical sales. Over the next few years, he gets rich, filthy rich. He's savvy enough not to flaunt his wealth. He launders his cash through land acquisition. This turns out to be a major blunder as his steady accumulation of millions of dollars' worth of agricultural acreage, despite having no visible means of support, eventually gets noticed by the Feds. The authorities stop by for a chat one day and the next thing he knows he's doing the duck walk, wearing bracelets and an orange jumpsuit. He spends the next 20+ years in prison educating himself about the Rico Act, whereby ill-gotten gains such as his are frowned upon.

These days he's reformed. He and his fifth wife and numerous children are making a real go of it. And I have a standing invitation to stay at their place.

The next day I roll into a one-horse town and stop for Gatorade. As I'm trying to get a second bottle of the stuff down my gullet, a prosperous-looking middle-aged woman finishes pumping guzzeline into her RV and wanders over for a chat. She asks me one question about my trip. I tell her a condensed version, which she uses as an opportunity to reciprocate. Before I can finish the second jug of Gatorade, she's telling me about *her* prison experience. Turns out, she spent 2 years behind bars for hoodwinking an elderly man into penis-enlargement surgery and bilking him and his wife out of a big fraction of their life savings. And then she tells me she's off to the nearest country club "trolling for fat cats." (I think that's what they call recidivism.)

As she burns through the first gallon of gas getting up to cruising speed, I try to put a positive spin on her story. I tell myself it could've been worse. She could have conned the poor fellow into penis-*reduction* surgery, in which case she'd probably still be behind bars.

The next day I initiate contact with a homeless guy. That's right, I accost him. Almost immediately, he starts telling me about run-ins with the law. It all got started when he spent 4 years in prison for a bank robbery he committed at age 18 — on the day he turned 18. In other words, he injudiciously waited till his birthday to commit the crime. Because he was of legal age at the time of the criminal act, he was tried as an adult and so he got hard time in prison rather than soft time in juvie. But he's over that. That's ancient history, water under the bridge.

What burns his bacon these days: cops routinely hassle him for vagrancy or loitering or sleeping in a public place — for being alive and homeless. And when they run the inevitable background check, they discover an outstanding warrant for violation of the open container law 11 years ago. Off he goes to jail. But that's not the bad part.

The bad part is this: they confiscate his dog, a pitbull. So each time he gets out of jail with a new court date he'll never honor, he has to walk to the pound (doggie jail) to get his dog back. Meanwhile, he's still broke. I tried to give him some cash but he wouldn't accept my offer, probably because I was a fellow traveler.

~

When I'm not consorting with ex-cons, I'm often fending off road angels, folks with a heart of gold who want to help me in some way. They want to be my impromptu host. They want to rescue me. The only problem with this is my fiercely self-reliant streak. So my natural reaction is to decline virtually all offers from kind strangers, politely of course. But I bring it upon myself, I realize, pedaling after midnight in the winter, in blizzards and in the subarctic.

Despite my reluctance, I do occasionally find myself accepting road magic.

Here's a little sampler:

A few years ago, I was at a Ryan Montbleau show in Portland, Maine. It was a Saturday night in December. As the band was doing the encore song, I scrambled to find my four panniers. Filing out with the crowd, I started thinking about where I might stealth-camp for the night, when a woman approached and offered me eggs (yes please), weed (no thanks), and her guest bedroom (sounds good). Stefani assured me she'd taken in a few fellow travelers and hadn't axe-murdered any of them. She wore my helmet as I pedaled us up the hill to her place. And we've been friends ever since, though I haven't met her lovely new husband yet. (I'll meet him when I couch-surf at their place next summer.)

A couple weeks later, I pedaled north to Unity, Maine, again for live music. My plan was to see Guy Davis that night and Railroad Earth the next night. I thought I'd head straight to the venue, a beautiful converted barn and property of Unity College, an environmental school with a teensy enrollment of crunchies and granolas and wannabe hipsters. But as I arrived in the village in a heavy snowstorm, I got waylaid by one Car Person after another. They kept stopping to let me, the poor misguided pedaler, know that *the* B&B was booked and there was no other conventional place to stay. They didn't know about my stealth-camping prowess, of course, so they offered to let me stay at their commune or their friend's place or with the town barber. That last option sounded intriguing, but I was in no hurry to find lodging and so I pedaled to the venue to volunteer for the next two days. Immediately, the woman running the performing arts center tried to take me under her wing. She got on her phone and made arrangements for me to bunk with Guy Davis in the flat upstairs reserved for the talent. I thought that was too much of an imposition on Guy and so I opted to stay with the barber and his wife. And so I did. And I will again. That is, if I don't stay at one of the communes or with an Amish family on the edge of town. This hospitality reflects the cooperative nature of the community. In Unity, the tiny town with the apropos moniker, the bike shop is a co-op as is the coffeehouse and even the dog grooming spa. Who knew?

Counterintuitively, as the flow of Car People increases, the incidence of road magic falls asymptotically toward zero. Random acts of kindness all but vanish. It's as if there's a hyberbolic dilution of individual altruistic tendencies with increasing n, the number of potential altruists available per unit time or distance pedaled. (Evolutionary ecologists have studied this phenomenon and shown, theoretically, that individuals are less likely to act altruistically under conditions of anonymity where the likelihood of benefiting through reciprocity or improved reputation is minimal.) So while realized altruism barely exists along busy roads, it's fairly common in depopulate places like the Yukon and Alaska where n is just a few per hour. In such places, consecutive drivers sometimes stop and offer this, that, and the other.

Here's a prime of example of back-to-back acts of road magic in a far-flung place, the Yukon, one of the greatest places on Earth.

There I was pedaling north by northwest through God's Navel in the brief autumn, with the steroidal Saint Elias Mountains on my left and bluer-than-blue Lake Kluane on my right, heading to Alaska, blissfully unaware of Car People till I was suddenly jolted by the sight of a car pulling over and two women flagging me down. One of the women — I'll call her Jessica Paparazza — had her digital camera clicking away on automatic. By the time I hit my brakes, she'd already captured dozens of unsanctioned images of me minding my own bidness. With the raw athleticism of an Olympian, she loped and bounded toward me, still clicking away and lobbing questions at me rapid fire. She offered me bananas and water and left-over pizza slices and implicit lifelong friendship. Her friend lobbed innuendos and then escalated to unambiguous offers of mock reproductive activities. I accepted Jessica's offers of bananas and lifelong friendship.

Still dazed by this close encounter with exuberant, altruistic Car People, about 10 minutes later a car passed me from behind and pulled over. A woman got out clutching two fistfuls of assorted power bars and telling me she had many more and she wanted me to take all of them. She explained that her friends in Florida had gifted her years' worth of power bars for her drive to Alaska and that she would never eat even one of them, having developed a lifelong aversion during her thru-hike on the Appalachian Trail. We immediately compared notes on our thru-hike experience and became instant friends. And then off she went, fulfilling a lifelong dream by moving to Alaska.

I pedaled on, weighed down by my embarrassment of power-bar riches. Twenty or so miles down the road I found a hand-written note on a sheet of cardboard. She'd left it to invite me to stay at her dream lodge if I ever made it to her new slice of heaven on Earth. I did. She gave me savory food and delightful company and a comfy sofa. We remain fast friends for life.

In Alaska, I was befriended by another road angel, a person of serenity, grace, and kindness. I'll call her Libby (wink). She and her fiancé put me up and spoil me rotten whenever I'm pedaling through Oregon. A few weeks from now, I'll pedal into Portland and surprise the two of them at a Timbers soccer match. And I may not-so-grudgingly accept their magic yet again.

When I'm not having close encounters with ex-cons or road angels, I seem to spend a lot of time in the company of singer-songwriters and bike mechanics, but that's another story.

How can you fit all of your stuff in those saddlebags?

Speaking of singer-songwriters, Greg Brown says, "Stuff is never enough, it just won't get you there."

The less lyrical answer is: all you need to do is be a minimalist and use ultralight gear. So what do I carry? Well, right now, my panniers contain: camping gear (ultralight sleeping bag, one-person tent, and short self-inflating pad), rain jacket, bike tools, air pump, iGadgets (phone and pad), solar charger, spare slime-filled tubes, chain lube and almost nothing else. In winter, I switch to a warmer bag and carry appropriate clothes.

Why are you doing this? Is it for a charity?

I'm raising money for Citizens Against Drivers, both sober and drunk.

Seriously, though, somewhere between 0 and 100% of the profits from the sales of this book will be donated to charity, according to how I'm feeling. But that's really a secondary motivation. I ride to be green, fit, healthy, sane, happy, and for the freedom and adventure. I ride to get from point A to point B. And I ride out of inertia; I keep forgetting to stop.

How can I get into your book?

That happens spontaneously, organically. It can't be forced.

But it usually helps if there's some outrageous behavior, like public nudity. It helps if you have prison stories. If you don't scandalize me or otherwise shock and appall me or blow me away with extreme kindness or virtuosity or deviance, you probably won't even make a cameo. Sorry. (Of course, mowing me down with your vehicle like a homicidal maniac, that works too.)

Have you ever wanted to race in the Tour de France?

Actually, I'm doing my own modest *Tour de Terre*.

Besides, isn't the Tour de France kinda ... cute? I mean, it lasts for 19 half-days and they cover a modest 2200 kilometers. I do the equivalent of 10 Tour de France rides each year — with loaded panniers, a steel frame, and a bloated midsection.

What do you think of Lance?

"Lance who?"

The unfortunate truth is: more often than you'd think, I'll be out for an evening of live music when I "attract" *that guy*, the one who is three sheets to the wind and thinks he's clever for calling me Lance, over and over again.

> "Hey, Lance, what are doing here, Lance?
> Yo, Lance, you cheating, lying sack of sh@t.
> Hey, Lance, my girlfriend wants your autograph.
> Hey, Lance, buy me a beer.
> Hey, Lance, wanna arm wrestle.
> Hey, Lance, I LOVE you, man.
> No hard feelings, Lance?"

To retaliate, I find out what this blowhard enjoys as a sober activity and I nickname him accordingly. If he's into golf, I call him "Tiger" at every opportunity. As in, "Hey Tiger, did you golf today? Hey Tiger, how's your short game?" That usually helps curtail the Lance nonsense, although sometimes the bouncer ends up rescuing the scrawny cyclist from the beefy yokel.

Have you ever done a triathlon?

No, I have one key limitation: I don't get enough oxygen when I ventilate liquid H_2O. And then comes the near drowning and the rescue. Who needs that? So I've never done a triathlon. But on a big day, I expend as much energy as a triathlete. Does that count?

The truth: I really have no interest whatsoever in racing. I don't mind watching other people do it — for a few minutes — but I don't want to do it myself.

Have you ever done the big group ride across the state?

Oh, you mean, like the Tour of California or the Tour of Maine, one of those annual rides for charity. No, I always have a scheduling conflict: I'm always riding my bike solo during those events. And I really do insist on being self-supported and choosing my own route each day, on the spur of the moment.

But I hear those rides are a lot of fun and usually for a good cause. And I'm tempted to do it once just for the social aspect. (I'll join the Google Buddhist Bicycle Pilgrimage next year, if I happen to be in San Francisco Bay Area at the right time.)

But what if you want to go to a concert or a ballgame or something?

I just go. I go to concerts at the Fillmore in San Francisco and baseball games at Fenway Park in Boston as well as other games and concerts here, there, and everywhere. I go to music festivals in the Sierra in California and in the northwoods of Maine and everywhere in between. I just go.

Be forewarned: If you do likewise, you're extremely likely to be the only attendee arriving by bicycle. And you'll surely trigger lots of fellow event-goers to ask incredulously, "You didn't ride your bike here, did you?!"

On the plus side, you'll probably make at least one spontaneous friend-for-life thanks to the fact that you're a conversation piece. The panniers, the helmet, the silly cycling clothes — your sartorial splendor — will attract someone's attention. And a scintillating conversation will ensue. And the next thing you know you're seated together behind the dugout at Fenway Park with the third-most exuberant person you've ever met. At least that's what happened to me last summer, when my flamboyant friend nouveau, a Serena Williams lookalike, kept a big wad of us thoroughly entertained. At one point, she stood to go for refreshments and her skirt got caught on one of the knobs on the chair back. This threw her off balance and she did a tumbling pirouette in front of several dozen witnesses, all of whom saw her underpants repeatedly and from every conceivable angle. But as quickly as she'd lost control, she saved face by saying, "I couldn't decide what to wear to my first Red Sox game ever. I had to wear pretty underwear, but I just kept thinking 'thong, no thong ... thong, no thong ... thong, no thong.' I'm so glad I didn't wear a thong." As she stood, she got a standing ovation.

You must have a good bike?

"Not really."

This question always surprises me. It's usually asked by someone who obviously isn't an avid cyclist or a big fan of activity in general. But that's no explanation, not really. What do they really mean? Do they honestly think that "good" bikes propel themselves?

Obviously, this question belies their lack of an intimate appreciation for the physics of cycling. Otherwise, they would know that the bicycle is the single most efficient mode of transportation ever devised. And even a crappy bike is an order of magnitude more efficient than a car. It's so efficient that it's feasible to sit backwards on the handlebars on a BMX bike and pedal across North America. (And people think *I'm* odd!)

How many gears does your bike have?

"A bunch, 27 I think, but I only use one at a time." (Less frequently, I'm asked how many gears my 10-speed has. I usually say "ten.")

How heavy is your bike?

"I'm not at liberty to say."

Actually, I routinely turn into truck weigh stations and, almost invariably, the bike and panniers and I tip the scales at 250 lbs (113 kg, 17.9 stones), presumably rounded to the nearest 10 or 50 lbs. The first time I weighed in like that I did so not because I was curious about how much I weighed but rather whether I would even trip the mechanism.

Recently, I weighed in at a bike shop and was shocked to learn that my bike and body and bags weighed a combined 310 pounds. I did the only sensible thing: I cut weight not by reducing my body fat but rather by giving away some extra gear. (I invoked the hiker rule, whereby if it's not essential and you haven't used it in the last 24 hours, you don't need it.) These days, I'm back down to 270.

What kind of bike do you ride?

"I dunno. It's dark green and has those funny curly handlebars. I think the frame's steel."

For the gear-heads among you who really would like to know, here's my current setup (in excruciating detail):

THE BIKE —

These days I'm riding a Surly Long Haul Trucker (19-inch frame). It's the standard model, not the elite one disc brakes, internal hubs, and a collapsible frame. The factory-issue extra spokes are missing. I lost them bushwhacking through a thicket at an oasis in the Anza-Borrego Desert — on a day I almost lost my life as well. (Worst case of dehydration and heat stroke I've ever had.)

Last time I bothered to notice, there were three rings on front and nine cogs on the cassette. Don't make me count the teeth. Just know that I have a grampy gear that lets me climb any grade, the steeper the better.

As for tires, I've developed a strong preference for Schwalbe Marathon Plus Tour (Performance Line SmartGuard), 700 x 35C (or 38C), with slime-filled tubes.

I find the bicycle to be far more efficient when I have pedals to push, so I almost always use them. These days

I'm using two KORE platform pedals (detachable with Allen hex key), with studs. (I don't use clip-in pedals because my balance is affected by HD and because I do lots of off-road riding.)

ACCESSORIES —

So as to see and be seen, I use as many as seven lights.

Headlights:

Primary: CYGLOLITE Metro, 300 lumens, rechargeable (USB). I prefer the 700-lumen model because it overcomes the invisible-gorilla problem by scorching the drivers' retinas. Unfortunately, that model has a fatal design flaw: it fails when the first raindrop comes within a meter or so of the seams in the housing. It magically sucks moisture from the air and self-destructs. And this is a problem not just because of the replacement cost and inconvenience, but because the light is an important safety feature for cycling in the rain, when drivers have reduced visibility and patience.

Secondary: flashing LED light mounted on handlebars.

Tertiary: flashing SL120 transduction light (mounted on front fork, with magnet mounted on spokes). It's made in Denmark, so of course it requires no batteries or AC or even solar power.

Tail lights:

Primary: CYGLOLITE Hotshot rechargeable (USB).
Secondary: ditto.
Tertiary: SL120 transduction flasher.

Quaternary: LED flasher attached to left pannier.

GPS: GARMIN Edge 800, which I use to navigate (often erroneously) and monitor my speed, cadence, heart rate, and power. I also monitor calories burned, slope, total ascent, total distance traveled, and distance to the next live music venue and/or taco truck. (I also navigate using my iPhone.)

Panniers (4): Ortlieb, yellow, waterproof

> Disclaimer: Ortliebs have failed to live up to their reputation for being indestructible only once in my experience. And that failure was arguably my fault. I jumped a curb and one of the improperly attached panniers popped off the rack and got caught in the spokes. The bag exploded like a piñata. I scrambled to gather my stuff as I held up traffic. That night, well after midnight, there was a loud knock on my door. I waited for the danger to abate. More knocking. Even louder. Finally, I went to the door: it was a man returning my wallet! (I offered him a reward. He said, "Thanks, but I already helped myself to two twenties.")

Rear-view mirror: Blackburn model designed for use with bar-end shifters, attached with Velcro strap. Essential equipment: I would no sooner ride without this particular mirror than I would ride with two flat tires (or missing pedals).

GEAR —

Clothes:
> Zoic Ether shorts, with a secret pocket that contains a special attention-grabbing cloth (intended for cleaning sunglasses) on an elasticized strap.

Pearl Izumi Elite shirt, neon yellow with reflectors.

Footwear:
Keen cycling sandals. I wear these sandals 365 days a year. In winter, I wear two pairs of socks (one wool and one waterproof) and a pair of neoprene cycling booties over them.

iGadgets:
iPhone: used for taking videos of menacing Car People, which potentially get uploaded to YouTube. iPad: used to write stories about Car People.

Solar charger:
Goal Zero Nomad 7 with 4 rechargeable AA batteries.

Safety equipment:
Bear Spray (capsaicin): used to attract bears, both black and brown, to my campsite. I carry this only when I'm in bear country.

Air horn/siren, Safety-Sport Admiral: used to scare the beejeepers out of the local bear each time he or she tries to evict me from "my" cabin, which of course happens to be situated deep within his or her homerange. Note: this is very effective on the first trial, but thereafter becomes increasingly ineffective as the bear's hearing losses mount. Caution: do not do as I did and test it indoors.

Sleeping bag, ultralite: MOUNTAIN HARDWARE Ultra Lamina 45/7.

Sleeping pad: THERMAREST Pro Plus Small.

Tent: BIG AGNES one-person, ultralite. Disclaimer: the product description mentions spaciousness. Let's just say it's more spacious than a sleeping bag. The truth is: I have to wriggle outside to change my facial expression. Usually, I carry no tent as I prefer to sleep under the stars. Currently, it's too rainy not to have a tent. (Sometimes I've used an ultralite HENNESSEY hammock.)

Hey, you asked....

How many bikes do you own?

I own two bikes, a Long-haul Trucker and a Pugsley. According to the snobs at velominati dot com, that's an inadequate number. (In my defense, the Pugsley should count as at least 10 bikes.) They claim the correct (optimal) number of bikes to own is $n+1$, where n is the current number, a positive integer that must be at least 3 (e.g., a high-performance road bike, a mountain bike, and an all-purpose around-town bike). Moreover, the accumulation of bikes should have an upper bound of c, your personal carrying capacity (i.e., maximal feasible number of bikes according to your credit card company or your boss or your partner).

If you find yourself with $c+1$ bicycles, you should revert to c tout suite, unless of course you decide through careful deliberation you'd rather be destitute and celibate anyway.

And if I may add one more rule, it goes without saying that c should be ratcheted upward by at least 1 each time you get a pay raise or lose a partner for reasons independent of your current n.

As decrepitude takes its toll, I plan on switching to a high-performance recumbent trike, perhaps a Catrike.

So, I'll soon own no *bi*cycles *per se*. (Don't tell the velominati.)

What's so great about the Pugsley?

"Glad you asked."

It's not just great, it's the greatest bike ever devised. I know Lance Whatshisname said "it's not about the bike," but he never rode a Pugsley!

The Pugsley casts a spell over you the first time you ride one. It's comically beastly, with 4-inch wide knobby tires. It's like a two-wheeled Hummer that gets *really* good mileage. It's utilitarian to the *n*th degree. And it even gives you cache among the Bicycle People, especially the grown boys. It taps into special centers in the adult brain devoted to the emotions of nostalgia, childlike joy, playfulness, and humor. It's fun and funny.

Be forewarned:

If you get a Pugsley and you don't live in Alaska or some other place where the Pugsley and similar bikes have become familiar, you will be overwhelmed with social interactions, almost as if you've just adopted a Pug puppy. You'll be interrupted. You'll be late for meetings.

My experience:

I spent all day every day hunkered in the corner of a coffeehouse where I worked on manuscripts for publication in peer-reviewed science journals (to see these publications, use Google Scholar and search for "Waite TA"). I was invisible, or nearly so — until I got the Pugsley. Suddenly, I was no longer free to peck away at the keyboard anonymously, alone with my thoughts. I was a minor celebrity.

With the Pugsley parked outside, I'd get interrupted several times a day. The typical scenario went like this. I'd realize someone was hovering nearby waiting for me to look up. It was nearly always a man in his 20s or 30s, who would say something like, "Dude, sorry to bother you, but I've been asking around and the baristas told me that's your bike out there, the Pugsley. It's awesome. Dude, can I take it for a spin?"

This alone makes the Pugsley unique. Not since I was a pre-teen has anyone ever asked to test ride any of my bikes.

"Of course," I'd say jokingly, "just leave something as collateral."

Every guy took me literally and offered something. Most of them handed me a laptop. One guy left his black lab. And another guy left his wife! I gave him the combination to the Kryptonite lock and his wife and I chatted as he walked out to the bike, unlocked it, threw his leg over the crossbar, looked down at the preposterous front tire and reacted in the universal way: he laughed. Hard. And then he started pedaling. And kept laughing. As he disappeared from view, his wife said, "Damn, he's not coming back!"

~

I bought the beastly Pugsley so I could adhere strictly to my inviolate green-lifestyle rule: thou shalt pedal every day and everywhere. No exceptions, aside from deaths and other major personal crises.

So, in preparation for overwintering at my off-the-grid, backwoods log cabin in Ontario, I bought the Pugsley. That way, I could pedal from my land to the nearest town, 15 miles each way, throughout the winter and do so without going on a road. I could travel on a continuous sheet of ice, pedaling across massive glacial lakes and the beaver ponds and flowages connecting them. It was a beautiful plan and it worked to perfection, even as the ice began to "rot" with the onset of spring.

Of course, I knew I'd eventually plunge through the ice on a beaver flowage. And so I did. But that was okay because the Pugsley floats! That's right, those enormous tires and waterproof panniers (containing extra air-filled bags) provide so much buoyancy that the moment you plunge through the ice you find yourself astraddle a most improbable raft.

After taking that refreshing plunge, I switched to pedaling the Pugsley along the muddy and flooded road. As you can imagine, the Pugsley is far and away the greatest amphibious vehicle ever devised. It's ideal for simply charging right on through any flooded section of the road. But you need to be prepared for the buoyancy factor. If the water is deep, the tires make contact with the pebbly substrate only intermittently. Basically, you bounce along the bottom, while trying to keep the pedals churning so you get some traction each time you touch down. Otherwise, you'll lose momentum and go kersplash into the frigid melt water.

Here's my favorite example:

I was pedaling to town along the single lane, unmaintained gravel road that runs between my land and that of my only "neighbor," Les Stroud, TV's

Survivorman. During "mud season" the road turns into a highly vicious slurry and is passable by Pugsley only. So I wasn't surprised to see Les and his son walking toward me. They'd wisely left their 4-wheel drive truck a couple miles away and were slogging along in their Wellies, when they suddenly saw me barreling down the mucky lane on the beastly Pugsley. I stopped for a chat.

Les hadn't seen my Pugsley yet. He was agog. Instantly smitten, he asked to take it for a test ride. I agreed, of course, especially since he was about to leave his son as collateral.

He hopped on and laughed. I offered him my helmet. He tried to wave me off. I insisted. While he was adjusting the helmet to his fat head — he is "TV's *Survivorman*" after all — I tried to give him a few pointers about pedaling through the overflow. I mentioned the buoyancy and the need to pedal continuously, even when not touching the bottom. He didn't seem very attentive.

So off he went laughing and pedaling straight for the water. Predictably, he plunged into the water, stopped pedaling, and went kersplash. Full-body immersion. The bike floated. Les did not.

His son, laughing like an 8-year-old who'd just seen his fallible dad do a stupid human trick, finally managed to say, "Dad, you forgot to pedal."

Les dragged the Pugsley back to us and asked for those tips again. He tried again, pedaled furiously all the way across the 250-foot span of standing water, and then pedaled back across. When I last saw him, he was trying to get a signal on his smart phone so he could buy a Pugsley.

You must be in really good shape?

"Not yet, but I'm getting there."

I'd be in better shape if I didn't do so much damn aerobically undemanding typing. I can feel my fitness waning incrementally as I type this sentence. Luckily, because cycling is extremely efficient as a mode of locomotion/transportation, I don't need to be in good shape to commute from coast to coast.

Of course, if I really cared about achieving peak fitness, I'd commute transcontinentally on my Pugsley. (Challenge accepted.)

What if you get sick or injured?

"Bite your tongue!"

While I'm traveling, I seem to have a mostly uncompromised immune system.

Does your crotch hurt?

"No, but thanks for asking."

Eventually, your crotch turns into leather, like a catcher's mitt left outside overwinter. But first stuff falls off. In fact, that's what happened to Lance's missing testicle. Sure, he lied and said it was cancer that caused it to go AWOL. But let's face it, he lied about everything, so I think we can safely assume that his testicular reduction was actually a case of recrudescence caused by too much grinding on the saddle.

Seriously, though, when neurological symptoms flare up, I wear two pairs of padded shorts. And occasionally when stuff's about to recrudesce from too much friction and pressure, I'll slather lube onto the pad a la the Tour de France boys.

I can't speak for extreme cyclists with complimentary genitalia, but I've heard murmurings of "very dark purple labia." And a friend of a friend claims that she and all of her extreme cycling friends in the greater DC/Baltimore metro region go to the same gynecologist because she — an extreme cyclist herself — knows how to interpret the symptoms.

Don't you get lonely?

"Not yet."

I'm lucky to have strong misanthropic tendencies, I guess. Most of the time I'm perfectly content to be solo or invisible, on my own, like I was in Alaska when I didn't see another great ape for up to 9 months at a stretch.

Don't you miss your family?

"You haven't met my family."

(I hereby half-heartedly apologize to my first-order relatives, a.k.a. sibs. It's just a joke.)

How can you afford this? You must be rich?

"Yes, I'm rich, just like you."

If you're anything like me, we're both in the 95th percentile globally. And unlike half of all people on Earth, we have more than a few dollars a day in purchase power.

But even compared with rich Yanks and Canucks, I'm particularly rich because I save about $40,000 per year by not owning a car or house. Consider this: my annual bills including mortgage, utilities, insurance, and so on sum to $0.00. The only monthly bill I have is for a cell phone. That's it. That's financial freedom.

Most people take it for granted, but the cost of typical American domesticity is way up here, I show by reaching for the sky. The cost of nomadism is way down here, I show by nearly touching the floor. The cost of my semi-nomadic lifestyle is about as close to the floor as you can get, without actually touching it. (Of course, it helps that my hooker budget remains forever fixed at zero.)

You must save a lot of money on gas?

"Never touch the stuff."

Another stumper. I'd like to launch into a diatribe. I'd start by explaining that saving money on the stuff I refuse to buy has nothing to do with my motive. But to be crash and limit my answer to the cash savings, I should simply say, "Yeah, about $4000 a year."

Seriously, by pedaling 20,000 miles annually, I save about $4000. I've already saved about $50,000 and over the next 30 years I should save another $120,000 (assuming $4 per gallon and 20 mpg).

But that's a gross underestimate of the true economic payoff. Just imagine the investment opportunity lost by wasting $4000 annually on gasoline. Investing that money in a 401K would yield $800,000 in 30 years, $1.5 million in 35 years, or $2.3 million in 40 years.

And that doesn't even account for the fortune you could amass by not purchasing, maintaining, insuring, and accessorizing cars. Assuming another $8000 wasted annually in that way, in 40 years you could have $6 million to squander on bicycles and Lycra and charities.

Did you get a DUI?

"No."

Look at that poor bastard, they think, he lost his license. To the typical Yank or Canuck, the car addiction is so systemic that it's inconceivable someone would use a bicycle for transportation of his or her own volition.

Do you even own a car?

"Nope, I divorced my last car over a decade ago. And I've been living happily ever since."

Are you nuts?

"Not yet, but I'm getting there."

Even though I'm losing my mind according to a hyperbolic decay function — that's mathspeak for really fast — I find I don't really miss it all that much. Seriously. So far, I'm no nuttier than the average vagabond, no madder than a Victorian Era hatter, and not nearly as crazy as a loon or a coot. I'd like to think I still have the sense that Darwin gave geese. Of course, as my sister will say when she reads this passage, "Oh, that's bragging, you *know* you're bat-shit crazy." But if you insist on labeling me, I have a strong preference for "quirky" or "eccentric."

For the record, I do have an admittedly odd obsession with failed bungee cords. The shoulders are strewn with them. Listen Car People, those things don't work. The Law of Entropy prevails and the things go sproing onto the shoulder and later, miles down the road, you can't figure out how you lost so much stuff from the roof or the trailer.

My advice: Learn to tie a proper knot. You don't even need to re-enlist in the scouts to remediate your basic knot-tying skills; these days, you can watch a YouTube instructional video for just about anything, including knot-tying. Better yet, you can take advantage of the free knot-tying app. In mere minutes, you can learn the bowline, three half hitches, clove hitch, etc. Applying this new skill will save you roughly $487 in failed bungee cords, plus thousands of dollars' worth of stuff that otherwise would have been lost on the roads over your lifetime. (You're welcome.)

Oh, I also have an unusual fixation on decrepit basketball hoops. I notice them. I like seeing them mangled and *sans* net, overgrown by massive live oaks, twisted to a comical angle by the sagging barn or the frost heave. Sometimes it's clear someone truly fastidious did a great job of putting the hoop in place — at exactly 12 feet.

In other words, if you could eavesdrop on my subvocal monologue as I pedal along, you might beg to differ with my assessment of my mental health. You might even think I'm certifiable. But, again, I prefer quirky or eccentric or intriguing or just plain weird.

Why do you have signatures on your helmet?

"It all started with Guy Davis. It's his fault."

A few years ago, I pedaled to Unity, Maine, in the dead for winter — for live music. I would hear Guy Davis, a famous blues guy, on Friday night and then join the dreadlock kids and bop to Railroad Earth on Saturday night.

Guy's performance was great. During the first set, he titillated the blue-haired benefactors, especially when he crooned "I'm your chocolate man."

At intermission, I sidled up to Guy and asked him to sign my helmet.

"Why should I sign your helmet, man?"

"We'll, never mind the fact that I pedaled 150 miles in the snow to see you play, the real reason is that I want to make a friend jealous. He's a former PhD student of mine, who plays blues guitar emulating your style, and you signed his guitar after a show in London a few years ago."

"Tiny white guy with dreadlocks?"

"Yes, you remember! His name's Eric. He was *my* protégé too!"

Guy grabs my helmet and autographs it, expertly adding a ★star after his signature. I immediately take a photo with my cell phone and send it to Eric.

Minutes later, my phone vibrates. Sure enough, it's a text message from Eric: "WTF, you get to hang with Guy?! I HATE YOU!"

I share Eric's message with Guy, who laughs and then suggests we make him really jealous by taking a selfie of the two of us. He mashes his cheek against mine and I click.

Less than a minute goes by before I get a reply. It says, "U r not my friend anymore. Tell Guy I hate him 2."

~

That's what got the ball rolling. Ever since, any singer-songwriter who sees the signatures on my helmet is likely to recognize one or more of the names and then ask to sign. So I don't ask them to sign, they offer, as in, "I want to sign right beside Lucy Kaplansky." Or hey, "It's Peter Mulvey, he's great!" Or "I toured with Ryan Montbleau last year."

Have you biked through all 50 states?

"All but the 50th ..."

You might surmise that I've avoided Hawaii because flying on a jet to Honolulu to tick off the last state would violate my green lifestyle principles. And you'd be right. Of course, if I were the least bit intrepid, I'd pedal to Hawaii. Before dismissing that idea as pure folly, check out the book, *Pedaling to Hawaii*. That's right, believe it or not, the author *pedaled* a boat across the open ocean — and survived to tell the tale.

These days I could pedal a Hobie Mirage kayak, with outriggers, right out of San Francisco Bay. Or I could make like the ultra-rowers who annually race from the coast of California to Hawaii. We'll see.

Have you seen any bears?

"Yes, 193 so far."

Have you been bitten by a dog?

"No, but I've been chased many times."

Occasionally, I sprint through a hotspot for free-ranging dogs. Native reservations and rural roads in Appalachia are ideal destinations if you're anxious to gauge your sprinting skills relative to those of pit bulls.

And in many rural landscapes, unleashed dogs become superabundant early each evening, right after their humans get home from work and set their dogs free to defecate and/or chase bicycles.

But the truth is: most of the dogs I encounter happen to be situated along dedicated bike paths. As a cyclist who wishes to maximize time spent away from Car People, it's always a relief to happen upon such a path. But this relief is often closely followed by mild disappointment because a big subset of Car People also happen to be Dog People. And these people love to drive their dogs to the nearest multi-use trail, where they proceed to violate every rule and regulation. They don't stay right. They don't keep their dogs on a lease. They don't seem to be aware of anything but satisfying their inexplicable drive to collect the feces of their pet, which of course begs the familiar question: who is the dominant individual in this hominid-canid relationship?

Which reminds me: the typical dog person "knows" humans cleverly created dogs through artificial selection, whereas the typical evolutionary ecologist hypothesizes that wolf ancestors of domestic dogs manipulated humans. Assuming (correctly) the tendency to be tame has a heritable basis, those individual wolves that happened to be tame enough to get food rewards from humans presumably had a considerable advantage in terms of lifetime reproductive success. If so, it might have taken only a few generations for domestic dogs — complete with floppy ears and curly tail and playfulness — to evolve.

Behavioral geneticists at Cornell University recently confirmed that selection for tameness per se leads to extremely rapid evolution for these attendant doggie traits. By simply allowing tame individuals to live amongst them, humans arguably got duped by incipient dogs and the familiar doggie traits arose as a byproduct of natural selection, not through a clever attempt to produce these traits through selective breeding. From this perspective, humans have been metaphorically picking up after defecating dogs for millennia.

While contemporary defecating canids seldom chase me, they do tend to dash in front or dangle their leash like a booby trap or try to incite play or otherwise get in the way. They often run loose while their humans keep them "under voice control." For the cyclist, this means that when the Car/Dog Person yells "come here, buddy," the dog — as if obeying a law of Newtonian physics — chooses a collision course with the bicycle roughly 98.7% of the time. It's uncanny.

Their humans are worse, of course. They don't defecate on the trail, but when I yell "on your left," they look over their left shoulder and consequently do a compensatory swerve to their left — in my way. Or they get startled and react in a most unpleasant way. And when I crash because they and their dogs force me to make an evasive maneuver and I lay there facedown with a broken thumb and a concussed brain and a mangled front wheel and twisted handlebars, they "forget" to apologize or respond in any decent way. Instead, reflecting their true underlying Car Person status, they indicate their sense of entitlement. It's inconceivable that they're culpable of anything, including their dog's deposit on the paved pathway.

Do you carry a gun?

"Nope."

You know what the pro-gun folks say: "Guns don't kill people; people with guns kill people." If I were to acquire a gun, I'd instantly become one of the people with guns. And I might use it in a fit of road rage.

Can I see your legs?

"You may look, but don't touch."

How much food do you carry?

"Usually none. Why, do you need some?"

Do you ever use "warm showers?"

"Hardly ever."

Because I insist of spontaneity and self-reliance, I almost never plan beyond my next meal. Exceptions have been cases where I happened to meet someone who happened to be a host and one thing led to another.

I have stayed at a few hiker hostels along the Appalachian Trail. That's fun but awkward because if you show up on a bicycle, hikers see you as a cheater. And of course you are! So I usually mention that I've done a thru-hike. That usually buys me a little "trail cred."

Why don't you get a motor?

"I *have* a motor. *I'm* the motor *and* the passenger."

Here's just one example of exchanges prompted by this rhetorical yet goading question:

In Alaska, just south of Denali National Park, I stealth-camped for the night, rose at first light, and pedaled hard. Hours later I rolled into the village of Willow. I pulled up to the grocery store. And disturbing hilarity ensued.

At the deli counter, I ordered two foot-long veggie subs "with everything" and then I watched the young fellow-who-won't-get-around-to-attempting-high-school do his artistry. His "method" for applying ingredients was to walk several steps to the counter behind him, reach both hands into the vat of choice, grab fistfuls of, say, jalapeño pepper slices, lift his dripping hands above the vat, do an about-face and drizzle his way back over to the sandwich assembly board, where he'd mash his latest "score" onto the precariously growing pile of sandwich built upon the bread-turned-back-into-dough.

Under the heading of TMI: The next day I had Willow's Revenge despite my enormously high tolerance for capsaicin. I'd overdosed on jalapeños just twice in my long illustrious career as a pepperphiliac, despite hundreds of megadoses. But I'd never consumed over a 100 slices in one evening, till that evening.

But better was the banter:

Before consenting to make the subs, he challenged me to justify my bike trip. He barked, "Why don't you get a friggin' motor?"

"I wouldn't get any exercise that way," I said.

"Seriously, what the fuck, why are you doing this?" he asked with real disgust in his voice.

I offered some lame comeback about health benefits and the physical challenge.

"That's total fucking bullshit!"

Then he asked who was financing my travels, suspecting a government handout, no doubt. I told him I was retired. He asked me how old I was. I told him, 52.

"Shit, I started working when I was 12 and I'll never get to retire."

Then he asked what I'd done for a career. I admitted it, "University professor."

"Great, you can teach me how to make a bomb!" he said way too enthusiastically.

Sure, I thought, that's what retired ecologists do. We pedal around the world seeking disenfranchised young men as protégés. We recruit them into our terrorist cell.

I told him my bomb-making skills were a bit rusty. He said not to worry because we could consult his father's copy of *The Anarchist Cookbook*, which for the uninitiated is controversial only partly because it contains recipes for explosives. He told me it's his favorite book, albeit the only one he's ever read. And then he told me about "these idiots in Iraq" (his words verbatim) who'd recently got caught with the ingredients for a weird kind of "dirty bomb." The ingredients were lots of Tang and lots of blasting caps. He was sure the bomb would be a dud, that the blasting caps would make some noise but probably wouldn't detonate the secondary explosive, Tang.

I suggested the mere fact that these "idiots" had the ingredients for a bomb — no matter how poor the design — *that* in and of itself is a potentially effective act of terrorism. After all, the goal of the terrorists is to terrorize their target, not to annihilate it.

He said, "Wow, you sure know a lot about terrorism!"

"Thanks," I said reflexively. And then I went off to convert my lower GI tract into a homemade dirty bomb.

Do you ride on the highway?

"No, I ride on a secret network of interconnected bike-only paths that only Bike People know about."

Actually, in the southwestern states, bicyclists are allowed to ride on interstate highways along stretches where no frontage road or reasonable alternative back road exists. In California, a sign on each on-ramp specifies that bicyclists must use the shoulder only — as if we'd venture out into the carpool lane if not for this helpful hint.

Do you need water or food?

"Yes, those are essential for survival."

Isn't it dangerous?

"Jeez, I hope not."

Yes and no. Life'll kill ya, after all. And I like to point out that my "profession" is safer than cab-driving, deep-sea fishing, smoke-jumping and so on.

Aren't you afraid of getting hit by a car?

"Deathly afraid."

At a primal level, that's what it's all about — not dying at the hands of one of the Car People. But I take special precautions to avoid that fate. And just as I would never dream of staying out of wilderness areas with bears afoot, I wouldn't dream of staying off the bike just because fellow humans operating their four-wheeled weapons create an omnipresent danger.

Have you ever been hit by a car?

"Yes, but only twice. And as you can see, I didn't get turned into fatally flattened fauna either time."

Actually, the first time I didn't technically get hit by the car. I went flying around a corner just as a driver failed to signal before aggressively pulling out of a parallel parking spot. To avoid crashing, I hit the brakes and went into a slide. The bike and I slid right under the vehicle, a four-wheel drive truck. The driver was shocked, to say the least. He lowered his window, leaned out and looked down at my face and said, "DUUUUUDE, you're under my truck!" He helped me get out. My bike and I were both fine. He apologized profusely and even gave me his business card — his name was Buck Link — in case I had any latent injuries and needed some insurance money to pay for medical expenses.

What do you do when you get a flat tire?

"I call AAA."

What do these people think, that I abandon the bike and hitchhike to the nearest town with a Walmart to buy a replacement?

Actually, I have tools, extra tubes, and a patch kit, of course. But these days, I use nothing but slime-filled tubes, so I hardly ever get a flat. These tubes are self-sealing, not self-healing, so gradually a puncture wound weakens to the threshold where the tube blows. When this happens, pedestrians may think you've vomited, but at least they'll give you a width berth.

How many tires have you gone through?

"That's a personal question."

I usually ride a set of tires till I start getting punctures and then I buy a new set at the next bike shop. On average, my tires probably last somewhere between 5,000 and 10,000 miles. (They don't last very long in the southwest, where the shoulders are strewn with blown-out truck tires. The impregnated wire mesh releases bits of thin wire that work their way through your tire and tube.)

What if you break down in the middle of nowhere and can't fix it yourself?

This happens rarely, maybe once every year or two. On a couple of occasions, I've hitchhiked to the nearest bike shop. One time I did this in Alaska, but when I finally found the teenaged guy I thought could get me back on the road, it turned out his bike shop, located in a plywood shack on a tertiary dirt road, wasn't really a bike shop. It was a front for his after-school weed-dealing business. We were both disappointed. So I then hitched a ride to Fairbanks and had an expert mechanic there replace my bottom bracket and the whole drive train and the dérailleur and so on.

On another occasion, I was pedaling through an Ojibwa rez in Ontario, Canada when I heard a pop and then another and another. Within minutes, I had *nine* broken spokes. (I'm in the habit of carrying one or two spare spokes, never nine.) I turned my bike upside down to look more pitiable while hitch-hiking. Nobody stopped, till finally a stretch limo pulled over. The driver took pity on me and offered me a free ride to the nearest bike shop. I loaded the bike and panniers in the trunk and got into the back seat with his legit passengers. Turned out, they were hookers headed home from their unofficial shift at the casino. To scandalize the man in tights, I suppose, they imitated the driver and offered me a "free ride." I played dumb.

~

On every other occasion where I lacked the parts to fix my bike, I've been able to pedal, more or less, to the nearest bike shop. One time I was screaming down a long descent in New Hampshire, having crossed the Appalachian Trail at the crest, when I hit a pothole and then another. This nearly finished off my rear wheel, which already had two broken spokes. Now with five broken spokes, the wheel had a major wobble. I trued it as well as I could, which is to say not well at all, and then detached the rear brakes so the wobbly wheel could turn. The bike was barely rideable, but somehow I managed to coax it another 60 miles along the narrow winding roads all the way to the border of Vermont, where I hoped to find a bike shop.

I wobbled into town at 4:53 PM and, sure enough, found a bike shop with a posted closing time of 5 PM. But I quickly discovered that this too, like the plywood shack in Alaska, wasn't really a bike shop, at least not in the conventional sense. And like the plywood shack shop, this one was "run" by a pubescent high school guy. But he wasn't selling weed. In fact, he wasn't selling anything at all, except via the internet. He was paid by an absentee owner to build up bicycles and put them in cardboard boxes to be picked up each eve and shipped to the buyers, elsewhere on Earth. So the shop was not set up to do repairs or to sell power gel shots and cycling gloves and helmets and such. I was out of luck, except for the fact that the kid thought I was "cool" and that my trek was "epic" and so he agreed to help me out. Next thing I knew he was cutting open a box, pulling out the just built-up bike, and stripping it almost back down to the frame. In no time, I would have two new wheels, two new tires (with tubes), a whole new drive train, and even a new rear derailleur. I was okay with this.

Within an hour, I was ready to ride. But first I had to figure out how to compensate him. He didn't have a cash register or a credit card reader. He'd never charged anyone for anything. I suggested a dollar amount, which he accepted. I paid him double that, figuring he could use a good tip as compensation for the grief his boss would surely give him.

~

On another occasion I managed to strip the threads on the bottom bracket and so had to pedal one-legged all the way to Hastings, Nebraska. And once again, I got bailed out at a bike shop that wasn't really a bike shop. My GPS initially gave me directions to a conventional shop but it was closed because it was Sunday and I was in the God-fearing heartland. So I followed directions to a second bike shop, out toward the edge of town, down a strictly residential street. The GPS told me I was "arriving on the left," but there was nothing vaguely resembling a commercial property. I did a U-turn and the GPS told me I was "arriving on the right." Naturally, I figured this was just another of the thousands of spurious businesses in the World According to Garmin.

But I was down to one pedal and determined to find help, so I knocked on a door to ask for directions or advice. Ann Breckner introduced herself and told me I'd come to the right place, that it really was an extremely cryptic bike shop. She said her husband, Bob, was out for a ride, but he'd be home soon and could probably help me.

Sure enough, a few minutes later Bob rolled in — on a Pugsley no less! Two hours later and after dissembling one bike after another from his personal collection of 20 or so, we finally managed to find a compatible part. And once again, I'd been rescued at a bike shop that wasn't — this one a garage without a sign, "run" by a velophiliac and a great guy to boot.

What did you do with all of your stuff? Is it in storage?

"What stuff? Stuff is never enough."

I was predisposed for a semi-nomadic life because I had precious little stuff to begin with. I divorced my house, gave away my books, donated some clothes to charity, and then hit the road, toad.

Do you have a smart phone?

"Nope, my phone's dumb. It does only what I tell it to do."

Actually, I did cave recently and join the iPeople. I don't have any cool apps yet, so I'm still not sure why I bought the damn thing, but at least I'm one of the iSheeple. Come to think of it, I should download some cycling-related apps.

Do you ever ride at night?

"Yes, nightly."

I really do ride, at least locally, almost nightly. (Last night, I rode to listen to a pair of dueting Western Screech-owls near John Muir Elementary School.) But sometimes I travel at night. In the desert, I sometimes make like a kangaroo rat during the hottest part of the day and resume activity in the evening, when the temperature drops by as much as 60 Fahrenheit degrees. And other times, when I feel energized or infatuated by having the roads to myself, I pedal all night. For example, when I leave Fenway Park late at night, I like to pedal back to Maine before sunrise. Eastern Massachusetts rivals any other place in the USA in the category of bike unfriendliness, but at night the roads effectively turn into bike trails and it's a breeze to pedal through the suburbs and up the coast to stealth-camping paradise.

How do know where you're going?

"I don't."

I do use a GPS, but it's sometimes more trouble than it's worth. Its algorithms are stubborn. If the thing thinks you shouldn't be on a given road because it's not the most direct route, it will tell you over and over again to turn. Or if it doesn't like your road because it's too heavy with traffic, it'll try to send you up and over mountain passes, along the ocean, and then back inland. Sometimes, you can save yourself less than a mile on a busy road by simply bypassing that stretch and traveling, say, 140 miles on the prescribed route. So, I use it warily. And I'm getting better at outsmarting its tiny brain.

What happens when you get to a big city?

"I take a cab."

Actually, cities are often the easiest and safest places to ride. Consider Los Angeles. You might imagine this is the single worst place in the USA for a cyclist. But the truth is you can arrive from the north in Malibu, get on the dedicated multi-use path near the Stinson Beach roller coaster, head south to "Muscle Beach," eventually to Huntington Beach, and then take a left onto the dedicated path along the Santa Ana River. This path takes you almost all the way to Riverside. That's about 140 miles through LA and Orange counties, with the vast majority away from cars.

You're doing this alone?

"Yes."

Do you ever ride with anyone?

"Hardly ever."

Long-distance hikers have a saying: hike your own hike. That doesn't imply you should hike solo. But it's a lot easier to hike your own hike — or ride your own ride — if you're not part of El Grupo. I prefer to bike alone. That way I can be as spontaneous as I want to be, and I want to be very spontaneous.

But there's a cost to pedaling solo. Even though my mode of transportation is more efficient than any other mode ever devised, the truth is that I could be a good deal more efficient if I rode with someone. I could draft now and then. I could be a self-serving pedaler in a pelaton, mimicking the behavior of marine mammals in pods or geese and pelicans in V's. I could minimize the influence of the drag-related term in the Bicycle Equation. And if I wanted to push the efficiency envelope, I could switch to a tandem bike. But if ever increasing efficiency were my goal, I'd probably switch to a recumbent trike with aerodynamic bubble windshield. And I just may, one of these days.

~

Of course, sometimes I do find myself spontaneously joined by a fellow cyclist. I'll be pedaling along and some wicked fast roadie — Dennis How comes to mind — will reel me in and chat me up. Sometimes a scintillating conversation ensues and I manage to match the roadie's speed for an hour or two. These chance encounters often make my day.

And sometimes I'm joined by a friend for a few hundred miles' worth of "vacation pedaling." (Isn't that what you do with all of your vacation time?)

What are you going to do next?

"This. Lots more pedaling."

Next I'll go to Denmark so I can learn how to pedal like a Dane. (I hope they have strawberry rhubarb pie in Denmark.) And then I plan to pedal from Copenhagen to Chennai, in southern India, to surprise my sister. (She won't be too surprised because she's come to expect my unannounced intrusions. Usually she learns of my visit by spotting my tent in her backyard.) And then I'll pedal across Mongolia to China and then Indonesia and Australia and so on.

When I get back to North America, I'll homestead on my land in Ontario for a thoroughly Thoreauvian stretch of 2 years, 2 months, 2 weeks, 2 hours, 2 minutes, and 2 seconds. I'll grow and gather my own food. I'll generate electricity by pedaling my Pugsley perched on a generator. I'll be truly off the grid.

And then I'll switch from pedaling Earth to paddling Earth. I'll become a hardcore voyageur, propelling myself everywhere in that other conveyance sublime, the canoe. But I'll probably opt for a Hobie Cat kayak so I'll have the option of continued pedaling. I'll be a pedalphile [*sic*] till the end.

How long are you going to keep doing this?

"Till my birthday, in the year 2059, when I turn 100."

Madame Calment pedaled her way to the century mark, and I think I can too. And assuming I stick to my plan of matching her longevity record of 122, I'll have 22 post-pedaling years to devote to non-pedaling passions.

~~~

Go pedal. There's nothing more to read here.

🚲 🚲 🚲 🚲 🚲

References and Recommendations

CHAPTER 1 –
For an entrée into evolutionary game theory as applied to airport security: Tambe, K. 2011. *Security and Game Theory: Algorithms, Deployed Systems, Lessons Learned.* Cambridge University Press.

CHAPTER 2 –
For a fuller treatment of the pros and cons of adopting a car-free lifestyle: Alvord, K. 2000. *Divorce Your Car!* New Society Publishers. 320 pp.

CHAPTER 3 –
To explore rankings of countries by happiness:
http://en.wikipedia.org/wiki/Satisfaction_with_Life_Index

To learn more than you ever wanted to know about Denmark's cycling culture:
http://denmark.dk/en/green-living/bicycle-culture/

CHAPTER 4 –
To learn more about the Terry Fox story check out the recent documentary, *Into the Wind* (2010):
http://espn.go.com/30for30/film?page=into-the-wind

CHAPTER 5 –
To learn more about Klaus and his *karnevalsorden* check out: http://www.rocktheroads.de/

CHAPTER 6 –
To see the "invisible gorilla" video:
http://www.youtube.com/watch?v=vJG698U2Mvo

To learn more about selective attention: Chabris C. and D. Simons. 2010. *The Invisible Gorilla.* Random House.

CHAPTER 7 –
For data on cycling mileage and fatalities in 10 developed countries see: WALCYNG, Report1. no.4, 1997, Lund University Sweden and Factum Austria.

For data on mortality by mode of travel in USA and Denmark:
http://en.wikipedia.org/wiki/Epidemiology_of_motor_vehic le_collisions
http://webcache.googleusercontent.com/search?q=cache:ht tp://www.peoplepoweredmovement.org/site/images/uplo ads/MakingCyclingIrresistible.pdf

For time series of cycling mortality in Denmark see:
http://ec.europa.eu/transport/road_safety/pdf/statistics/d acota/bfs2010_dacota-swov-1-3-cyclists.pdf
http://www.etsc.eu/documents/BIKE_PAL_Safety_Ranking. pdf

CHAPTER 8 –
For mortality rates of dangerous job:
http://jobs.aol.com/articles/2013/11/12/the-15-most-dangerous-jobs-in-america/

To join the Church of the Flying Spaghetti Monster go to: http://www.venganza.org/

CHAPTER 9 –
For evidence of cardiovascular benefits of active commuting see: Hamer, M. and Y. Chida. 2008. Active commuting and cardiovascular risk: A meta-analytic review. *Preventive Medicine* 46: 9-13.

For compilations of life expectancy estimates:
http://www.worldlifeexpectancy.com/world-health-rankings
http://www.worldlifeexpectancy.com/history-of-life-expectancy

http://www.worldlifeexpectancy.com/usa-cause-of-death-by-age-and-gender

For forecast of drop in life expectancy in USA due to obesity: Olshansky et al. 2005. *New Engl. J. Med.* 352: 1138-1145.

CHAPTER 10 –
To learn more about the Finnish cohort study:
Sarna et al. 1993. Increased life expectancy of world class male athletes. *Med. Sci. Sports Exercise* 25: 237-244.
Sarna et al. 1997. Health status of former elite athletes. The Finnish experience. *Aging* 9: 35-41.

For evidence of improved longevity in Tour de France participants: Sanchis-Gomar et al. 2011. Increased average longevity among the "Tour de France" cyclists. *Int. J. Sports Med.* 32: 644-647.

For a review of 14 papers: Teramoto & Bungum. 2010. Mortality and longevity of elite athletes. *J. Sci. Med. Sport* 13: 410-416.

To learn more about the life-history tradeoff between fecundity and mortality and the inspirational case of Madame Calment see: Promislow D. 1998. Longevity and the barren aristocrat. *Nature* 396: 719-720.

CHAPTER 11 –
For a look at emerging evidence of the stress associated with commuting: Evans et al. 2002. The morning rush hour predictability and commuter stress. Envir. Behav. 34: 521-530.

For an entrée into the formal literature on the adaptiveness of stress in wild animals see: Thaker et al.

2010. Stress and aversive learning in a wild vertebrate: the role of corticosterone in mediating escape from a novel stressor. Am. Nat. 175: 50–60.

For an introduction to Darwinian medicine see: Nesse, R.M. 2001. The smoke detector principle. *Ann. New York Acad. Sci.* 935: 75-85.

CHAPTER 12 –
To see how Americans spend their money check out:
http://mentalfloss.com/article/31222/numbers-how-americans-spend-their-money

For a review paper promoting putative pharmacological benefits of exercise: Vina *et al.* 2012. Exercise acts as a drug: the pharmacological benefits of exercise. *Brit. J. Pharmacol.* 167: 1-12.

For recent evidence of dopamine imbalance in persons with Huntington's disease: Chen *et al.* 2013. Dopamine imbalance in Huntington's disease: a mechanism for the lack of behavioral flexibility. *Frontiers Neurosci.* 7: 114.

CHAPTER 13 –
To see the list of countries by ecological footprint (with key background information):
http://en.wikipedia.org/wiki/List_of_countries_by_ecological_footprint

To see annotation to the list of top 10 countries by bicycle ownership per capita:
http://top10hell.com/top-10-countries-with-most-bicycles-per-capita/

CHAPTER 14 –

To read Muir's description of his hike to Yosemite see his book, My First Summer in the Sierra.

For evidence that climate warming has impacted small-mammal communities in Yosemite National Park see: Moritz et al. 2008. Science 322: 261-264.

CHAPTER 15 –
To see an example of the attempt to optimize flight efficiency of drones by mimicking the soar-and-glide mode of hawks: Qi Y. and Y. Zhao. 2005. Energy-efficient trajectories of unmanned aerial vehicles flying through thermals. *J. Aerospace Eng.* 18: 84-92.

CHAPTER 16 –
For an introduction to the physics of cycling see: http://en.wikipedia.org/wiki/Bicycle_performance

For a similar exploration of cycling physics (that inspired some of my examples) see: Reid, J.S. 2013. *Physics of Cycling.* 23 pp. http://homepages.abdn.ac.uk/nph120/meteo/cycling.pdf

To see the derivation of the bicycle equation and to learn from the master see: Wilson, D.G. 2004. *Bicycling Science.* MIT Press. 485 pp.

CHAPTER 17 –
For any primary reference on arcane details I've conveniently overlooked in any chapter, please contact me at: tom.waite.1@gmail.com

About the Book

You just read the book and now you want to read *about* the book? That sounds like procrastination to me. You're squandering precious pedaling time. For the last time, I urge you to go pedal.

But while I have your attention I should say these stories describe real events and so any resemblance to the truth was intentional. Inevitably, as with the telling of any tale, some slippage has occurred. The resultant corruption though amounts to minor embellishment, not outright invention. This stuff really happened.

About the Author

To date, Tom Waite has written two other books that also fall within the emerging subgenre of eco-geek adventure humor, *The Laughalachian Trail* and *WILD with Latitude*. They're wildly entertaining. Or so he claims.

Currently, Tom's off pedaling round Earth a few dozen times. Don't wait up. (He'll be hard to find as he'll be stopping off ever so briefly at many undisclosed locations, but you can always reach him at: tom.waite.1@gmail.com.) Rumor has it he's making faster-than-glacial progress on his next self-imposed writing assignment. The working title is something other than *Chicken, Hookers, and Scotch.* Stay tuned.

18008227R00173

Made in the USA
San Bernardino, CA
23 December 2014